D0328150

Praise for The Wagamama Bride

Liane Wakabayashi's journey to a profound acceptance of faith takes us from London via New York to Tokyo, where love is found and not quite lost, then home to Jerusalem. Written with honesty and humor, this is a memoir that I couldn't put down.

GAYE ROWLEY, PhD, author of *An Imperial Concubine's Tale,* and translator of *In the Shelter of the Pine*

With a persistent desire to explore her own spirituality, mostly through her roots in Judaism, Liane Wakabayashi takes us on a journey into another culture, in its most intimate manifestation —marriage and family. This is a memoir full of love, scintillating conversations, memorable people, art, food, sorrow and joy, the author's discovery of how to be human in the modern world.

REBECCA OTOWA, author of *At Home in Japan*

Liane Wakabayashi shares her inner process of finding what she needs to be happy and true to her ideals while showing us all the obstacles that prevent her from doing so. I found myself rooting for her to get through each step. I will not say how it all ends up, but I will say I'd be interested in reading a sequel someday.

EDWARD LEVINSON, author of *Whisper of the Land*

Liane Wakabayashi's moving memoir tells a life-affirming tale about how we can live an authentic life as we navigate what we owe to others—and to ourselves.

ANN TASHI SLATER, author of the forthcoming memoir, *Paradise Lands*

The heart wants what the heart wants, but how difficult it can be to reconcile the conflicting desires of the mind and soul in Liane Wakabayashi's interfaith and intercultural family! Her deeply engaging transnational and transformational story will move—and maybe even change—you."

SUZANNE KAMATA, author of *Squeaky Wheels: Travels with my Daughter by Train, Plane, Metro, Tuk-tuk and Wheelchair*

The Wagamama Bride is a witty and delightful memoir that explores how two people from different cultures learn almost to stay together and accept each others' differences. A must-read for anyone interested in the personal and the spirit.

EVERETT KENNEDY BROWN, author of the forthcoming memoir, Kyoto Dreamtime

Like the Fiddler on the Roof talking to God, Liane Wakabayashi, though increasingly immersed in her new Japanese family, culture, and religion, is drawn in the opposite direction. Sharing her deepest inner and interpersonal predicaments and their resolutions, the writer teaches us what courage and honesty to oneself are about.

RACHEL COSIJINS-PLUMP, PhD, Japanese Media Studies

With openness and humor, *The Wagamama Bride* delivers the message that a Torah-true way of life is within every Jew's reach, even in Japan!

REBBETZIN NECHAMA DINA HENDEL, Chabad of Baka, Jerusalem

THE WAGAMAMA BRIDE

THE WAGAMAMA BRIDE

A Jewish Family Saga Made in Japan

LIANE GRUNBERG WAKABAYASHI

GOSHEN BOOKS

THE WAGAMAMA BRIDE

A Jewish Family Saga Made in Japan

A memoir by Liane Grunberg Wakabayashi

Copyright 2021 All Rights Reserved.

No part of this manuscript may be used, copied, translated, or distributed without written permission of the author.

For questions and comments, please contact: hello@goshenbooks.com

Disclaimer: This memoir is a work of creative nonfiction based on true events and real people. Some names have been changed to protect the privacy of dear family and friends. The events in *The Wagamama Bride* were recalled from letters, published articles, conversations with friends and family members, and from the author's personal journals.

Published by Goshen Books of Jerusalem, Miami and Tokyo

ISBN: 978-0-578-84404-6

Library of Congress Control Number: 2021906956

Cover design by Hatsumi Tonegawa

Cover art and calligraphy by Liane Grunberg Wakabayashi

Second Edition

Contents

For my mother, my muse,
Adrianne Lebensbaum

A lamp for my feet is your word
and a light for my path.
—Psalm 119

Japanese, Hebrew and Yiddish words in *The Wagamama Bride* appear in their original languages in italics, with English translation.

The Wagamama Bride

Foreword

A WINDMILL IN WIMBLEDON

*Listen, daughter, and observe
and incline your ear;
and forget your people
and your father's house.*
—Psalm 45

It's difficult fasting in Jerusalem, but in Wimbledon, surrounded by generous slices of chocolate layer cake, it was nearly impossible. My mother speared a bite, popped it between her lips and my mouth watered. Talia, my sister, passed plates over the white tablecloth, and the Maidenhead branch of our family dug in. The only thing that landed on my bone china plate were squares of sunshine from the pane glass windows.

"You sure do pick your moments to make a point, dear. Is fasting on Yom Kippur not good enough for you?"

I shrugged. I kept my mouth shut. I used to match my mother's way of speaking, word by feisty word. But I didn't have the heart to do so now that she had such little time left. So instead, I tried humoring my mother. I explained myself and threw a few facts in.

"Tisha B'Av is a day of mourning," I said. "The First and Second Temples, the Holy of Holies in Jerusalem, were destroyed on this day. The Jews were expelled from Spain on Tisha B'Av, too. Fasting is never fun, Mom. But it's kind of nice to have one day to be miserable. It takes the pressure off being depressed the rest of the year."

I detected a hint of a smile. My mother and I once shared a fondness for the ironic. But when you're doing your best to hide your pain, even a smile takes effort.

My mother had done everything in her power to make me in her image, a Conservative Jew, the yogis of Judaism. My mother was very flexible in her Jewish practice, except for one sticking point—marrying out.

"Never in my wildest dreams did I imagine you would move to Tokyo, marry a Japanese man who had no interest in converting to Judaism, and become Orthodox."

"Mom, I've been moving in this direction for years."

"Yes, dear, I know. Chabad has done wonders for you and the kids."

A Chabad House had appeared in the middle of Tokyo, soon after I became a mother for the first time. Chabad was literally a home, a shul, a sliding open door in Tokyo. On the other side waited a full-bearded Israeli Rabbi or two, and their fresh-faced, wig-wearing wives. Like so many wayward Jews who stumble upon the worldwide Chabad movement—there are centers like this one in every major city—I was enticed by the warm welcome and a nonjudgmental attitude. It felt nothing short of a miracle that these young, charming Chassids from Crown Heights and Kfar Chabad had set up shop—spiritually speaking —in Japan's capital, the city I called home.

"Liane, what about poor Ichiro? He's been left out in the cold by all this religiosity, I'm afraid," my mother said, pausing to cough. What started as a slow, hacking cough turned so watery and deep, it sounded as if it came from a bottomless well, and it terrified me.

My mother's cough came with the devastating diagnosis of lung cancer. It had spread to her bones—but that wasn't going to stop her from traveling. Not even a death sentence was going to prevent her from escaping the oppressive heat of the West Palm Beach country club she called home. I had flown over from Tokyo, wanting my children, Shoshana and Akiva, to be with her and be reminded that they had an interesting family not only in Japan, but where she was born, in England, too.

My uncle Graham had set out the bone china, the best silver and the cut crystal glasses. Shoshana, my nineteen-year-old daughter, and Akiva, my fifteen-year-old son, were old enough to appreciate that something in this household was way out of the box compared to Japanese family normalcy. How many eighty-three-year-old bachelor uncles in Japan are going to shop, cook, and clean up for a houseful of relatives?

My cousins, Justine, the archaeologist, and Sir Hugh, the politician of the family—the MP from York—had brought along a box of photographs. In one black-and-white photo from the 1920s, Hugh's grandmother Cecily—my grandfather's older sister—struck a pose as only an actress can do, humorously respectable in a "kimono" that looked more like a bathrobe. Kimonos are crisp. But Cecily's costume for a performance of *The Mikado* was droopy.

I had to laugh. "Whoever made that costume didn't realize that kimonos never drag on the floor!"

I was the costume buff of the family—having interned at The Metropolitan Museum of New York's Costume Institute while in high school, where I dissected antique dresses the way medical school students dissect cadavers. I had to know what was behind every seam. My mother aspired to become an actress and had graduated with high ambitions from Guildhall

School of Drama in London. My uncle was a West End ticket agent who drove up to see every new show, and a good many re-runs, too.

We were, it would be fair to say, a family of ultra-serious theatre-goers. But Torah scholars? Rabbis? Not one. Shabbat-followers? I couldn't think of a single close relative.

I shared DNA with the Maidenhead branch of the family through a great-grandfather, Avraham Cohen. I know it doesn't sound like much, but in a small family that gets smaller and smaller with every generation, this relative could have been the beginning of our mass assimilation and marrying out. Great-grandfather Avraham, in the early 1900s, left his wife, Sarah—I'm not making this up—and parted from my grandfather before he was old enough to even remember his father's voice.

What father does that? Unless Avraham had died when my grandfather was a boy. But nobody visited his grave. Nobody even knows where he lies. I don't think his children ever forgave him. My grandfather, David, rid himself of all connection with Avraham Cohen by changing his name to Richard Dennie. His older brother Harry never married. His older sister Cecily retired her floppy kimono when she married a wealthy older man in the audience, a diamond broker. In this way, my family could claim Maidenhead, with its great churches and tree-lined avenues, as their own and forget that only a generation earlier they had been Latvians, hailing from Dvinsk.

Avraham Cohen was—I'd like to fancy—from the priestly Kohanim ancestry, tracing the male lineage, generation by generation, to Moses's brother, Aaron. But I'm only speculating, just as I'm guessing that a great-great-grandfather of mine could even have been a Rabbi. I want to imagine Avraham standing with his prayer shawl over his head on Sabbath, with his hands together for the priestly blessing reserved for Kohanim, even though I know that my own grandfather never did.

The explanation for how I could have married a Japanese

man begins with this Avraham. He deserted Sarah, his wife, leaving his children and their children, and now me, three generations later, with a lifetime to ponder the consequences of marrying out—an abomination to Richard and my grandmother Betty Dennie's way of thinking.

Where did Avraham Cohen vanish to? This question was a safe one for dinner table conversation, something for me and my cousins to ponder. The question also kept us from engaging a more difficult and relevant topic—the near-complete loss of Judaism in our family. I had married a man of Buddhist-Shinto persuasion. Uncle Graham had never married. Only Talia, my sister, had continued the chain, marrying a Reform Jew.

I held in my hand the death certificate that Justine had brought along. It was handwritten in cursive lettering on paper as old as parchment. Now we had a date for poor Avraham's demise.

When the last photograph had been laid to rest back in its box, I pointed across the street to Wimbledon Common and asked if anyone wanted to join me. Both my teenagers, Shoshana and Akiva, rolled their eyes and returned to their phones.

I left the flat alone, heading toward the traffic light, crossing Parkside Avenue to enter a peaceful forest. I walked up a dirt path wide enough for a white horse and its rider to trot past.

To see my invincible mother weakening before my eyes was harder than the fasting itself. I needed this fresh air. The foliage became thicker, the leaves darker, and then suddenly I saw what looked like a tunnel of light on the forest path. Moving toward it, then through it, I came out into a field of sunshine. I spotted a windmill ahead with a stout silhouette, its white blades spinning slowly. Each step forward took me back in time. I could almost hear my grandfather ambling behind me, beseeching me with his wooden cane not to run too far ahead. "Yoo-hoo! Yoo-hoo, my darling! You'll get lost!"

The windmill was stacked onto an octagonal brick house. I approached the café at its base. Rocket Lollies were on the ice cream menu—just as I had remembered. I craved the sweet syrup, and I succumbed—red juice dribbling down to my chin—even though it was the fasting day of Tisha B'Av. That's the thing about returning to a Jewish way of life, far beyond anything practiced in my family for generations. Once you let your guard down, it's easy to slip back to the old self who didn't know or care about a Torah-led way of life. But I do care now. Judaism offers remedies for just about everything that needs a cure, whether it's losing two temples or your mother. Not that it's ever easy to follow Torah. There are always the two voices inside. One says: "Restraint brings you closer to God!" The other says: "Go for the Rocket Lolly!"

Chapter One

TESTING THE WATERS IN TOKYO

From the heavens, He looks down.
He sees all mankind
from his dwelling place.
—Psalm 33

On September 27th, 1987, I traded New York City for Tokyo, where I had assumed that single Jewish men were as rare as pandas. But nothing could have been further from the truth. *Bastas,* young Israeli vendors, fresh from army discharge, stood in a row outside of Ebisu train station, peddling trinkets from Thailand. I paused in front of a table laid out attractively with silver rings.

"*Ma nishma?* How are you?" the vendor said.

"*B'seder.* Okay," I said, as I felt his eyes fall to my necklace.

We got to chatting.

I learned that he was in Tokyo to save up money. Then he planned to hang out in cheaper countries in Southeast Asia. He looked so innocent, with soft blue-grey eyes set close together, brown wavy hair, and pale skin with a few freckles. His nose rose like Mount Fuji.

For a second, I thought I was looking at myself in the mirror. But selling on the streets of Tokyo wasn't exactly legal, and he could get into trouble. He smiled at me. Nice white teeth. Yet the *yakuza*, Japan's gangsters who acted as if they owned Tokyo's plazas, could have rearranged his upper bite in one knockout, if he didn't pay them real rent.

"Sterling silver. I guarantee you the best quality. You like brown stones? Tiger's Eye. Or blue stones? Lapis Lazuli. Every ring 50 percent off."

He wanted to talk business. Okay. It was a start. A deep green stone pendant, set in silver, dangled beneath his Adam's apple. His biceps bulged through his black t-shirt. I was ready to slip blue Lapis Lazuli on my finger when he squinted, and his smile disappeared just as a van pulled up to the curb.

A pinky-less man pointed at the vendor through the van window. I saw the murderous look in his eyes. That's when I split. I merged with the crowds of evening rush hour commuters heading into the train station. Could it be that I was attracted to him just because he was Jewish?

I was the product of five generations of *Haskalah*, Jewish women who took off their corsets to do their bit in shaping the European Enlightenment. They rolled up their sleeves, raised their hems, and moved into the workforce. Grandma Betty's first job had been playing the piano in the days of silent movies with her sister Vie. She went on to get a teaching license and taught at a private boys' school. On both my mother's side in England and my father's in Romania, the brightest ones traded religion for education and careers. My mother had two aunts who wore flapper dresses and cloche hats and carried great fans of feathers when they appeared as showgirls in London's West End.

It was my Grandma Betty who didn't like this move to

Tokyo one bit. She had never forgiven me for "shacking up," as she called it, with the love of my life in New York: a tall, blond curly-haired Roman Catholic potter who had me laughing as nobody ever had. He went on to marry a nice Catholic girl. Now I was giving Betty Dennie something new to worry about. "This year in Tokyo. Next year it will be the moon," she quipped in a letter.

My grandmother spent the extra few pence to make sure her letters arrived from Wimbledon to Tokyo by airmail, an extravagance she allowed herself in states of emergency.

April 1988

Wimbledon, Parkside SW19

Dear Liane,

I'm afraid I don't understand your present obsession with Japan. I hope this will subside and you will concentrate on interests nearer home, where there must be many opportunities.

As I've frequently suggested, I'd be pleased to hear that you had become interested in one of the many Jewish organizations where Jewish youth gather and you would probably have met eligible men by now, instead of wasting so many years so fruitlessly. I'm afraid you'll ignore any suggestion I make of that nature, so perhaps I'm wasting my time. I'll never understand why your parents have never shown similar interest in your welfare. Anyhow, the card for Granddad that you sent March 19 —on his birthday—arrived only three weeks late. It seems it was returned to you as insufficiently stamped, due, I suppose, to the weight of the booklet you enclosed.

I must confess that I couldn't find any interest in reading your article, or even the rest of the booklet. Did you ever receive the article I sent by a local authoress I know who wrote an interesting piece on Japanese life that was far more readable? A light touch always makes it more interesting. Anyway, I must now attend to all my own problems.

Love from Grandma and Granddad

Wasting so many years, fruitlessly! In a subsequent letter, she compared my sorry state with Princess Diana's, who was two years younger than I, married to a prince, and—to my grandmother's way of thinking—happy in her role of stay-at-home royalty, with two perfectly adorable sons.

I had been engaged to the potter. We met when he was a sub-chef, and I was waiting tables at a Catskills kosher resort called Golden Acres Farm. When we broke up, it was because my father had sent him, as an engagement gift, a book about the dangers of intermarriage with Jews.

It sent the poor man packing fast. He was smart to see what I refused to admit: that marriage between a Jew and a non-Jew would be a soul-wrenching exercise in losing identity. I roamed from relationship to relationship, trying to hook up with Jews. But things never worked out.

My grandmother's message had been harsh, but to my way of thinking, not to be taken seriously. A friend, much older than I but younger than my grandmother, once told me that one must marry a man who loves you more than you love him. It will guarantee that he stays. To take a man or leave him—that's power, I thought, and I etched those words into my heart.

If only my grandmother had been a little more reserved in her criticism, generous in her praise—who knows? I may have thought of myself as a bit more lovable and been more open to her suggestions.

Meanwhile, the accordion folder where I held these letters grew thick with aerogrammes from New York, where my mother sent letters offering nothing but encouragement. "A year in Japan will be marvelous for you. But remember, dear, all work and no play applies more than ever."

I couldn't help but crack a smile as I read on.

"It sounds as if a little lite relief is needed in your life."

Coke Lite. That was her drink.

"But apart from renting Woody Allen movies and cultivating funny friends, hobbies, and pursuits, I don't know what to suggest." This is what mothers and grandmothers did—I assumed. It was a family's God-given right to lead lives above reproach and to advise. And it was my right to ignore them, as need be.

Conde Nast Traveler Magazine had sent me to Tokyo to write about department stores. The magazine was so new that the first issue hadn't appeared, and I realized when I got to Tokyo that I had no idea what tone of an article they expected me to produce. I was so anxious writing draft after draft that I actually lost the roundtrip portion of a first-class ticket provided by Japan Airlines. With twenty-twenty hindsight, this proved to be not such a terrible thing.

The Japan Times hired me as a copyeditor and gave me a platform to write about artists working in Tokyo's small foreign community. Japan Airlines generously reissued the return ticket for a year later. I loved the craziness of working for *The Japan Times*. We were housed in a temporary Quonset hut, while a pink post-modern office tower was being constructed next door. Our desks were crammed together, smokers and nonsmokers, the neatniks with the hoarders, including the editor who choked up the air conditioning vents with stacks of old newspapers he couldn't bare to part with. We were a united nation of editors, proofreaders, journalists, and section chiefs from the US, the UK, Australia, New Zealand, Canada, the Philippines, led by Japanese executives and a zipper company called Nifco, which had recently taken over the newspaper. I sat with six others on the international news desk, watching sumo tournaments on television monitors while we tapped out headlines and photo captions for the front pages. Emperor Hirohito passed away at 88. A ferry carrying more passengers than the Titanic sunk in the Philippines. Japan sends its war apologies to the Korean state. And so it went.

Most Westerners on staff wore shoes. The Japanese padded around the office in slippers. I loved the insanely laidback newsroom culture. You could be walking around in next to pajamas and nobody would bat an eye. I wore sneakers so that I could explore Tokyo after my shift, reviewing as many department store art exhibitions as I could. I felt like I'd gone to heaven when I got to interview my New York City hero, the artist Red Grooms when he came to Tokyo for a major retrospective featuring his life-size train cars and the hilarious cast of New York characters he had riding them. Red Grooms art could bring on the pangs of homesickness too.

My mother had warned me against my tendency to overwork. Like mother, like daughter, we couldn't help ourselves. In addition to holding down a full-time job as grants administrator for a big foundation in New York City, my mother had somehow gotten involved with parolees.

"The other thing which I'm quite shattered by," she continues in her letter, "is that I've been in training for over a year to be a mentor to a young mother coming out of prison. I was 'linked' to my mentee mid-March and made, or I thought we made, a dual commitment. She has been out only 3-4 weeks on a work release program (even stricter than parole which should have been granted next October) and suffice it to say she vanished yesterday. Standing me up in the process but worse, much worse, leaving her five-year-old son bereft once again of his mother and perhaps the greatest victim of all. And a family that was really behind her and worried frantic. I find it almost unbearable to think of her 'on the street' again (jargon for using drugs, you know), and God knows what else. The success rate of the Women Care program is extremely high—over 95 percent of the mentees do make it, so it is hard to accept that my Carmen is one of the doomed five-percent. I worry about her all the time."

. . .

I SLID CLOSED the shoji screen and placed my mother's letter in the folder. She felt the heartbreak of a child bereft of a mother. Reading between the lines, I saw that she herself was now a mother bereft of a child. She knew what words couldn't say—that she was losing me to Japan.

The house I called home now was tranquil, blessed with one of those Zen gardens you see in a Japanese calendar, not a leaf out of place. I had answered an ad for a secondhand bicycle, following directions to a soaring tiled roof that flared like a skirt over a cozy, wooden cottage. The house was hidden in an intimate garden blessed with a gurgling carp pond and colorful trees ripening with lemons, plums and persimmons. To the Europeans who sold me the bicycle, I joked that I would take the house, too.

As it turned out, the couple was moving to Spain, and if I wanted the house, it was mine. The rent was the equivalent of my salary at *The Japan Times*. No problem, I thought. I advertised for a roommate, offered the *tatami* room facing the garden, while I took the maid's room facing the street. Someone in heaven was watching over me. He had sent down his realtor and found me a paradise I couldn't refuse.

I FLEW to Hokkaido's largest city, Sapporo, to cover a story for *The Japan Times*. This was the annual Sapporo Snow Festival, held on one of the coldest weeks of the year, in early February. Snow buried the park that ran through the center of the city. Sapporo's main promenade was transformed into an outdoor gallery of giant snow and ice sculptures. Units from Japan's Self-Defense Forces, being forbidden by constitutional law to fight, brandished their creativity instead. I trudged through the snow, admiring the icy Taj Mahal, the Forbidden City, and other fantastic replicas of World Heritage sites. The last thing I was thinking about was stumbling upon a Jewish guy here, which is probably why it happened.

The Snow Festival had attracted a number of foreigners, grouped by country, who were competing in an international snow sculpture competition. I stopped in front of a grouping of elongated, ghostly figures, quite unlike the cartoon mascots in the posters advertising the Sapporo Snow Festival. These figures reminded me of the artist Edvard Munch. They looked heavenward, with mouths agape, as if they were going to scream. A friendly hand stopped patting the snow to wave at me. *"Ma nishmah?"*

How are you doing? Did I really hear that in Hebrew? I watched as padded ski gloves worked in circular motion, lifting curvaceous human forms out of the snow. *Kol beseder,* I said. A-Okay. The Israeli Team, representing a country known more for its parched deserts than its snow, had won the international competition.

I congratulated the artist, who said his name was Samson. Biblical Samson had been a judge, a warrior, a hairy sort of guy, whose strength came from his tresses. This Samson wore his hair long. I could just imagine bringing home a guy like Samson to meet my mother—or, even better, to Grandma Betty, who'd condemned previous boyfriends she had seen in photographs by appearance alone. It seemed nobody was ever good enough, especially boyfriends branded by her as "Salvation Army rejects"—sight unseen. But I was curious. Even a bad relationship can make for a very interesting story.

We found a park bench, where Samson and I spoke over *amazake,* a steaming hot and fermented sweet beverage that warmed us up to conversation.

"You know, we ought to have an exhibition of Israeli artists in Tokyo," I proposed, suggesting an exhibition at Tokyo's one and only Jewish Community Center. Samson was in the business of creating art. Would a little collaboration be so bad?

Samson wrote down phone numbers for his Israeli artist friends—and as an afterthought he added an acquaintance, Lalenya, a French-Israeli who resided in Tokyo. I phoned Samson's friends, and they were more than happy to participate, but when I called Lalenya, she turned me down.

"*Schlep* my canvases? You want me to drag my paintings to the Jewish Community Center? I have better things to do than waste my time. Absolutely not."

"It's just for a day!"

"Even more reason to say no. I'm not a *meshugenah.*"

"No, I never meant to insinuate that you're a nut case!"

Lalenya's husky voice, her French accent, spiced with Yiddish, commanded respect. I'd never spoken to anyone like her—power, fierce intelligence and charm wrapped up in her unique package. Lalenya didn't hang up the phone. Instead, she switched the topic to me. She wanted to know why I had left New York City for Tokyo.

"I came to write a magazine story about blockbuster art exhibitions in Tokyo's department stores. Imagine walking into Macy's and riding the elevator to the top floor. Instead of seeing a sales floor of bedding and luggage, the doors open to an exhibition ticket booth, presenting masterpieces from top museums around the world."

"Come on, Liane. You don't move halfway around the world just for research."

"Wait a minute! I did my master's thesis on this subject," I protested. It was unnerving that someone I had never met could sense ulterior motives better than I could myself. Lalenya invited me to come for tea the next day. Her street in Nishi-Azabu was like so many streets in Tokyo, a mix of genteel ugliness and conspicuous wealth wedged so close together, there wasn't room for even a tree in between. A condominium with huge glass windows saluted drab tenements with poky windows, built to put a roof over the heads of World War II survivors. Lalenya's home was an original, a long caravan with two doors on opposite ends. I knocked on a thin, plywood door.

No answer. "Wrong door!" she shouted.

Lalenya came out into the street, black, wavy hair expanding and contracting in the wind, Issey Miyake pleated pantaloons billowing around her girth, and a cigarette between her fingers. She waved me into her atelier, cluttered with canvases and smelling of turpentine. I caught my breath in front of a large painting of an avant-garde Butoh dancer, mouth open wide in angst. I was uncomfortable with the confrontational look in the Butoh dancer's eyes, an expression of human madness and suffering. I assumed this was the language of the rarified Butoh dance world.

I took a seat on a *zabuton*, one of the flat square cushions scattered on a tatami floor. On a small, low dining table, a reddish-brown teapot and unmatched teacups jockeyed for space with a large ashtray. Soon another person opened the door. This was her husband Shotaro, who greeted Lalenya with laughter so deep I had to know what he was saying.

"Shotaro says I'm *wagamama*," Lalenya translated, "because I told him that I won't be bothered with exhibiting my paintings at the Jewish Community Center." I tried hard to follow Lalenya as she wove a conversation from perfectly fluent English, French, Japanese, and Hebrew. "What does *wagamama* mean?" I asked. "A kind of mama? A mother?" She kindly paused to translate for me into English. "*Wagamama* means selfish."

"Yes, I'm *wagamama*. I say what I feel. Nobody will stop me because I speak the truth. People are afraid of hearing the truth in this society. But that's the *Japonais* problem, not mine!"

I wondered why this lioness was living in Tokyo if she felt this way, never imagining that I would one day find myself in the predicament of being called *wagamama* too.

Lalenya popped a cigarette in her mouth, then added, upon further reflection. "*Wagamama* means to be strong and independent. A foreign wife married to a Japanese man must be *waga-mama* to survive here."

"Got you," I smiled. We were on the same wavelength.

But something bothered me. "Do these marriages between Japanese and *wagamama* brides really last?"

She accepted the lighter Shotaro brought to her lips and shrugged. That was the last Lalenya offered to say on the subject. She offered me a cigarette, too. I propped it between my fingers and wondered what kind of a foreign woman would find love and compatibility with a man from such a different culture. Lalenya had been in Tokyo for a decade. I put any possible red flag out of my mind. I was still feeling like a newbie after fifteen months in Tokyo and pretty much enjoyed the feeling of not belonging. I saw myself as a wired-up writer, working in a newsroom, where every encounter held potential for a good story. I was not thinking ahead.

MAKING small talk in a cigarette-filled fog, I felt as if I'd stumbled onto the Left Bank of a dimly lit, night-café society that I had been searching for in New York City but never found. Even if Lalenya's friends didn't speak the same language, these artists joked with one another effortlessly and understood each other.

Lalenya set out antique red lacquer plates on the small table, followed by dinner. I helped myself to *onigiri*, salmon-filled rice balls, stringy black *hijiki* seaweed salad, pickled yellow *takuan* radish, and Camembert cheese, a meal with no logic or planning. Everyone simply brought what they themselves were in the mood to eat. Lalenya smoked and translated snippets of conversation, which I jotted down. I had many questions, but Lalenya quickly tired of them. She held up her hand like a stop sign.

"Enough with the questions! Get out of your brain! Feel your body!" She plugged her mouth with her cigarette, and with her two hands freed she pressed her thumbs into my sore shoulders and stiff neck.

"What are you doing?" I asked in surprise. Random massage didn't fit with what I imagined happening in café society.

"This is called *shiatsu* massage," Lalenya replied.

"My neck feels on fire!" I tried to wriggle my shoulders free, but Lalenya's thumbs wouldn't let go.

"You may be in a bit of pain today, but by tomorrow you'll feel great."

"It's too strong for me," I said.

"You'll need strength to stay in Japan. In this society we must roar like lions!"

I shook out my aching shoulders. "What if I can't be a lion?"

"Then you'll learn how to bleat like a sheep. Meh, meh."

Weeks later, I was standing by the great sliding glass doors of the Jewish Community Center. I reached for a hammer and stretched up on my toes to nail a hook into a linen-covered wall. Lalenya had joined this exhibition of six Israeli artists after all. Paintings and sculptures cascaded down two flights of stairs to the entrance.

I had no idea that my new friend was about to return to France, but the painting she sold was a clue that all was not well in her marriage. The painting depicted a row of penises hanging to dry on a clothesline. She had had enough of Japan and its men. Perhaps Lalenya wanted her young Jewish-Japanese daughter to grow up in a more accepting environment. She was going home to Strasbourg.

I should have taken note. I wish I had probed Lalenya about the heartache of raising a child born of a Jewish woman in Japan. But I didn't know that I would one day be in her position.

"We are in Japan to lead, not to be led, and if we can't be ourselves here, we ought to leave," she sighed, while the packers came to wrap up her canvases.

Lalenya offered a parting gift to me. It was a phone number

she jotted on a slip of paper. She urged me to visit her friend, who ran his own shiatsu clinic.

"He is a serious teacher and a student of traditional Oriental medicine," Lalenya said, explaining that the *Shu Han Run*, a trove of wisdom written thousands of years ago by the Yellow Emperor, was being practiced at the White Crane Clinic run by her friend. Sensing a good story, I wrote the phone number in my diary.

Chapter Two

TAPPED BY THE TAOIST

From His dwelling place He surveys
all the inhabitants of the earth.
It is He who fashions the hearts of them all;
He notes all their doings.
—Psalm 33

In Tokyo, I was in adventure mode, so I figured why not go all the way and try Traditional Oriental Medicine as well? I followed Lalenya's handwritten map to reach the White Crane eastern medicine clinic, on the second floor of a mint-green, tile-covered building. Tall camellia bushes, blossoming with waxy red flowers, stood sentinel from a long balcony. I didn't know what to expect of a Taoist clinic, but the abundance of nature was inviting.

Inside the clinic, a receptionist with shiny long straight hair, a model of fitness and intimidating good health, wearing a white nurse's uniform, handed me a key to a locker and told me to change into a pale-green surgical gown and red polyester basketball trunks—an odd combination if ever there was one. The receptionist then escorted me into the treatment room.

Therapists were moving around with implements I'd never seen before, like cupping tools to stimulate the back, and heating lamps to warm the stomach. Cigar-shaped burning moxa sticks clouded the room with smoky herbs to stimulate energy lines in the body that you can't see or even prove exist. Skinny, bearded therapists dressed in martial arts uniforms, white tops and black bottoms, stooped over narrow massage beds lined in a row. Patients covered in large towels lay in corpse pose, and I climbed up onto a massage table, resting between layers of pink toweling, and waited my turn to be seen by Incho *Sensei*, the clinic chief, and Lalenya's respected friend. I felt so quiet inside I could hear myself breathe.

When Incho Sensei approached me, he smiled warmly. He was wearing black pantaloons and a crisp white blouse, like the others, as if he'd fallen through a rabbit hole and walked out of a feudal samurai household—a farmhouse held up with time-varnished dark wood beams and sliding paper doors over-looking rice fields. He had a wisp of a beard. His salt-and-pepper hair was greased and tied in a ponytail. He could have passed for a television star on a popular Sunday night history drama—except we were in a room with fluorescent lighting and concrete walls. The only thing missing was his sword.

Incho Sensei was accompanied by Ichiro, a carbon copy of himself but younger, and with a fresher wisp of beard. "Hello, my name Ichiro, I, the translation."

I grinned from ear to ear. "You're a very fine translation," I winked back.

He spoke with a charming, lilting accent, as if he had learned to speak English while smoking grass on the beaches of southern India.

Ichiro smiled and bowed. I liked his manners. A real gentle-man. His master placed his right hand in the air, over the pink towel that covered me. His fingers moved like marionettes over my belly. Ichiro explained that Incho's hand was responding to the heat within me. In this way, Incho Sensei diagnosed that I had a tired intestine. I was overindulging in sweets, and daily stress was affecting my liver more than a bottle of wine. And I didn't even drink! Well, hardly. It was all a bit overwhelming, like being a contestant on the game show *This is Your Life*. Incho Sensei appeared to know me inside out.

When Incho Sensei finished the exam, he turned me over to Ichiro for treatment. As he moved closer, I saw that his square glasses were hitched to a rather attractive face, bright and round as the moon. He had a black widow's peak that pointed to a scar between sparse eyebrows. His beard was short, or maybe it was young. When Ichiro smiled, I wondered why his parents had never bothered to fix his teeth.

"Ichiro meaning first-born son, the serious one, so you can trusting me," he chuckled, delighted by his attempt to joke in English.

"Ah, the first fruit of your father's manhood," I laughed back.

"Fruit making body cold," he said.

Well, he didn't get my sense of humor. So much for first-born son jokes.

"Incho saying your condition not good, not bad. But he reading you're tired."

"Burned out," I admitted, as I thought about all the late nights that I'd spent typing up articles. It was my biggest dread that I would not meet a newspaper deadline, and *The Japan Times* would have empty columns on its arts and education pages.

"Burned what?" he asks.

"'Burned out' means exhausted."

"Ah! You meaning culture shock?"

His words surprised me. Culture shock. I thought that a frenetic pace of working to build up a newspaper portfolio, given the opportunity, was what any self-respecting writer would do.

Perhaps Lalenya had been right. I didn't know how to relax. Ichiro pressed deeply into the base of my spine.

"Ouch," I said.

"Shiatsu good for circulation."

"I'm living outside my comfort zone. Maybe you're right. I'm an illiterate in Japan, and that is a culture shock." I paused to let the truth sink in. "It's humbling to have to ask for help."

"So you don't liking ask people for help?" Ichiro said, as his elbow dug deep into my buttocks. Touch without pleasure. This was my introduction to shiatsu.

"No, I don't like to ask for help. But I accept it. Look, I'm here at the White Crane Clinic today, aren't I?"

Ichiro put a finger across his mustached lip and studied me the way you would eye a beached baby whale. Curiosity mixed with pity.

"Look, I'm afraid of needles," I said, as I pushed away the needle between his fingers.

"Okay, no needles." He said it with such finality that I was stunned. He didn't try to persuade me at all.

"You look disappointing," he said, and he was right.

Disappointing. This way of talking was cute and innocent. He was tall and thin as a rail, and I could just make out through his thick glasses that he had beautiful pale-brown eyes, wide as almonds.

"I thought you would try to sell me on the benefits of acupuncture."

"No needing to rush."

I returned a few days later. This time, Incho Sensei initiated me to acupuncture, needling around my lungs. Thin needles tingled, but it didn't hurt, I told Ichiro, who was translating again. He tugged on his wispy beard, as he searched for the words in English to explain simply the complex Taoist ideas behind the White Crane Clinic's approach, not only to shiatsu, but to the much more comprehensive field of Traditional Oriental Medicine.

According to the Chinese philosopher Lao Tsu, the author of the Taoist classic, *Tao Tse Ching*, all of life could be understood from a direct observation of nature. Many things looked like opposites, male and female, hot and cold, black and white. But they were all really related, and neither had meaning without the other.

"The Taoist symbol represent opposites, yin and yang, that complementing each other and making a whole. Together they making harmony. You coming from America, a *yang* culture. Americans friendly, opinionated, and individualistic. We Japanese, we shy *yin* people, and get along in society because we working in groups.

"You see, we both needing each other!" Ichiro said as he returned my locker key, brushing his hand lightly against mine.

What an interesting man. I was six weeks short of my thirtieth birthday. My younger sister, Talia, had just announced her engagement. My mother had announced hers to Leon, husband number two. And my marriage prospects were dwindling—according to my grandmother.

On my next visit to the White Crane Clinic, again Ichiro brushed his hand lightly in mine when he returned the locker key. This time, I felt a flutter in my heart. No, stop being ridiculous, I told myself. He probably repeated this casual gesture every time he handed a locker key to a patient. Even the clerk at the convenience store brushed my hand when he handed back my change.

I continued going for treatments that were bringing me into balance. I didn't feel as compelled to work nonstop. I started giving myself a break on Friday nights, the eve of Shabbat, by lighting candles. It was a pleasure to speak without the computer buzzing in front of me, and instead sitting down for roast chicken, potatoes, salads, with new friends at the Jewish Community Center in Hiroo.

Visits to the White Crane Clinic became more frequent. This society was as obsessed about work as me, and I noticed that shiatsu was a common refuge for the overworked. Three times a week, as I lay on a narrow bed, with thin needles coming every which way out of my skin, Ichiro challenged me with a thinking so different from anything I'd ever heard before.

"We Taoists training to building our energy with daily meditation, chi-gong, prayer, sometime fasting."

"That sounds like a pretty tough routine," I said.

"What do you training with?" he asked.

"Excuse me?"

"Everyone training at something."

"Okay, I train at writing," I responded cheekily.

Ichiro volleyed right back. "That's your work, no? What about spiritual growth?"

"Writing—there's always room for improvement," I said, for in truth the written words didn't just appear on demand. I had to excavate and sometimes dynamite them out of me. Yet I couldn't not write. Newspaper articles were my keys to a happy, meaningful life.

Ichiro nodded. He seemed to understand.

He said he needed to dig along my spine with a hard, wooden tool in order to release deep, cruddy stuff. Toxins. Stress. Muscle tension. Even undigested food. I felt as if not only my stuffing, but a coat of armor was being released.

He was all ears, and I noticed how quickly he picked up English, a lot more quickly than my Japanese was coming along. I found the language daunting. He asked all sorts of personal questions, which I only realized much later weren't personal at all.

"Are you like sweets?"

"Cakes are what make life worth living."

"I feeling same way exactly. Sugar releasing stress very nicely, but also making blood acidinized."

"Acidic? Do you mean oxidized?"

"Yes, *acidinized*," he answered, as if he hadn't heard me. "An overly acidinized diet causing many problems, like weight gain, diabetes, and cancer."

"What do you eat instead? Prunes?" I quipped.

He laughed. "Okay, I seeing you serious. You making jokes because you wanting your doubts taken away."

"What can I do to make my blood more alkaline?"

"You liking rice?"

"It's okay. But I have no idea how to cook rice properly, so I never make it."

"At the White Crane Clinic, we eating brown rice."

A man with curly hair and a bushy beard appeared in the treatment booth.

"Here's Honda Sensei, my *sempai*, my senior. He brainwashed that only brown rice good for you. He also follower of George Ohsawa, the founder of macrobiotics—a way of life, not just way of eating. Brown rice very important."

"But against Japanese society's way of thinking now. Most people eat white rice—because of Ichiro's grandfather," Honda said.

"What did he do?" I asked.

"My grandfather inventing the rice polish machine. His machine taking off hard part, the hull, and underneath the bran, and making white rice cheap so everyone can enjoy, not just upper classes."

"Yes, and taking the vitamins and minerals with them. The white rice we eat today has no nutritional value," Honda trolled.

"I know Honda Sensei, he liking white rice, too. We spending so much time together at the clinic that even he saying stupid thing, he like a hairy wife to me."

A hairy wife. How poetic.

"My parents' generation, growing up in the war years, time when they only have to eating brown rice."

After the treatment session, I walked a few blocks to Shinjuku, to Kinokuniya Bookstore's top floor, with its haven for books in English. I found what I was looking for, an English copy of George Ohsawa's *Macrobiotics: An Invitation to Health and Happiness*. At home, I curled up under the covers of my futon, opened to the first page, and read: "It seems to me that man's ultimate desire is happiness. I rarely find a person, however, whose life is really happy. Even a happy person rarely can continue to be happy more than a year or two, without having a car accident, a divorce, a separation, heart attack, or cancer. If he is happy for about ten years, he must be kept in a museum because such a person has become extinct in our society."

I closed my eyes and imagined visiting The Metropolitan Museum and meeting this macrobiotic specimen of good health in tie-dyed robes and a tiara in the corner of the Costume Institute. I laughed.

As I read on, Ohsawa borrowed a line from Aristotle that sounded so familiar, and such a famous line from the Jewish sages as well, that I stopped to read it again: "The happy life leaves nothing to be desired."

This too is one of the most accepted of all Jewish principles, if not the foundation of Torah itself: "Who is truly happy? The one who is content with what she has." I paused to ask myself: Was I happy? Was I really happy? Would I have left New York City for Tokyo if I had been that happy?

My parents had recently divorced and were starting over with new partners. I was alone that last April before I left for Japan, heading into Central Park with my tennis racket in one hand and my Walkman in the other. My body was in New York City but the rest of me was already on the far side of the Pacific, as I recited basic Japanese phrases. "*Watashi wa Americajin desu*, I am an American," I said over and over again.

A woman dressed head to toe in black, carrying her sheathed dry cleaning, jolted me back by pointing to my racket. I pulled the headphones out of my ears and repeated the Japanese sentence: "*Dozo, yoroshiku onegai shimasu.* Pleased to meet you." I smiled, and so did she.

"Pleased to meet you, too," she said, and then told me her name was Didi. She asked if I wanted a tennis partner.

"Are you good?" Didi asked.

"I'm okay for a volley," I replied.

"How's your serve?"

"It sucks. How about yours?"

"Never got the hang of it."

Very cool. Our eyes met. We both had outlined our blue eyes in black kohl, all the better to be seen with. I laughed and so did she. We were not strangers.

Didi had well-chiseled Eastern European features, a fully developed nose, and a nice, even smile. Maybe she had spotted the silver Star of David around my neck. I didn't miss her six-point star of gold. She dug into a buttery soft satchel, pulled out a chilled bottle of Perrier, and handed it to me. She asked if I'd mind waiting.

"Got to get the pants back in the closet," Didi explained. I could see through the cellophane that they were calfskin. They must have cost her a fortune.

I waited on a park bench. I pressed the play button and returned to my Japanese lesson. Friends, let alone tennis partners, had been hard to come by in New York City and in a matter of months I would be leaving for Tokyo. Didi had come along, out of the blue, to reach out to me. Who was I to turn her down? But it did occur to me that I may be crazy to sit on a park bench waiting for someone I didn't even know to return when I had so much Japanese ahead of me to learn.

Well, Didi did reappear, as promised, dressed in tennis whites and carrying a lightweight Wilson racket, just like the one I had brought with me. This time, Didi pointed out the coincidence and I laughed. We walked over to the courts to play a few friendly sets, no scorekeeping. We lobbed balls back and forth. Some went over the net. Others flew high over the fence, sending us running into the park to search for them. An hour later, invigorated but spent, we collapsed on a bench to talk.

"Who in their right mind walks up to a complete stranger in Central Park and proposes a game of tennis? You have guts! How did you know I don't bite?" I wiped the sweat from my forehead.

"Intuition," Didi said with astounding confidence. She told me she worked for a big theatre producer. Everyone knew his name. And who did I work for? Fritz Jacobi, the public relations director at Columbia Business School, who was a dear mentor to me. Didi told me she lived in a studio overlooking Central Park. I told her I lived in a Brooklyn Heights studio facing the afternoon light.

"Didi, you have *chutzpah*. I'm trying to make it as a journalist, but the thing I hate most is making cold calls to set up interviews. I'm always afraid someone will say no."

"Do they?" she asked.

"Not really. It's just fear in my imagination, I guess."

"Look, what's the worst that can happen? You just get a no. Speaking of which, what are you doing Friday night? Want to join me for Shabbat dinner at my Rabbi's house?"

It was my turn to decline. "Very funny. That's the last thing I want to do!"

"There is nothing sadder than sitting around a Shabbat table like a lost soul, with nothing to say to a bunch of people who are just as tongue-tied and awkward in forced singles situations," I said, not realizing I would eat my own words years later at one Shabbat table after the other.

Didi raised her groomed eyebrows. She shook her cascading

dark curls. "Well, you poor deprived thing," she said. "Shabbat is mind-blowing. No two Shabbats are ever alike."

Hmm. Didi had taught me another interesting lesson: that the one who says no doesn't necessarily get the last word.

Would I have run away from any realistic chance of meeting a Jewish husband back home if I was happy with my lot? In Tokyo, it was easy to minimize Judaism and ignore it as a prerequisite for marriage. The more demands I put on myself to lead an interesting writer's life, the more I wanted to live outside the zone of the familiar.

AFTER I FINISHED READING George Ohsawa's book, I told Ichiro my honest impression. "I want my creature comforts. Macrobiotics is too austere for me. Just apples, *mikan* tangerines, a handful of raisins, miso soup, and brown rice? No sugar, no meat, no eggs, and no cheese—what's left to eat? Air?"

"Air is very tasty," Ichiro joked. "What if you discovering even more delicious foods than what you giving up?"

"How?" I didn't know how to identify lotus and burdock, the most common root vegetables used in macrobiotic cooking after the humble carrot.

"You just needing a few cooking lessons to learning macrobiotic way of eating," Ichiro said. He took my pulse and asked me to stick out my tongue. He put a thermometer under my armpit.

"Blood circulation not good in your feet," he said as he felt my icy toes. "You know the definition of an enlightened person? Somebody who happy, no matter what the situation. They not bothered by suffering or pain." He swiveled a heat lamp over my feet.

"When are you going to enlighten me?" I joked.

"I can't enlightening you."

Oh, my goodness. He thought I meant it.

"But if you letting me, I showing you how to cooking brown rice."

This grammatically challenged man wanted to teach me how to cook the staple of the war years—brown rice. I fell for it. I love cooking and trying out new recipes, and the prospect of broadening my diet with root vegetables simmered in soy sauce and sake proved irresistible to my calorie-counting mind.

I met Ichiro at Jiyugaoka train station on his rare day off. He told me he worked seven days a week, but it was not as bad as it seemed. "I taking day of rest once every six weeks," he said. "That's crazy," I said. For whom in their right mind is going to use a precious holiday to stand in someone's kitchen? Unless he thinks of me as more than a patient.

We climbed the hill with the shopping split between us and the heavy tiled roof of my beautiful home peeped over the trees. "You finding this house by some magic?" he asked.

"Yes, it was," I smiled, recalling how I'd answered an ad for a second-hand bicycle and ended up taking over the rental lease on the house, too. When opportunities came to me, I didn't hesitate. My mother would have called me reckless and extravagant. But what she didn't know never hurt her.

A row of azalea bushes, groomed into spheres, separated the road from the property. We entered the path leading up to an artful *matsu*, a bent-over pine tree, arching toward the slatted front door. "We're home," I said. Ichiro plucked a ripe *biwa* growing over the door.

"Heaven preparing dessert for us."

I smiled. Ichiro had a way of saying the very things that I'd been thinking. I turned the key and a flush of energy rose within me. It was as if I knew Ichiro from somewhere else, as if we had met before in another life. I had a strong feeling overcome me, followed by these words: *You have things to do together, lessons to complete.* I inhaled the fresh air, scented, fruity and enticing after a summer rain. I didn't know where these thoughts of knowing Ichiro before were coming from. This wasn't rational. If we had gone through many lives together, where was the proof? I had never heard my parents talk about past lives. For them, this life was more than enough. But I had followed my intuition to Tokyo, with its risks and upheavals, and that wasn't exactly rational either.

I turned the key and the wooden doors slid open. We took off our shoes in the *genkan*, the foyer. Ichiro bent down for the guest slippers, and on the rebound he noticed the mezuzah on the door.

"What's this?" he asked.

"Oh, it's a way of marking a Jewish home, protecting the family, making the space sacred. Inside the mezuzah, there's a rolled up, tiny scroll that's been handwritten."

"What it say?"

I wish an answer would have rolled off my tongue as smoothly as his Taoist explanations. But I had no idea. His curiosity came from a genuine desire to know. What a strange thing, that a Taoist would probe me for answers to my Jewish faith that I couldn't deliver but made me want to know.

I showed Ichiro down the hallway to the *zashiki*, the formal guest room cushioned in tatami mat flooring and we strode over to a corridor with glass doors facing the garden. I slid open paper shoji screens to reveal the small lemon tree shaded under the persimmon. Together we watched a red cardinal land on a stone pagoda lantern, then disappear into the branches of the persimmon tree.

"Very beautiful," Ichiro cried, as a pole draped with towels, socks, bras, and panties swayed in the wind. I threw my hands in the air and swooped the laundry off the pole as discreetly as I could.

"You becoming native! Very good!" Ichiro said approvingly over my choice to hang laundry rather than use the dryer. "Shall I showing you proper way to make green tea?" he said, changing the subject deftly. I led him to the kitchen, where Ichiro demonstrated the proper way of pouring hot water over the tea leaves before the kettle reaches the boiling point.

"You're a great teacher—paying attention to the most minute detail. Even the temperature of the tea water!"

Initially, I found it charming and helpful to be told how to do things the way I assumed he had observed his mother doing. He touched me to the core by sharing her secrets.

"Thank you very much," he responded, before offering me his next instructional observation. "A classic house like this one coming from Zen Buddhism."

Ichiro told me this wooden house's spiritual dimensions, something I had not to know about before. He spoke about a journey that started at the front door, moving from stone flooring to wood halls, and finally to bedrooms covered in tatami as if it were an adventure from the public to intimate spaces.

"This is the first time I think in Zen terms of this sweet cottage I'm renting from my landlady."

"Strong to weak, hard to soft, permanent to disposable—a house with its own natural spirit," Ichiro explains. "Traditional houses with gardens like yours rare. They knocking down, land dividing and—"

"I know, I know! Mrs. Shima, my landlady, has heart problems. She could go any day, and then where would I go?"

Returning to New York City was not something I wanted to do soon. I had given up the lease to my cosy but airless Brooklyn Heights studio. My parents had divorced, and our small house in Great Neck had been sold. I felt as if I had been picked up and deposited in Tokyo by an invisible hand that belonged to a power even greater than *Conde Nast Traveler* magazine—dare I say God? For what purpose, or for how long, I had no idea.

I could have sat all afternoon with Ichiro, watching the

sunshine travel above the trees from the porch, but he had come to teach me. After draining the teapot, we moved back to the kitchen.

"You having a *tawashi?*" he asked.

"A what?"

"A brush to abolishing dirty burdock."

"Abolish slavery! Abolish nuclear weapons! But dirt we simply get rid of!"

His English was like an aphrodisiac that made me peal with laughter, fragrant with innocence. His cooking, too, was seductive. I watched Ichiro cut the burdock roots into matchsticks and simmer them in a frying pan with fine cut carrot. While the brown and orange vegetables softened and merged, he garnished the miso soup with thin green spring onions and white bamboo sprouts. Then Ichiro ladled perfectly steamed and tender, almost nutty, brown rice into bowls. To all appearances, this man was a masterful chef.

"If this is macrobiotics, I'm a convert," I said, as I put down my chopsticks after the final bite.

Ichiro put down his chopsticks, too, and stretched his long legs on the tatami. "*Ii nee.* You living like a queen here, don't you?"

"A queen without a king," I sighed.

His eyes fixed on the goldfish, darting and flashing in a small pond outdoors. He popped a cigarette into his mouth, cupping his hands against a change of wind.

❀

Chapter Three

THE COURTSHIP

And the sun is like a groom
departing his bridal chamber,
happy as a warrior to run on course.
—Psalm 19

A t my next visit to the White Crane Clinic, I discovered that Ichiro's nickname was the Prince. With a name like that, I wondered what could be his family background. He sure exuded confidence. When he was in the treatment room, there was a happy buzz that was hard to pinpoint. I only discovered on the day he was absent that this human commotion originated from Ichiro himself. His guffaws were greater, his voice louder, and his speech was faster than the other therapists. On the day he was absent, Enya played over the speakers, and a soundtrack that normally lifted me up actually got on my nerves without Ichiro's laughter in the foreground. That very night, Ichiro called me to apologize.

"I sorry I not able treating you today. My grandmother passing away."

I hardly knew what to say. Therapists don't usually call their patients at home to apologize for cancelling an appointment. "It sounds serious. Is she in the hospital?"

"No, she passing away. She having a stroke because of high blood pressure and doesn't listening to her doctor warning about salty diet."

I got it. Ichiro was referring to the past. "I'm so sorry."

"I like to inviting you to the funeral," he blurted out.

Hmm, a date with a coffin. That would be something. I was tempted to say yes, but I hadn't even met his parents. "I'm sorry, but I can't," I said. The funeral coincided with big transitions. I had just quit my job on the international desk at *The Japan Times*. I was about to be starting an intensive course in Japanese in the mornings and editing for a translation house in the afternoons.

"You're a journalist. Japanese funeral quite interesting," he said. "We believing that Amida—another name for Buddha—coming with his attendants to greet dying person and escort him at death."

"Escort him where?" This was becoming interesting.

"We reborning in a place called the Pure Land in the West, where we listening to the teachings of Amida in order to become Buddhas."

Reincarnation. That I could handle. I explained to Ichiro that Jews too had their own Amida, and it was a standing prayer.

This was odd. I wondered if there was a connection between 3,500-year-old Judaism and the Amida Buddhism, originating near Kyoto 800 years ago.

"Amida, meaning 'upright,' is the most sacred of Jewish prayers, when you pour out your heart and ask God for anything you need—forgiveness, healing, and peace."

"You have lots to teaching me. I never meet another Jew except for Lalenya," Ichiro said.

Ichiro's openness to Judaism was surprising and led me to proposing that we go to a Shabbat lunch at the Jewish Community Center. The Shabbat after his grandmother's cremation, we took seats overlooking the Community Center swimming pool, which was empty of swimmers because, as I explained to Ichiro, Jews don't swim on the Sabbath. I visualized the next date poolside: strip down, apply sunblock, and dive in.

"Why don't you swimming on the Sabbath?" Ichiro asked, while we gazed down at a rectangular turquoise pool surrounded by empty chaise lounges.

"It's not just swimming. It's study, work, sports, TV, movies, you name it."

"*Taihen.*"

"Yes, it's difficult! That's why I don't do it!" I laughed, never imagining that one day I would fall in love with Shabbat precisely because there were no work demands and especially no screens to check.

Following tradition, we found empty seats together and after a blessing over the wine, we got up to join a line for washing hands. We chatted as we returned to our seats, oblivious to a few glares. Someone shushed us. So we shut up until the Rabbi blessed the challah. Afterward, he passed around thick slices of moist, honey-tinted bread, tempting as cake, and we were free to speak again.

"Should I?"

I was following Ichiro's recommendations for a macrobiotic diet and therefore in a quandary about whether to go ahead and enjoy the challah. George Ohsawa railed against refined white sugar and white flour and discouraged eggs. I used to love challah. But sitting by Ichiro, not only my shiatsu therapist, but my macrobiotic counselor, I hesitated. "Come on," Ichiro said. "Becoming too rigid about diet, not healthy either."

He had a point. I tried biting into the sweet challah, but I couldn't go further. I had been feeling more energetic without the refined flours and sugars. Ichiro didn't see any apparent contradiction here between being a macrobiotic follower at the White Crane Clinic and a challah-eater in a Jewish setting. This flexibility worked for him, and I admired him for that. He ate slice after slice of challah. He then doled neat little hills of egg salad, potato, and tuna salads onto his plate until the roast chicken arrived.

"This is the Shabbat? I loving rest on *Oshogatsu*, Japanese New Year. How often are you do Shabbat?"

"Every Friday night from sundown until Saturday night sundown."

He looked surprised. "Every week Jew doing this? That's amazing. But why?"

"Do you want the long reason or the short?" I replied.

Eynat, a university professor with glasses and a birdlike trill in her voice, helped me out. Pointing at the pinhole lights, or perhaps the heavens above the ceiling, she explained to Ichiro that since God created the world in six days, and rested on the seventh, the Jewish people followed God's lead and observed a day of rest, too.

I turned to Ichiro and nodded in recognition. "Eynat is a scholar, an expert on Jewish history, culture, and law. She probably knows more about my own religion than I do."

"You bringing me here today, so this important to you. Being Jew not just brain knowledge. It something you carrying in your heart, no?"

I admitted my mixed feelings. "You either accept your family's values, or you rebel against them."

"You thinking like a rebel?"

My grandmother's harsh letter came to mind. "Not really, but some members of my family have made me out to be so."

His next admission caught me off-guard. "I rebelling, too."

He told me that his parents wanted him to follow his father's and his grandfather's footsteps, and become an engineer so that he could someday take over the family rice polishing company. He got accepted into engineering college and went.

"But once I getting there, I more interesting read Dostoyevsky than study mechanical engineering. After two years, I quitting."

"Just like that? You quit college?" I was stunned. I couldn't imagine quitting midstream. With money tight in our family, scraping together college tuition had been no joke, and quitting was not an option.

"Well—I didn't attending many classes," he chuckled while stroking a few wisps of sparse beard. "But I reading all the time till I getting idea to travel. I wanting to find the source of Buddhism, so I go to Nepal, Sri Lanka, Bangladesh, and India.

"Death is main reason families go to temple in Japan. But Buddhism not just for funerals. So in India I learning more about Shakyamuni Gautama, founder of Buddhism. He born in foothills of Nepal to a family of royalty and not allowed out of palace grounds because his father, the King, wanting him to see only pleasureful life. When he becoming an adult, he do so anyway, and he shocked when he seeing real life. He seeing an old man, a sick man, a corpse, and a yogi for first time. That made him deciding to leave his family, becoming a wanderer, then he sitting under Bodhi tree for seven weeks, meditating to escape *samsara*, the endless cycle of birth and rebirth. There he became Buddha. He experiencing *satori*, enlightenment."

Enlightenment. Now that's an ambitious life goal.

"A state of eternal peace and equanimity didn't sound so bad —and just think of the teaching credentials!"

"Yes, teaching is noble profession. I finding a Buddhist priest and he teaching me this: 'Only repeating name of the Buddha with all your heart, whether walking or standing, sitting or lying; never cease for a moment. This the practice which results in salvation.'"

Those words sounded so familiar. "Each night before I sleep, I recite the *Shema*, which says the same thing, to love God, with all your heart, with all your soul, and with all your might. 'Teach these commandments thoroughly to your children and speak of them while you sit in your home, while you walk on the way, when you retire and when you arise.'"

"You calling your way Judaism and I call mine Buddhism, the Tao, and of course, all cosmic wisdom coming from the same source. We having this choice to finding God wherever we going, whatever happening, the good and not so good."

So much to process here. I had no idea that prayers found in the thousands of years of Jewish liturgy would show up in the Buddhist practice.

"Did you find a good teacher in your travels?" I asked.

"I finding the best," Ichiro said.

I expected Ichiro to name Sai Baba, Osho, Iyengar, an Indian guru or yogi of such renown that even I knew the name.

"I having two gurus, Hepatitis and Malaria," he said, with lips tightening. "I getting very sick in India, so I go back to Japan early. I lying in bed at my parents' house. My parents taking me to Tokyo University Hospital, but even the doctors can't finding cure. Finally, my parents meeting an acupuncturist, and he telling me to eat two small macrobiotic meals every day and run ten kilometers. I getting cured, even though it not easy to eating and running in that condition. I trying my best. That's how I coming to be interesting in Eastern Medicine. I wanting to understand the consciousness that brings healing."

"Wow, your parents love you so much to have searched the way they did. That was some ordeal to go through," I said, as I looked into his healthy eyes and couldn't imagine him sick.

"Yes, my mother and father great parents. I took you to meeting them if you like."

I was so preoccupied with decoding our conversation that I didn't realize other conversations were going on around us.

"Jews never say rules!" Neal was a Tokyo University doctoral student in ichthyology and wore a kippah adorned with goldfish. Besides knowing a lot about goldfish, Neal knew a lot about Torah law, too.

"Rules, commandments, what's the difference?" Someone across the table gestured as he waved a slab of salmon from the tip of his fork.

"They're *mitzvot*—good deeds. Kindnesses. Each time we practice a mitzvah, we strengthen our bond to *Hashem*, our God. A mitzvah is about common decency and self-respect, you know, the Golden Rule: Do not do unto others as you wouldn't want them to do unto you."

"Quite right. I know it in my brain. But I've never felt it here," I said, pointing to my heart. I turned to Ichiro and put down my napkin. "I'm clueless how to even begin. Torah has so many rules—613 commandments."

A burst of song cut off our conversation. This was the *Birchat Hamazon*, the blessings after the meal. I didn't know the words to catchy melodies that went on and on, page after page. Everyone else at the table seemed to know the tunes, could read the words in Hebrew, and participation seemed like rollicking fun if you could sing along. But I couldn't, and so Ichiro and I just sat there, discovering something else we had in common.

When the singing was over, Neal offered Ichiro a sweeping summary of what it means to be Jewish. "Each week, we read a different *parsha,* a chapter from the Torah, the Five Books of Moses. Torah tells the stories of the founding of the Jewish family through Abraham, Isaac, and Jacob. Our forefathers go through superhuman trials that pit brother against brother, wives against each other, and wander as strangers in foreign lands. We learn how different their destinies will turn out when they hear the voice of God, put their trust in Him, and follow His commandments. These are more than stories though. They're spiritual lessons in how to find happiness in any tough and seemingly impossible situation, and, to fear God."

"You meaning to humble yourself before God?" Ichiro asked.

"Yes, exactly," said Neal. "It's not enough to put our absolute faith in the soul of all souls, the creator of all living things, we have to love God no matter what."

"Easier said than done," I interjected.

"It easy!" Ichiro said. "All you needing is a master! At the White Crane Clinic, my master calling this way of learning the Tao—first you doing, then you asking why. Eventually understanding coming through abdomen knowledge."

"Yup, feel it in your gut. Then follow and then you'll understand!" Neal exclaimed. "Torah says the same!"

Judaism's precepts were no stranger to Ichiro. That was eye-opening. And for me, to hear words of Eastern philosophy that resonated in Jewish thinking was a surprise as well. There is so much to read in Torah, to study, to apply in daily life, that observant Jews spend their entire lives learning the Five Books, chapter by chapter, in an orderly, week-to-week progression throughout the year.

"On a scale of one to ten, where you on Torah journey?" Ichiro asked, assuming, that I knew more than I did. I had never even considered such a question before, so I paused. I drummed my fingers on the white tablecloth. "I'm not observant. I don't go to synagogue each week. I don't read Torah each week, not by a long shot. But all right. I don't want to give myself a one out of ten. I was born to Jewish parents. After elementary school, my mother drove me twice a week and on Sundays to Hebrew school at Forest Hills Jewish Center. I had a bat mitzvah in Great Neck at Temple Israel. Okay? I'll give myself a three."

Ichiro burst out laughing through crooked teeth. "A three?"

"I'm just being truthful," I protested. "I don't recall a single thing I learned."

"You just not meeting your teacher yet."

Ichiro's way of looking at life was mind-blowing to me. In one conversation he could completely reframe my childhood memories of suffering through Jewish education and help me realize that faith was important to me. While dessert was served, I continued to reflect on Ichiro's way of thinking while he spoke animatedly to Neal, the man with the fish on his kippah. Was it that simple? Did I only need to meet the right teacher for my wall against Jewish learning to come down?

"I wasn't against any religion, but I seeing value in listening to my master. It good training put my own desires second, and follow his way."

"So you're never tempted to go against Incho?"

"Of course! All the time! I challenging him every day!" Ichiro said as he bit into a cube of cake. "I tempted to running away, but when you're on a spiritual path you can't anymore."

"Why not?"

"Because I wanting to learn how to be humble."

"Is that what Taoist's believe? To be humble? I think Lalenya had a word for it. Weak. Being like a sheep."

"Oh, no! When you seeing everything that happening in life for learning, you never needing to get upset. So instead of being unhappy, just accepting that you creating every situation for your own growth, that's being humble. And we have a word for the opposite."

"Which is?"

I noticed that our table companions had moved on. A couple were talking about where to find an apartment within walking distance of the synagogue, naming a rental fee that made Ichiro choke on his tea. I overheard another couple discuss their next scuba diving trip off the beaches of Phuket. I listened, but there was no way to access these conversations. A platter heaped with watermelon and grapes arrived, and it was time to pass the fruit salad.

Over the weeks, I became interested in learning to meditate. Ichiro told me that Zen meditation practiced diligently could lead to enlightenment. So why not try?

From the tile-roofed hall of Tokeiin Temple in Shizuoka, I wrote an article about my first authentic Zen experience, an introductory seminar. The clack of wooden blocks meant it was dinnertime. Swatting mosquitos could only be visualized and not acted upon. In order to understand Ichiro better, I wanted to understand Buddhism's spiritual strength—peaceful meditation. When our teacher, Nishijima Sensei, unwrapped three little bowls, I copied him. When he set them out in descending size order on a raggedy *daibukin* cloth, I copied him again. Two servers silently doled out a macrobiotic and strikingly kosher meal of golden miso soup afloat with bean sprouts, a side of salty yellow pickles made from radishes, and a bowl of honest to goodness, steamed brown rice.

Zen translates as "just sitting." I assumed I knew all about sitting. From a young age, I had to join my family sitting in the synagogue—and only sit. My eyes glazed over at the Hebrew text, and the English translation didn't move me any closer to communion with God. Perhaps Zen would bring me closer to Ichiro's soul of all souls.

I sat alone with my thoughts on a brown velvet cushion with a white stucco wall in front of me. Between the shoji screen's orderly squares of rice paper, noisy cicadas clung to light and dark green leaves. I straightened my back, fixed my tongue to the roof of my mouth, and waited. When I had taken as much as I could bear, I raised my hand to catch the priest's attention. "Excuse me! Aren't there some sort of rules I should be following? Nothing is happening."

The priest offered a patient smile, no doubt cultivated over years of hearing the same question. His hand disappeared into a crease in his brown robes. "If you practice day by day, then you'll come to understand you've made some kind of tower out of your accumulated efforts. This is the Buddhist way."

It's here that I discover that I can't construct a Buddhist tower to God. But a weekend at a Zen temple does nudge me toward the realization that my own spiritual tower to God could be through the Torah. If only I had a teacher to learn from. If only I could find my own guide. How nice it would be, to meet a Rabbi, or better yet, a Rebbetzin, the wife of a Rabbi, who could help me find my own spiritual direction.

❀

Chapter Four

IN-LAWS AND TEACHERS

For you, O God,
have heard my vows,
You have granted the heritage
of those who fear your Name.
—Psalm 61

My English born and raised mother, Adrianne, with her clipped London accent, got engaged six weeks after meeting Carol, a Romanian of Ashkenazi and Sephardic descent who rolled his r's. Carol was from a small town with 14,000 Jews on the Danube River in Romania. Here, Eastern Europe's flat wheat-growing plains stretched for miles, and synagogues were clustered in Braila's grand town center built by the wealthy Ottoman Turks.

My parents met at a Hanukkah party in Montreal in 1958, where my mother recalled: "Coming as I did from a very gentile and genteel part of London, I was astonished and delighted at the abundant evidence of a vibrant Jewish community in Montreal. I rejoiced in the myriad kosher butchers, the Jewish delis, the Judaica shops, the numerous synagogues and varied Jewish centers. Away from the harsh and critical atmosphere of my home in London, I felt like a bird let out of a cage. At last I was free to breathe. I was truly my own person and in charge of my own life. I knew that no matter what was in store for me on this huge new continent, the potential was vast and exciting and I was GOING to make a go of it."

Reading between the lines now, I understand what "making a go" meant to my mother. Coming from a not especially obser-vant background, Canada represented to her a chance to live proudly as a Jew—an act of pride that I found hard to relate to until I got to Japan. Then it crystalized for me: growing up in New York City, the second largest Jewish population in the world, I just couldn't appreciate what it must have been like for my mother to grow up in a city where you are the micro-minority—that is until I moved to Tokyo.

"Friends of mine in London had urged me to contact a friend of theirs, who lived in Montreal. Not having anything much to do with my time, I soon gave him a ring. I loved his American-sounding accent! But we were never destined to meet. He told me he was engaged to be married. However, he had a friend called Peter. Could he give Peter my number? He could and he did and a few days later an equally charismatic sounding guy called me up. He had been invited to a Hanukkah party at the weekend and would I like to come? He explained that he would have a pretty, young French girl on his other arm! A bit perplexed by this sudden turn of events, I turned to my friend Helen, who had enticed me to join her in this adventure to Canada, and, in a stage whisper, urged me to go.

"We drove to somebody's apartment in another part of town. There were young Jews from all over, I remember: America, France, Poland, and Romania. I took off my coat and stepped into the living room, absolutely packed with people. One of the first I laid eyes on was your father. There he was on the sofa, squeezed in by two extremely stout young women, with an expression on his face of a trapped puppy dog. He was studying to be an engineer. More importantly to me, he was extremely good looking, with a wonderful Charles Boyer-ish way of speech." Since they were both Jewish, there was nothing but unfettered joy and celebration on both sides of the Atlantic when my parents announced their engagement on February 4th, my mother's birthday. At least that's how the story was told. Sadly, famous actor Charles Boyer met his doom playing an ill-fated game of Russian Roulette not long after.

My parents had been raised in secular homes at opposite ends of Europe, roughly equidistant from Nazi Germany. They had both grown up in families physically unscathed in the war years, but had internalized the dire lesson of survival passed down by their parents: blend in, call yourself and your children by gentile names, change your last name so it doesn't sound too obviously Jewish, get well-educated, and cleave to the newspaper rather than the Torah. But for heaven's sake, marry a Jew! As I look back now, I see that despite my parents not having much in the way of Torah learning, neither one of them would ever consider marriage to a non-Jew—the way I did. For my parents, marriage was the red line. The chuppah set the boundaries.

My openness to a relationship with a man whose face looked more like the Buddha's than Moses's happened fast, in a matter of weeks. Ichiro massaged my sore shoulders with confident fingers and a hearty laugh. Love may mean the same thing in both our languages, but marriage? It never occurred to me to ask him for a definition or provide him with one of my own.

It was *Tanabata*, July 7th, a day with a special meaning in the Japanese calendar. Tanabata celebrates two celestial lovers who reunite on this day of the year. Princess Orihime, who was a weaver of fine cloth, and Hikoboshi, a heavenly cowherd, were permitted by Orihime's father Tenmei, the Sky King, to meet Hikoboshi on the seventh day of the seventh month, if she worked hard to finish her weaving. The myth wasn't lost on me. Ichiro and I had met by the front doors of a Shinjuku station department store under Tanabata streamers on a hot evening when somehow he had gotten permission from his Sky King to leave the clinic early enough to invite me for dinner at his favorite Indian restaurant.

We ate *sag panir,* with spinach and cauliflower-potato curries, from small metal bowls in a mall festooned for Tanabata, with colorful strips of paper hung from wires suspended overhead. The streamers were optical illusions, pillars of paper that looked solid but flew apart at the slightest breeze. The strands brushed my hair as they groomed the air. Later that night, I found myself sitting in Ichiro's cozy room. A giant neon Sanyo sign beamed in from the night sky above his balcony. Ichiro offered me a seat on a *zabuton,* a well-padded cushion, the lone object on his tatami floor. He set two blue-white teacups on a small tray before us. He poured me green tea at just the right temperature.

Ichiro clinked my cup and said: *"Kampai."*

I returned the good wishes in Hebrew. *"L'chaim.* To life."

To all appearances, Ichiro lived austerely. The only piece of furniture was a beaten-up school desk that shouldered a book-shelf with European classics such as Herman Hesse, Jean-Paul Sartre, Fyodor Dostoevsky, Virginia Woolf, and Oscar Wilde. His books in translation were nearly identical to my college required reading lists, and this was somehow reassuring. If we didn't share the same cultural background, at least our paths had converged in literature.

"Is this always the way you live?"

He rested his bearded chin in his hand to consider how to answer this. He mentioned a former girlfriend, someone his parents had refused to meet, and how weeks earlier he had ended it and moved back home. That was the first and the last I'd ever hear about Rikako.

"She was much older than me, divorced with kids."

"Well, this time, you've met a gaijin. I'm a foreigner in your parents' eyes. You're okay with that—but will they be okay?"

Ichiro set a teacup down and started filling it to the midpoint. "All right, is the cup half-full or half-empty, now?"

"Half-full," I replied, "but what does that have to do with your parents?"

"If you're positive, they'll be positive," he said simply. "The cup half-full meaning that there's hope."

I felt at peace sitting on Ichiro's floor, breathing in the fragrance of six new tatami mats, fresh as newly cut grass. He lived on the fifth floor of his family's apartment building, but this room looked like the kind found much closer to the ground and hidden behind trees, in a traditional inn, a *ryokan*. The walls of Ichiro's room were plastered in putty green stucco. The sliding windows were hidden behind a shoji screen, a grid of wood covered with paper. I brought tea to my lips, closed my eyes to imagine myself in old Tokyo, Edo, with its rickshaws, peddlers, parasols, and near absence of Westerners. Ichiro sat on his heels, his white sashed shirt falling lazily over loose black pants. I had fallen for a man at home with traditions that appealed to my romantic sensibilities and ecological leanings. I saw no excesses here.

"There is much for me to learn from you," I said.

"Is that so?" Ichiro asked. He took off his glasses, and I saw his almond eyes were studying me with intensity. "I'm not usual. You're not usual, either."

"Even before I met you, I felt so at home in Tokyo."

His eyes grew wide.

"I would love to feel settled," I said.

Ichiro took me in his arms on soft tatami and planted a kiss on my lips. Above us, a photograph of a man with a trimmed moustache, dressed up in a black tuxedo, gazed down at us.

"Who's he?" I said abruptly, sitting up as if there were three of us in the room.

"That's my grandfather on the day he knighted by Emperor Hirohito for his engineering inventions," Ichiro explained. "Tomorrow let's meeting him."

The next morning, Ichiro took me to meet grandfather, who was hospitalized. While Ichiro held his grandfather's hand, he spoke in English for my sake. "Grandpa, it's me, Ichiro. I bringing with me someone I wanting you to meet. Her name is Liane-san, and she from New York. And, she Jewish and a journalist, and I'd like to marrying her."

Things were moving fast. We had briefly spoken about marriage in that vague, abstract way you look into a hazy sunrise but can't make out a single detail. I couldn't see the future, but I sensed it intuitively. The future on the horizon with Ichiro held promise. I could feel it, the beckoning hand that had drawn me to Japan was now beckoning me further into marriage.

There was no response. Ichiro's grandfather was skin and bones, resting in a deep sleep in well-ironed pajamas.

"He never talking much. My grandfather liking to sit on his drafting board, working quietly by himself, except for Sunday night when he watching samurai Taiga drama on NHK television. He coming to Tokyo from Shizuoka, with just a *furoshiki* holding his clothes when he thirteen years old." Ichiro lifted one arm, to mime the bundle his grandfather must have been carrying as he turned directly to speak to him again.

"I'm sorry, Ojiisan. I feeding you brown rice in the hospital, but I did it because I wanting you to recover. Maybe I didn't such a good idea for the inventor of the rice polishing machine to eating brown rice. But I wanting did my best for you."

Grandpa was in no condition to respond, especially since

Ichiro was speaking to him in English, a language he didn't speak even when he was conscious. Ichiro guided me to his grandfather's hand, so warm for such a weak man.

"Would you giving me your permission?" For a split second he seemed to come alive. Ichiro's grandfather uttered a *rah* sound so loudly I thought he'd leap out of bed next.

"That yes!" Ichiro said, as he laid his hand over mine and his grandfather's.

Years later, I would learn that *rah* is actually a Hebrew word, which means evil. What if his spirit addressed us in the Hebrew language? I shudder to think. This is how the most important decision of my life was made. Ichiro had asked me to accept is difficult work life and I had said yes. I had asked this Japanese man who knew next to nothing about the Jewish people whether he could accept me and my unfamiliar traditions.

"We have a lot to learn about each other," I said.

"But we can do it! Anything possible when we setting our minds to it!"

I loved Ichiro for his positivity. His passion for spiritual growth was so new to me. I'd never met a man who had so few possessions and so little interest in the material world, yet was happy. I was open to having his enthusiasm rub off on me.

I WANTED my mother to be the first to know what Ichiro's unconscious grandfather now knew, so I called on a Sunday night, which was Sunday morning in New York.

"Who did the proposing?" she wanted to know, as I heard her yawn in the bedroom.

"Mom! What kind of a question is that?"

"An important one," she replied in a groggy voice.

Her opinion mattered. I wanted her to be on board with my decision. If she had been one to give blessings, I'd have asked for that too.

This was the first time my mother heard about Ichiro. I said I would be happy to marry him, and he kind of jumped on the idea of marriage as soon as I brought it up. "But for heaven's sake," my mother said, "what have you got in common with a Japanese man?"

I glanced at the bearded Taoist lolling on the tatami, elbow holding up his chin as he tipped his head in the direction of the phone. "I think he fits me perfectly," I said.

"But what does he see in you, my dear?" I heard exasperation in her voice.

Whew. I paused to count to ten and ignore this question. If she saw me through the prism of her ideals, and I could not match up, then she could sigh in relief that she didn't have to marry me and vice versa. I laughed because sometimes that's the only thing to do when you're angry. This, too, I learned from Ichiro. It didn't come naturally to me. I'm not much of a faker. But why give her the upper hand when I could zap the negativity with ripples of laughter.

"I'm simply asking a normal question," she said.

"Ichiro thinks it's his lucky break to find a woman in Tokyo — Japanese or foreign— interested in the subject he cares about most, which is spiritual growth."

My mother interjected. "Well, you do have your own religion. I hope you're not going to forget that you are Jewish, after all."

"Oh, Mom." I rolled my eyes. "Judaism, Buddhism, the Tao— it's all the same God."

I heard my mother sigh as her tea kettle shrieked. "Look dear. It's your life to do with as you wish. But if I were you, I'd think carefully about making your life with someone from such a different background from yours."

"Mom, I love him. He inspires me to think more deeply about the purpose of life than ever before."

"Love, shmove. You don't just marry the man. You marry into a culture and the traditions of his country."

She was right. My mother could see ahead to potential problems I refused to entertain, because she herself knew firsthand. I wasn't just putting myself in a position to take from his culture. Something was being asked of me, too. I would in some way be giving back. But at what price, I would have no idea until I became a mother myself.

When she realized that no amount of coercion was going to change my mind, she dropped the campaign to dissuade me. I put the phone down, I took a walk around the block, let off some steam, then called my father. Carol was a pragmatic civil engineer and had recently remarried a Romanian physician, Dr. Sidi Tuchfeld. Both marriages, he pointed out, were to Jewish women.

"We Jews marry Jews for a reason," he said.

I told my father that Ichiro was a kind man, from a respectable family. "He has a serious profession—he practices shiatsu." "Maybe he can help your bursitis," I added.

"He's a masseuse?" my father asked, ignoring the other attributes.

"No, Dad, what he does is called shiatsu."

"It's a tragedy," my father said, as if both Ichiro's career and his bursitis were one and the same. He rattled off Deuteronomy 7:3-4, a passage from the Torah I wondered if he had learned by heart in rehearsal for this day.

"'You shall not intermarry with them: you shall not give your daughter to his son, and you shall not take his daughter for your son, for he will cause your child to turn away from me and they will worship the gods of others.'"

My parents had played tennis together on the public courts in Great Neck, driven into Manhattan to see Broadway shows, and had regular date nights at the movies. They invited their Holocaust survivor friends over for Saturday night house parties featuring my favorite cake, sponge topped with peach halves straight from the can. My parents had a great social life, but they weren't happy with each other. I had to take sides or get caught in the crossfire of two strong personalities raised on opposite ends of Europe.

"I'm a child from a broken home."

"We divorced when you were twenty-five—you hadn't lived home for years," he corrected.

"What's the tragedy if I've found a non-Jewish man with whom I feel safe?"

"Your decision is your decision, and I'm not going to tell you who to marry. You'll have the rest of your life to ponder what being Jewish actually means, especially after you have children."

"You really think there's such a great big divide between a Jew and non-Jew?"

According to my father, there was. If only he could have been a fly on the wall to that first Shabbat lunch at the Jewish Community Center and had discovered along with me that Jews and Japanese may have more in common than we ever fathomed.

"Have you heard of the Lost Tribe theory? It's the talk of the dinner table when I go to the Jewish Community Center."

I heard him pour coffee. It had to be Taster's Choice straight out of the jar. He drank a lunatic ten cups a day. There was a long skeptical silence.

"The Japanese people may very well be among the lost tribes of Israel," I said.

He guffawed. "So you're saying he's Jewish? I wouldn't rule it out, but let's stay with the facts. Torah decrees that a child born to a Jewish mother will be Jewish. Your children will be legally Jewish no matter what. I encourage you to give them a full Jewish education."

I broke into a smile and turned away from the phone to flash Ichiro the victory sign. This was so like my Dad—to look into his crystal ball, and see the worst possible outcome, then decide how to fix it before the disaster happened.

Later, Ichiro offered his own prediction. I was going to prove my father wrong. If it meant that much to me, he would support my Jewish identity but not follow it himself. I thought that was kind and generous of him. He showed himself to be the ultimate magnanimous mensch.

Another nagging thought arose. My cousins had married non-Jews. Even my great-aunts on both parents' sides had married non-Jews. And so be it that these marriages had resulted in divorce, in their children marrying non-Jews too, or not marrying at all. Instead of multiplying in numbers, our family had been dividing with each generation. By marrying Ichiro, I was following the family tradition, or so I thought. I couldn't imagine being singled out to continue the Jewish chain. I refused to believe that a post-war American Jew's puny existence had anything do with the destiny of the Jewish people. And from my new nest in Japan, it wasn't as if I was entirely off the Jewish hook. But my task would simply be to pass along the rudiments of Jewish pride that had been handed down by my parents to me.

ICHIRO'S GRANDFATHER passed away quietly in the hospital. This funeral I did attend. The priest chanted sutras interspersed with street addresses and biographical details. Ichiro, being the oldest son, sat next to his father on folding chairs that occupied the length of the porch of the *Honjo*—the main temple. He was surrounded by more uncles, aunts, and cousins than I could count.

From the priest, I learned that the grandfather was of samurai descent. His ancestors were in service to Oyamada, one of the ten war ministers of Takeda Shingen, the shogun who united Japan and then switched the nation's capital from Kyoto to Tokyo. Ichiro's grandfather was born in 1904 in Shizuoka, the priest continued, to a father who died when he was an infant. His mother, who remarried, birthed twelve more children, and then sent her oldest son to Tokyo to pursue a trade after he finished elementary school. Ichiro's grandfather had apprenticed in the house of a draftsman, where he taught himself mechanical engineering, the priest continued.

I found myself among hundreds of men and women dressed in near-identical black suits, standing outside in drizzling rain, waiting to pay their respects. Women were attired in stiff black crepe dresses, topped by rows of pearls. Hundreds of black umbrellas formed a canopy over the garden. A scaly, grey rooftop rose like a pyramid over the main temple. Green topiary shaped into spheres were fresh as mint; the periwinkle blue hydrangea bushes were even more vivid and beautiful in the rain.

Peering beyond the porch, I saw the sliding wooden doors to the temple were flung open to reveal gold leaf decorations trailing down from the ceiling, and underneath was a large, gold statue of Buddha. I asked myself: can you really live with this? As a Jew, can you in your heart of hearts visit a temple that displays a golden idol of Buddha?

I pushed the thought out of my head. The Ten Commandments make it clear that idol worshipping is a no-no. But I didn't have to worship the Buddha. I didn't even have to look at him. My camera, with its telephoto lens, dangled from a strap on my shoulder. It weighed on me as I abandoned all desire to photograph a funeral where I was invited not as a journalist, a tourist, or a gawker. The sensation of holding the old man's frail warm hand in mine was too fresh in my memory.

I joined a long line of people, waited nervously for my turn, not sure exactly what was expected of me when I approached three trays on a table. The tray I stood before was full of ashes of incense—I think. I reached for the powdery incense and brought it above my eyes, as I had seen Ichiro and his family do. I bowed once to the priest, who struck a huge, mournful gong, then I bowed once more, making eye contact with Ichiro and his parents, my mouth in a straight line.

Getting the expression on my face right, not too sad, not too happy, was no easy feat. A pretty, blonde woman with fine Irish features set in a round face was looking me straight in the eye. With the barest hint of a smile, she sent me reassuring vibes. Maybe she was a mirage. The funeral ended with a taxi drive to the crematorium, where the blonde woman actually reappeared. So I wasn't making this up. She introduced herself as the wife of Ichiro's youngest uncle. They lived in California and had flown over for the funeral.

"The secret *is* out of the bag?" I was surprised.

"Hard to keep a secret, in this family." Bonnie smiled. I watched her take her turn in picking up extra-long chopsticks, designed for transferring smoldering human ashes to their final resting place in an urn. A Jewish funeral ends with shovels of dirt onto a casket. I took a deep breath. There ought to be lightning bolts from heaven, warning me to leap onto the next 747 bound for New York, if I was heading in the wrong direction. But if this was the life meant for me, I expected that God would send me a sign.

WHEN THE TIME came to meet Ichiro's parents, they were caught up in the Buddhist version of sitting shiva, the mourning period, which continued for forty-nine days.

To reach his parents' home, we took the staircase. He turned the key in his parents' door and shouted, "*Tadaima,* I'm home!" So now I got it: this was his real home, and that studio of his was just his sleeping quarters. Interesting. I was expecting his parents to live in a Spartan flat like Ichiro's. I assumed his values must have come from his family background. Well, in fact, the opposite was true. The *genkan*, a spacious foyer, was paved with black stones. Recessed pinhole lighting illuminated a built-in cabinet made from a very blond varnished wood decorated with a fine blue-and-white porcelain vase. I felt as if I were entering a museum—and I felt right at home.

I heard slippers padding down a corridor in that same light wood that had similarly been polished to a sheen. Ichiro's parents appeared in the *genkan* to greet us. Elegantly attired in crisp neutral colors, the pair harmonized with their formal surroundings. We bowed to each other respectfully. Nothing touchy-feely, just the lowering of heads and warm smiles on the rebound. I got the impression that I was welcome, and I felt such relief I wanted to hug them. But I didn't, because I didn't want to shock them, or worse, give them the impression I had no manners. They guided me into the *kyakuma*, the formal tatami room reserved for entertaining guests.

I took a seat on a white *zabuton*, sitting *seiza* style, the formal way, with my legs tucked underneath me, which made my back straight. But after a few minutes, my legs cramped. Ichiro said something in Japanese that made his parents laugh. Ichiro's mother told me to sit however I wanted.

An episode of a TV sitcom comedy I watched as a teenager popped into my head. In *Love American Style*, the grown daughter brought home a bear to her parents and introduced him as her new boyfriend. The parents were so appalled, they told their daughter that anyone would be better than this bear. So, on her next visit, she brought home a human, a Hells Angels biker. He had long hair and a scruffy beard. He was pierced and tattooed. He wore black leather from head to toe. But at least he was not a bear.

I wondered whether I was Ichiro's better-than-a-bear new girlfriend. But this fear was allayed as soon as Ichiro began translating.

"We heard from Ichiro that you are interested in Japanese art."

"Yes," I nodded, tickled that they were more interested in what we might have in common than in the differences.

His father pointed to a painting of two young women facing each other in pastel kimono, set in an impressive, gold frame. Ichiro's mother asked what I thought.

"They're looking at each other as if they are mirrors, admiring themselves in each other's beauty."

She smiled. "Yes! That's what I thought when I first saw it. We choose the art together." It was by Ryohei Miwa, a masterpiece by a revered Kyoto painter.

Ichiro's father slapped his knee. "Women see such different things than men do. These *maiko-san* are young geisha waiting for their male clients to appear!"

My future father-in-law wanted me to know that this painting came from Matsuzakaya Department Store, and when he did, my hand went up to my mouth as if I'd just hit some jackpot. Ichiro was the son of a department store art collector. This had to be one more sign from God.

He pointed to a doll displayed in the *tokonoma*, the gleaming wood-floored alcove a step above the tatami flooring where we sat. On display was a doll which bore an uncanny resemblance to Ichiro as he probably looked as an infant. This doll had wide cheekbones, enormous brown eyes, and a reverse Mount Fuji peak pointing down from his forehead. Ichiro's father's personal buyer at Matsuzakaya discovered this doll-like sculpture soon after Ichiro was born. The marvels of having your own personal buyer!

"As the oldest son, the *chonan*, Ichiro has many responsibilities," his mother explained, as the apparent wealth and status of this family quickly sank in against a backdrop of gold leaf sliding doors that ran the length of the room. He will one day take over the management of the family business in rice polishing machines, and he will follow the Buddhist tradition of visiting the cemetery each month to pray for his ancestor's souls. That means he must live in Japan. As Ichiro's wife, this will be your responsibility, too."

My, oh my. Ichiro's mother sure didn't waste any time getting to the job description: a wife to the firstborn had responsibilities, status, and duties. A life forever in Japan. So interesting, I thought, to be a fly on the wall to their way of life. But to actually become one of them? To live in Japan for the rest of my life? Maybe, growing up, I had seen too many movies of the fumbling outsider, who narrates his own neurotic double life. It could be a meaningful rite of passage. But a passage to what, I had no idea.

"Come on, Mom," Ichiro interrupted. "Give Liane getting to know us chance before you telling expectation."

Good for Ichiro to stand up for me.

"We hear that you're Jewish," his mother smiled. "People used to call me the Jew of my village because I was good with money."

My jaw dropped. This was meant as a compliment, no doubt. But I had to correct her. "Some Jewish families, yes, but not mine. My father arrived by boat as a refugee from communist Romania to Haifa, and then on to Montreal, when he was twenty-two and penniless. My grandparents were supposed to join him, but my grandfather had a heart attack during immigration, dying on board a ship off the coast of Ireland. My father had to start working before completing his engineering degree, and he scraped out a salaryman's living all his life."

"*Taihen*, sorry to hear that," Ichiro's parents said in low voices in unison. Then, suddenly changing the subject, his father held up a cloth sack. He asked me to guess what was inside. I had no idea. "It's cash. It's the inheritance tax on Ichiro's grandfather's estate that we have to pay to the government.

That's life! Money comes in. Money goes out. He left us all well provided for."

Ichiro's father's willingness to talk about money surprised me. Growing up on one of the few working-class streets in Great Neck, I always saw money as the lurker of doom. There was never enough of it, and so it seemed that money was the root cause of disagreements between my parents. Children can only speculate, but they gave me the impression that the less money was talked about, the better.

Ichiro's mother had cooked up a storm. She served a tasty dinner of crispy deep-fried tempura, rice, and lots of little salads portioned out in tiny bowls of different shapes. Ichiro whispered something to his mother. His mother said something to Ichiro, then handed me a crisp 10,000 yen note.

I was touched. Ichiro was subsisting on an apprentice's stipend, and it could take months if not years before he moved up the ranks at the White Crane Clinic. He even had his own name for his parents' generosity. He called it cosmic circulation. "I don't borrow from my parents. Money circulates," he said, as he headed toward the kitchen, rolled up his sleeves, and gestured to me to grab a dish towel.

"I think we call it give and take," I said, following his lead and thinking to myself, how lucky I am to be entering this harmonious home.

OUR WEDDING DATE at the Imperial Hotel was decided by my future in-laws. The Imperial Hotel had been built like a fortress by its architect, Frank Lloyd Wright, and survived the Great Earthquake of 1923. But it had been rebuilt and reopened in the mid 1980s, complying with the latest earthquake standards. Ichiro's parents chose the South Peacock Room at the height of cherry blossom season, and a banquet hall with brown brick walls, fluted art deco pillars, and geometric sconces.

"Some of my friends coming to the wedding are macrobiotic," I said to the in-laws one night, as they discussed the proper size, color, and cut of filet mignon to serve to wedding guests. They were agonizing over meat, and I was perturbed that there was beef on the menu at all.

"I see, but our guests expect to eat something gorgeous," Ichiro's mother explained.

I proposed a vegetarian entrée straight from the macrobiotic cookbook. I asked for whole wheat rolls served with the soup, and for soy milk when tea and coffee were served. But going vegetarian, I was told, was like stiffing the guests—who by custom would bring envelopes stuffed with money.

When Ichiro's mother grasped how much my participation in the menu planning meant to me—a nod to the macrobiotic first date that had brought Ichiro and me together—she said with good-natured acceptance, "Okay, we'll do our best."

We raked over every square inch of potential conflict before the wedding. This give and take in the preparations brought me close to both of Ichiro's parents. I felt their respect and if I didn't get my way, I appreciated that I would get a courteous reason why.

The next big hurdle was the guest list. I wanted my married friends to come with their spouses. This, I was gently told, was not the custom.

"Why not? Wedding celebrations in America are always done with couples and families joining in!"

"Not in Japan! The guests bring big money to help pay for the hotel expenses. If another family member comes, they have to prepare double the gift money." I flashed back to my sister Talia's wedding, months earlier in Brooklyn. Not only had the bride and groom danced cheek to cheek, Ichiro and I had celebrated with scores of other couples on the dance floor, too.

There would be no whooping it up. No dancing. No rock band. Instead, there would be speeches. Lots of them. As we sat at his parents' dining table, the guest lists and speech givers were decided: a very long one for his side of the family and a very short one for mine.

The future in-laws may have been surprised by my demands, out of left field, but in a gentle way, they would remind me that marriage to Ichiro required that I make an effort to do as the Japanese do. Ichiro's parents had an impressive capacity to put themselves in my shoes and to see my requests as a foreign newcomer to their family might. I tried to put myself in their shoes, too, by realizing this was their way of honoring me in front of their important friends and family. It never occurred to me that this royal treatment as honorable guest would have a downside. Once an honorable guest, always an honorable guest.

Something was off. But intuition is essentially patient. It whispers, rather than picks up a megaphone. The whispers I could ignore. I was determined to go through with this wedding and prove that it could work out just fine and that we would live happily ever after. My mother was so busy with wedding preparations—the Japan trip of a lifetime she called it— and helping me out from the New York end that the last thing I could do was even hint to her that I had doubts.

My Dear Liane,

I called Kleinfeld's. They had ordered swatches for both shoes and headdress but were about to ship it to your friend Ginny's house in New Jersey! What a mess that would have been! The shoes will be sent to my apartment and I took delivery of your headdress at the office today. Since Talia is flying directly to Tokyo, I shall ask her to bring them both with her.

I was so glad when you told me that you plan to wear contacts on your wedding day. Are you going to have your hair shaped and wear a little makeup (especially your eyes)?

May I also suggest that your crystal necklace from Ichiro, lovely though it is, does not go with your bridal dress. It might be v. nice to wear Grandma's pearls (and how happy she would have been to know of this.) I also think that small pretty earrings of gold or pearl would give a softer effect than nothing on the ears. Maybe you could borrow these from a friend? I thought your hands look wonderful when manicured, by the way. Yes, I know I am sticking my motherly neck out (and yes, you are right that no one else in the world will, since no one else, understandably, gives a hoot, unlike a Mum), but I am sure you want to do yourself justice on your big day.

By hook or by crook, my mother was going to leave a mark on my wedding after all. She was coming from love, saying what she thought was best for me. It was the family way of communicating, harmless if you've grown up with this manner of unbridled speech, but devastating if you're suddenly thrown in the deep end of a pool of non-stop opinions, as Ichiro was about to discover.

I discussed her demands, calling them suggestions to Ichiro's mother, and I got the sense that my future mother-in-law may have been taking notes, too, strengthening her resolve to speak up and let the rest of the family know that she had preferences and sensitivities, too. Ichiro's father had the annoying habit of smoking at the dining room table. A heavy smoker, one day he simply took the elevator to the garage to smoke. And that's where he would light up from that day forward, after Ichiro's mother had set her own boundaries.

My future mother-in-law spoke up about another issue that had been on her mind: sleeping arrangements. Until we were married, she wished that boys sleep with boys and girls with girls. She and I would share many nights sleeping side-by-side on futons that my future mother-in-law laid out in the guest room, while Ichiro slept on the other side of a gilded paper door with his father. In a way, I felt honored. Ichiro's parents brought dignity and their own conditions to our pre-married life. They knew that we were living together on the other side of Tokyo, but in their home, our courtship reverted to old-fashioned mores. And I liked this too. I felt no barriers to loving these in-laws, to participating in their lives because we spoke our minds to each other. I knew where I stood with them, and it wasn't long before I had my own front door key and a pillow stuffed with buckwheat hulls to rest my head.

A month before the wedding, across town in Midorigaoka, my front doorbell rang. It pealed like church bells—quite the self-important chime for an old wooden cottage, as if humor-ously announcing the arrival of a king or a queen. I had very few unexpected visitors, except for Mrs. Shima, my landlady, who didn't bother to ring. She just came in whenever she jolly well pleased to stock my refrigerator with a pot full of chicken curry.

I slid apart the wooden doors. A woman bowed in greet-ing. She was old enough to be my mother. She wore just a hint of makeup, her hair lacquered black, cut and blown styl-ishly short. I bowed back. She looked like so many women in this hilly green neighborhood of Midorigaoka, wearing neutral coordinates that hugged a fit body. I stood there in jeans and a gauze embroidered Indian shirt. The neighbor told me she lived in the house behind ours and that she had heard about me through Mrs. Shima. She had stopped by to invite me over. This was highly unusual for a neighbor to not only reach out in friendship, but with an invitation to enter her home.

A few days later, I walked around the corner, rang the bell, and sat in my neighbor's living room, which she had decorated with wall-to-wall beige carpet, off-white lace curtains, and an L-shaped beige leather sofa, where we sat at opposite ends with the Limoges teapot on the coffee table in front of us. I wondered what I was going to say to my neighbor in my limited Japanese.

"Lovely home. Beige is relaxing," I began, smiling when I

realized that her neutral living room bore an uncanny resemblance to my mother's hush-toned décor back on Long Island.

"Oh, do you like it? Our previous home was a traditional
ikenya, a bungalow with tatami floors and sliding paper doors.
We loved it, but it was so cold in the winter!"

"I know. Exactly! This is how I live now!"

"So," she said, getting to the point of our meeting, "I heard
that you're getting married. I want to wish you my warmest
congratulations."

"*Arigato gozaimashita*, thank you very much," I answered in
my limited Japanese.

"Will it be a Christian wedding or a Shinto wedding?"

I laughed. What to answer? That the Imperial Hotel didn't
do Jewish weddings? The Imperial Hotel offered church and
shrine ceremonies—certainly no synagogue. Then again, it
might not have been a bad idea, a nod to the American businesswoman, Ruth Handler, born of Jewish-Polish parents, who
created the iconic Barbie Doll during an extended stay at the
Imperial Hotel in 1959.

"Shinto," I said.

She shook her head enthusiastically, as if she was actually
thanking me for something.

Which, it turned out, she was.

"What a coincidence! My husband is the Shinto priest at the
Imperial Hotel! The only hotel in Tokyo that offers Shinto
weddings is the Imperial! He does all the weddings with my son
—a priest in training, fifth generation in the family—so surely
they will be honored to do yours."

"Oh my God!" I exclaimed.

This neighbor had casually invited me for tea, where I found
out in the most limited Japanese imaginable that her husband
was going to marry Ichiro and me. Goosebumps rose on my
arms. I had been silently praying for a sign from God to either
go ahead with this wedding or send me the rescue helicopter.

And here, I thought, it indeed was heaven's way of giving me the go-ahead with a Shinto priest whom I shared backyard wall with—even though the wedding was happening clear across town. She had appeared in the nick of time to allay my concerns.

"Would it be an insult if I didn't wear the *tsunokakushi*, the headdress designed to hide a bride's horns of jealousy? It's been a long road to convince the rest of the world that Jews don't have horns. How ironic would it be, if I had to hide my horns in a Shinto wedding?"

She assured me I could do away with the *tsunokakoshi* and matching white kimono. A western-style wedding dress would do.

"Great. I want to do the right thing."

"For starters," she added.

"And then?"

"You'd better change once—it's the custom. So why not put on a kimono?"

"Will there be idols?"

"No, not at all. Shintoism prohibits idols."

Hallelujah. I would later learn that although Shintoism reveres thousands of gods, not one is visible to the naked eye.

I took this, most gratefully, as a divine thumbs-up.

But to cover both bases, I called the Jewish Community Center, spoke to the Rabbi, and felt him out about doing a Jewish wedding for us, too. He wanted to know whether Ichiro was willing to convert to Judaism.

"No," I answered.

"Then I can't marry you," the Rabbi said apologetically.

I put down the phone, miffed, but rules were rules—*mitzvot*, the Rabbi called them. I was still determined, though, so I called my Israeli friend Zohara, a theatre costume designer.

"Shall we go for a Jewish-y wedding?" I asked.

"Why not? It will be the best we can do," Zohara replied.

I called my mother to get her reaction. "What do you think? Is there any point in doing a Jewish ceremony if it's not official?" I asked her.

"It's a nice gesture," she said, adding that she thought my father would be pleased.

"Just a gesture?" I asked as catering bills and rental hall charges danced in my head.

"Ichiro and his parents will understand that the Jewish faith matters to you," she said.

It did matter. I should have been over the moon at the prospect of such a prestigious wedding, French haute cuisine wedding fare, maybe even the friendly ghost of its original architect Frank Lloyd Wright sauntering through the corridors. But I was not completely at peace. Something wasn't right, and I refused to entertain the thought that it was the marriage itself.

❀

Chapter Five

HIS AND HERS WEDDINGS

Give me understanding
and I will keep Your Torah,
and preserve it with my whole heart.
—Psalm 119

Zohara made a fine Rabbi. She stood before Ichiro and me with a prayer book in her hands, wearing flowing wine-colored robes. My father Carol, my stepfather-to-be Leon, Ichiro's father Toshihiko, and Ichiro's younger brother Masahide held up a large bolt of white cloth. I nodded in appreciation to my friend Karen, who had not only flown in from New York for the wedding. She had run all over Tokyo searching for the fabric to make this improvised chuppah.

Zohara read the wedding benedictions in Hebrew. Ichiro and I sipped from the same wineglass. I looked up at the basement ceiling. No bolt of lightning came to strike us down. I couldn't help noticing the look of mourning in my father's eyes as he watched Ichiro slip the gold band onto my finger. My mother modeled to him the stiff upper lip.

My father took a cloth napkin and wrapped it around a glass goblet.

"Even in happy times, we must remember the destruction of the Second Temple in Jerusalem 2,000 years ago," my father began.

"Why he choosing to telling us now?" Ichiro whispered in my ear.

"Because we Jews are still in mourning, waiting for the Messiah to arrive," my father explained. "Then, when he does, with God's help we can rebuild the Holy Temple in Jerusalem. Amen."

I stood next to Ichiro under the beautiful lace veil that Pauline, my mother's older cousin, with whom she shared the mysterious grandfather Avraham, had worn over her hair to her wedding at St. Peter's Church just east of Maidenhead.

Ichiro smashed the glass goblet with his shoe heel. Zohara pronounced us man and wife. My mother smiled at my mother-in-law. My father handed Ichiro's father a drink. My family had met their match in Ichiro's broad-minded and adventurous parents. With the chuppah above us, I visualized that bright sunny horizon.

THE FOLLOWING DAY, Sunday April 7th, we emerged from the subway station, and ran the last hundred meters to the Imperial Hotel with our umbrellas tossing and turning against torrential rains.

"What a day to get married," I muttered as I brushed off raindrops from my warm winter coat.

"Rain bringing good luck to marriage. It meaning wedding will last," Ichiro said. I smiled, grateful for his positivity, as we rushed through the lobby, decked out a fantastic display of *sakura* cherry blossoms. The arrangement was set on a table at the approach to the grand staircase. Branches with pink flowering petals had been packed into a vase to create the optical illusion of a cherry blossom bush, a feat that only a master flower arranger could pull off. As we stood before the cherry blossoms, Ichiro recalled a *kotowaza,* an old Japanese saying. "Marriage like a knot. When it getting wet, it became very hard to untie."

From the pink carnations grown in greenhouses, to the classical string quartet playing Vivaldi, almost everything in our Imperial Hotel tying of the knot had come out of a hotel showroom catalogue. It was a point-and-pay wedding of the highest order, with Ichiro's parents doing most of the pointing and practically all of the paying from the gift money brought by the guests. We were not going to receive any of it. If that didn't send up a red flag, it should have, but I didn't say a word about the financial arrangements to my parents.

"You should be so thrilled," my mother whispered as she adjusted my pearl tiara in the bridal dressing room.

I'm not much of an actress and I think she saw the tears that came to my eyes after I put on the Yumi Katsura designer gown, a confection of Thai silk with puffy long sleeves and a huge bow and train at the derriere. There was no backing out now. All that remained was faith—that I was going with the right gut instinct, a sunny horizon. I clutched my bouquet of trailing white orchids. Ichiro walked alongside me in a black tuxedo as we entered a Shinto shrine somewhere in the bowels of the Imperial Hotel. We came before a cedar altar offering tangerines, and nothing else, because, true to what Ichiro had told me, Shintoism rejects statuary and forbids idol worship as much as Judaism does.

The Shinto priest and his tall son—my neighbors—bowed to us slowly, one in a regal purple robe, the other in wizard-like lime green, topped off by impressive headgear that was soft, black and helmet-like. Ichiro translated what the priest was saying, something about our marriage being a union of our two cultures. I nodded seeing the obvious, that this was my union to *their* culture.

Our families sat opposite each other on facing pews. Parents, sisters, brother, cousins, aunts, and uncles scrutinized our every move as Ichiro and I traded three rounds of sake, which we drank from red lacquer dishes—something that could be described as a hybrid between a cup and a plate. A shrill flute hailed us ceremoniously. My father peered through his thick aviator lenses, adjusted his tuxedo bow tie, his mouth creasing toward his chin. My mother and my sister Talia wore matching black velvet cocktail dresses with princess necklines, slender waists and gathered skirts, which they had coincidentally snapped up on separate shopping trips. I thought to myself, how incredible—this could only happen between a mother and daughter on the same wavelength.

Mom's fiancé, Leon, squinted through his bifocals, and my eighty-year-old Great Aunt Vicky—on my father's side—adjusted the little silver pillbox hat and floor-length Lamé Sheath gown that she had sewn for the occasion. My divorced parents and their spouses had rallied to support me, doing the right thing by wearing black in accordance with Japanese wedding custom, and looking to all appearances like a jolly united front.

We moved to the South Peacock Room for the banquet. Ichiro and I took our seats at the dais, just us and our *nakodo*, the go-betweens. It was still a custom when we married for those who truly or symbolically made the marriage match to be the only ones given the honor of joining the bride and groom on the dais. Go-betweens are typically a happily married older couple. Our go-betweens were middle aged and married, but not to each other. These two were actually meeting for the very first time on the dais because our real go-between, the president of the Columbia University Alumni Association of Japan and my first friend in Tokyo, had been rushed to the hospital with fourth stage cancer. Now how about that to start a wedding off auspiciously, I said to myself. I looked out onto our guests, sitting elegantly attired in dark suits and kimonos. Our wedding guests were mostly men of Ichiro's father's generation. I was reminded of the annual dinners I had worked in New York, while on staff at Columbia Business School. I would greet the future business leaders of America, mostly men, with a smattering of women. The round tables, the fine tableware, the waiters in tuxedoes were all so familiar, it was almost déjà vu except for Vivaldi's Four Seasons playing in the background.

Ichiro's master, Incho Sensei, was the first to speak at the podium. He talked about the Taoist way of life that I would be joining. As it was a rather complex life, Incho spoke and spoke, while the wine goblets remained empty and the plates stone cold. I peered into the faces of Ichiro's aunts and uncles, his cousins, his brother and sister, who listened with eyes closed. Perhaps they were used to these long speeches, but I certainly was not. I became a drowsy fly on the wall, finding it increasingly hard to stay awake for my own wedding.

Ichiro leaned over, whispering in my ear sweet wakeup music. "I couldn't wait to take you in my arms."

A glass clinked on the far side of the room, signaling that it was speech time again. Karen, my dear friend had come from New York. She cleared her throat as she took the podium.

"I have shared laughs and adventures with Liane in New York, London, and Tokyo—all the cities Liane has called home. When I recall those early days we shared in glitzy Manhattan, when nervously starting my first job in the public relations department of the Museum of Broadcasting, I was welcomed by a smart, impish woman with an easy smile, buoyant self-confidence and a quick, take no prisoners sense of humor that put me at ease immediately."

It meant a lot to have my best friend in the world remind me not only of the life I had left but to make the best of myself in this marriage, too. Then Karen pulled out of her purse a wrinkled, old napkin, and my mouth dropped open. "Don't tell me you saved that?" I gasped.

"Sure did," Karen smiled as she began: "I do declare that I, Liane Grunberg, will never, ever marry a Japanese man."

The room burst into laughter.

Liane, you are embarking on an interesting life, a fascinating marriage."

I joined the laughter because I thought, how ludicrous. Why would I have written such a thing? Under the influence of a glass of wine?

My mother appeared at the dais to snap close-ups. She planted a kiss on my *nakodo* Yoko's cheek and whispered in my ear, as if mind-reading what I needed to hear. "Yoko would never have agreed to be here for you if she didn't believe in the chances of this marriage's success."

"Mom, you're right. Yoko is a true friend," I whispered back. "But what does she know about foreign marriages? This is a wild experiment for all of us."

My mother shot me a look of concern. "Strewth. Don't tell me you're having misgivings."

"Mom, if I can't say it to you, who can I tell?"

AN ATTENDANT APPROACHED and escorted me out down the hall and back to the dressing room to change into my kimono. I raised my arms and was speedily transformed by two wardrobe assistants and a makeup artist. They layered me up in a bright red kimono, lavishly embroidered with white cranes, a rare bird considered an auspicious symbol of prosperity and longevity. They darkened my eyebrows and reddened my lips so I barely recognized myself in the mirror.

Ichiro emerged from the groom's dressing room layered up in a *haori,* a hip-length kimono woven in silk and layered over *hakama,* wide, pleated trousers. Together we made a grand return to our guests in the South Peacock Room. I had stood erect like a pillar, while Ichiro bowed deeply upon entering the hall. By the time I realized what was happening, the cameras had already captured that embarrassing moment of missing my queue

Ichiro's friends from as far back as junior high school formed a chorus line. I took my place with Ichiro at the center, swaying in my kimono with arms around men I didn't know and would never see again. Afterwards, we returned to our seats to watch the ice cream be set on fire. Finally, it was time to take our places on the farewell reception line. I bowed, Ichiro bowed, and both his parents and mine formed a line by the doors, where we could exchange a few pleasant words with our guests and thank them for helping us get our marriage off to a good start. I had heard stories about foreign brides being shunned by their Japanese groom's relatives, doomed to marry at City Hall, if at all. This Imperial Hotel wedding sure was a powerful start. But could I sustain their expectations? A friend of Ichiro's father, a politician, paused to chat. "Very nice to know that you are Jewish."

"Really? Thank you so much! How kind of you to notice!"

"Have you read *The Japanese and the Jews*? It's a book by Isaiah Ben-Dasan and a huge bestseller in Japan."

"Oh, I didn't know that."

"Yes," the politician continued. "I read that a Jew never reveals his savings, insurance policies, and other provisions for the future. Ben-Dasan explained that if nobody in the family knows how well-off the member is, it is impossible for anyone to tell secrets that might be damaging. You see, we Japanese and Jews are the same after all!" He laughed so hard I thought his spleen was going to fall out of his tuxedo.

I began perspiring in the stiff, tight obi sash over my kimono. "Come ask me in twenty-five years," I replied—for in truth, the stereotype of the rich, secretive Jew was not one I could relate to. My father had been a civil engineer for Con Ed, the energy company of New York City. He had chosen lifetime employment for the sake of sleeping better at night. My mother had been a grants administrator at the Ford Foundation. And thank God, with two healthy parents still in their fifties, I knew nothing about wills, estates and secrets carried to the grave.

Spending a night in the Honeymoon Suite at the Imperial Hotel was one of the perks included in our wedding package. Through windows facing Hibiya Park's treetops, my mother came in to inspect the view and the king size bed where Ichiro and I would spend the night. When she had finally gone, I couldn't wait to slip off my kimono and let it drop onto the carpet.

"Wait," he said.

He stepped into the bathroom to fill the jacuzzi.

I followed him in, thinking I would brush my teeth first. But the hotel toothbrushes, in fact, all the toiletries, were missing.

"That's funny. The toiletries aren't here. Would you please call the bellhop, sweetie?"

"It's after midnight. We disturbing the hotel staff."

"But that's their job!"

"It's not nice we request staff after midnight," Ichiro said.

"Sorry, but I'm calling," I said, one hand on the room phone.

"Why not we enjoy the paradox?" he said.

"Excuse me?"

"Tonight we living like king and queen of paradox. We staying in gorgeous suite at Imperial Hotel. We having every comfort that we don't even using, like big screen and movies we not watching. I thinking heaven bringing down small discomfort—no toothbrushes preparing us for notice what really matters!"

"Which is?"

"We getting married!"

"I don't want to be the queen of paradox. Paradoxes make me anxious," I said, as I picked up the phone and dialed the Front Desk.

"You Jewish! I Japanese! We having rare chance to becoming masters of paradox," Ichiro continued. I put back on the wedding kimono and, holding it together with one hand, waited for the knock on the door. When the bellhop arrived in cap and uniform with gold buttons, he bowed as he handed me a new set of toiletries. He didn't seem put out at all. Maybe he was grateful that I had broken up a long boring night.

The next morning, I mentioned to my mother the missing toothbrush incident and she turned pink. "Sorry dear, I must confess that I did help myself to a souvenir. Imperial Hotel toiletries will be such a conversation starter back home."

"That's okay, Mom," I said, grinning from ear to ear. "Better you than the bellhop. As Ichiro likes to say, it's just one more of life's lessons to not get upset over the small stuff."

"Darling, remember he's your husband now. Not your teacher."

My mother had a point. But I had married my *sensei*, my teacher, for better or worse.

Chapter Six

ENTERING THEIR HOUSE

All honor awaits the princess
within the palace
greater than golden settings in her raiment.
—Psalm 45

I chiro and I were like the star-crossed *Tanabata* lovers of the Star Festival. Like these lovers who could only meet when their stars crossed one day a year on July 7th, our crossing was restricted to the hours between midnight and breakfast. Ichiro told me that the time apart was good for us, that our relationship would grow because our souls didn't measure time by the clock. Ichiro reminded me of the Tanabata lovers' punishment for abandoning their respective weaving and cow herding missions so soon after they married.

One evening, as I entered the in-laws' dining room alone—Ichiro was working—my father-in-law greeted me with a howl of laughter directed at the chrysanthemums I had bought.

"Chrysanthemums are for the cemetery! You put them in the holders in front of the tombstone! Next time I visit my parents' grave, I'll show you how!"

"Well, that's the last time I shop for flowers at the supermarket," I said after realizing the gift I had brought was a gift for the dead. I had fallen into the trap for foreigners shopping for flowers on a tight budget. That got my mother-in-law laughing, too.

"I see you're interested in flowers. Would you like to learn *ikebana*—flower arranging?" my mother-in-law asked. She placed my chrysanthemums in a cut glass crystal vase, fanned out the yellow, white, red, orange, and purple flowers to study the effect. Then she took the chrysanthemums back out of the vase and cut the stems to varying lengths to create a harmonious arrangement. I appreciated the care she went to, making the best of my innocent gaff. She didn't want to embarrass me, while my father-in-law spoke more directly. He had summed me up accurately as the kind of daughter-in-law who would rather hear the truth in order to learn from mistakes. I appreciated them both.

"Yes, I'd love to learn," I replied.

Ichiro's mother was a longtime student of the Sogetsu style of *ikebana*, famous for its presentations that were more sculptural than floral. She had on permanent display at home a photograph of floppy lotus leaves peeking out of flattened tin cans, created for Sogetsu's annual flower arranging exhibition at Takashimaya department store

Speaking Japanese, until now, had been a major effort, but at my first *ikebana* lesson, all I had to do was parrot whatever my mother-in-law said. When she said: "*Shin, soe, hikae,*" I responded: "Long, medium, and short." I trimmed leaves from a stem to better show off a perfumed lily with hot pink pistil that she told me was called Casablanca. Her botanical knowledge was vast, and I was eager to learn what she knew. She said *kirei*, pretty. I parroted *kirei* back. The volley was pleasing. The flower arranger's vocabulary was pleasant to the ear, and I got the impression that my mother-in-law enjoyed teaching me as much as I enjoyed learning.

She showed me how to use a *kenzan*, an essential flower arranger's tool. It's a prickly cube that catches stems and holds them in place so that flowers can tilt at impossibly beautiful angles. She stood back with ikebana scissors in her hand, nodded, and again said *kirei*—though I wasn't sure if she was admiring my arrangement or her own. So that night, as I brushed my long, brown hair and popped the contact lenses out of my eyes, I asked Ichiro whether it was natural to say, "*Kirei*, this is beautiful," about one's own ikebana creations.

"No, it's not usual, but my mother not shy to saying what's on her mind with you. She never doing that with her friends."

"Why wouldn't she say what's on her mind with her friends?"

"There are social rules."

"So she can feel less constrained in her conversation with me?"

"Exactly. You're foreigner. That's why she feeling so comfortable around you."

It was an honor to be both a foreigner and warmly accepted into the family. Western women don't always luck out this way with their Japanese families, and I wanted to show my appreciation by appearing with a small gift. Ichiro's mother had invited me during the lesson to call her Okaasan, meaning mother, and I readily agreed. Flower arranging became the bridge between us as week by week, I absorbed *ikebana* lessons without feeling as if I were even being taught. Okaasan left me to unfurl whatever I brought wrapped from the florist's freezer and play with the blossoming branches. She gave me complete freedom to design my own patch of garden in a wide, flat vase. Ikebana became a meditation on life, a way of finding my own harmony in the gaps between asymmetrically cut branches and flowers. As my Japanese started to improve, my confidence grew not only to speak about flowers, but to ask Okaasan to tell me more about her firstborn son.

"Ichiro doesn't really talk much about the past," I said one day, as I stood by the kitchen sink, running water over a welt I'd managed to get from holding the ikebana scissors wrong. Using the scissors safely was the hardest thing to learn in ikebana, because I suppose my mind was on other things.

"Ichiro told me he went trekking in Nepal after dropping out of college. I heard that you didn't recognize each other at Narita Airport because he had become so thin—and you had—err—gained some weight. He told me he didn't want to worry you from Calcutta, after he had contracted hepatitis. You must have suffered not knowing where he was, whether he was even alive?"

I was hoping to coax out of Okaasan stories about Ichiro. But she looked past me with a pleasant mask of indifference. "That was long ago. Ichiro didn't know if he really wanted to join his father and grandfather in running the rice polishing factory. Times were changing fast, and it became harder to manufacture in Japan when Taiwan and Korea began giving us competition by making the machines cheaper. We couldn't compete with their cheap labor force."

"But you must have been in shock? Wasn't it expected that the firstborn son would enter and eventually take over the family business?"

Okaasan nodded. "Of course, but you better ask Ichiro these questions." She wouldn't offer a seed to sow in the garden of newlywed curiosity. She left it to me to pull out of her son *his* version of his life story. The problem was, Ichiro didn't like to talk about his past. He preferred to deflect the conversation away from himself.

I had grown up accustomed to dinner being family time. We would watch the Huntley and Brinkley Seven O'Clock News on NBC, with conversation between the commercials. This was downright hard not having shared meals with Ichiro. I wasn't single anymore, but loneliness had followed me into marriage. The dinner table, I imagined, was where he would cross into my world through salads and quiches, lasagnas and pizza that I would make especially for him. But to Ichiro, food was food, just fuel for the greater things in life—to do with spiritual growth. His habit was to come home after eating dinner with the staff at the clinic. Instead of eating by myself. I was grateful when Ichiro's parents invited me over to share a meal with them.

"A husband should be the bread-maker, right?" Ichiro said between a spoonful of custard, a late-night solo treat he brought home from the convenience store.

"I watching my father always giving his salary to my mother. She deciding, too, how much my father keeping in pocket as money. But since you American, we not having to follow our parents' way. We starting life together, so we are freedom!"

"Freedom?" I didn't understand.

He was rarely home before midnight. He couldn't leave work early without getting permission from Incho. He wouldn't ask for a weekend off or a vacation, even though he was on an apprentice's salary, a wage that trainees could barely live on. Freedom was not what I was feeling at all.

"What do you thinking about financially support both of us for a while? I wanting to give my salary back to my boss."

"You what?"

I went to the kitchen to wash my teak chopsticks, a wedding gift packaged as a set of two, but Ichiro's set still remained in the box.

"Your boss, Incho, doesn't need your salary, but I do."

"It looking stupid," Ichiro admitted, as I stared out the window at the drizzling rain.

"Sorry, it's idiotic," I said, biting my lip as I watched the raindrops come faster. I felt a tirade rise in my throat: "I've just been hired by a translation house at nearly double the salary I had been making at *The Japan Times*. I am finally able to save some money, and instead, you're asking me to support you, while you work at the clinic seven days a week?"

"I want to humble myself before you," Ichiro said, as he lit a cigarette. "We're growing if I won't bread-winning."

"You could start with quitting smoking."

"I'll do that—and more, too!" Ichiro opened the glass garden doors to put out his cigarette in the rain. "If I not the breadwinner anymore, I having to listening to you. Come on, let's trying for just one year. If we succeeding here, we can surely achieving lots in our marriage in the future," he said, stuffing his cigarette back into his pack.

I asked Ichiro to give me a few days to think it over. This felt like the biggest financial decision of my life and a test. I called New York to consult with my mother, but she was out of reach, away on a cruise to Alaska with Leon, craning her neck at the Northern Lights. So, I called my father instead. Lately he had been painting scenes of New York City skyscrapers in vivid watercolors, outlining the East River skyline with a black pen and the triangular edges of a coat hanger. He sounded distracted, or maybe he had simply let go of worrying about me.

"What do you think, Dad? Is it strange that Ichiro wants me to be the provider for a year?"

"You're married, now. It's between you and Ichiro. As always, you can count on me for an eighty-dollar check on your birthday."

I was stunned by his bluntness. He wasn't going to bail me out if I needed it. When my mother returned from seeing the

Aurora Borealis, refreshed and euphoric from the "light show of all light shows," she didn't mince her words. "Darling, I hate to tell you this, but you're on the verge of being taken advantage of."

"Mom!" I couldn't believe it was true.

"Why is it okay for him to not contribute to the household?"

Should I tell her what Ichiro had told me? That his parents were going to provide for whatever I needed from now on? Entering Ichiro's family, I wouldn't have to worry about money because of "cosmic circulation," as he called it. In other words, he asked, and his parents gave.

"But what about the wedding? The gift money that went to pay for the hotel bills? You didn't see a single yen of it," she said.

I winced. She was right.

"My mother couldn't contain herself. "I am afraid, my dear child, that you are being very, very naïve."

There is nothing like criticism, or what I perceive as such, to make me run and do the opposite. So, I decided to forge ahead with Ichiro's request and become the breadwinner for a year—and, I suppose, win their respect. Not that I didn't worry about our yearlong experiment. Or that this money could have provided a nest egg in the future if we had wanted to purchase our own home. On the morning I was about to pay Ichiro's share of the rent, as well as my own, he handed me a white envelope.

"Here's a gift from my parents. They not wanting you stress out over money." I looked into the envelope to find Ichiro's portion of the rent, a wad of ten fresh 10,000 yen notes.

"Thank you," I said quietly, wishing this game would end before it began. But over the next twelve months, I paid the rent. Ichiro followed through on his intention, returning his paycheck to his master. He quit smoking. He began taking out the garbage, shopping for groceries, and helping me air the heavy futons under the eaves of the veranda—all in all, making his presence felt around the house. One morning, I heard a strange noise from the garden. Ichiro was beating the futons with my tennis racket.

"What do you think you're doing?" I said, reaching to grab the racket out of his hands.

"I finding in the closet. It looking like you never using your tennis racket."

I thought back to my last game in Central Park with Didi. I missed my tennis partner and I missed the game. We had lost touch, and all that remained of the volleys was this racket.

"Do you even know what a tennis racket is for?"

"Of course! I playing tennis with my mother when I was a teenager."

"Will you play with me now?" I asked.

"Sorry, no time. Lots of people I'm sure playing tennis with you."

"But I want to play with you," I said softly.

A memory surfaced of my parents playing tennis on Great Neck's public courts. I heard my mother's laughter as she tugged at her short white skirt and balls magically dropped out of the deep pockets of my father's white shorts. He whammed them above, or just as frequently, into the net. My parents loved everything about the game, from the tennis wear itself to the friendly competition that comes from two amateurs doing their best to get the ball into each other's court. And over the years, with lessons, I had learned to love playing tennis, too.

I sat on the cool wooden veranda floor and wrapped my arms around my knees. A sparrow flew sympathetically to the nearby birdbath. Ichiro came and joined me, too.

"I'm sorry," he said.

"It's okay. You had no way of knowing what tennis meant to me. Beating the futon with the racket stirred up memories."

"You're in Tokyo, now," he said. "You choosing this life outside your comfort zone."

"I know," I said, "But when do you cross into my world? When will you do something just for the sake of seeing me light up with happiness?"

"Happiness never coming from outside," Ichiro said.

But I disagreed. We volleyed words like tennis balls until the match ended with Ichiro hearing me. He took my hurt to heart and proposed a delayed honeymoon to London to meet my grandparents. We had married in April and arrived in London in June.

My grandparents stood waiting outside the entrance to their block of apartments at the stately Albermarle, where they had lived for nearly forty years. A few years earlier, they had lost everything to a fire and had to start their lives over from scratch, well into their late eighties. I don't remember my grandparents grumbling about their losses. Grandma Betty had managed to salvage a few curled photographs from the wreckage while the flat was gutted and rebuilt, and ever practical and budget minded, she had furnished the redone flat on a shoestring budget.

She wore for the occasion a green wool winter coat trimmed with mink collar and cuffs. My grandfather, struggling with dementia, was propped up by my grandmother's tiny hand while leaning on a cane. My grandmother called for a cab to take us to the center of Wimbledon. Ichiro offered Grandad Dick his arm too. "Well, Ichiro. We see Liane has crossed into your world. Jolly good of you to come visit us and cross into ours."

It was his sweet gesture, an earnest attempt by Ichiro to know my maternal family: assimilated Jews, builders of the Reform synagogue of Wimbledon, and opinionated to a fault.

We got into the taxi for the short trip to Wimbledon Village and dinner at my grandparents' favorite restaurant—which served fish and chips. But seeing the special of the day was Beef Bourguignon, at a very attractive price, my grandmother ordered that instead.

When her meal arrived, she grabbed the waiter's arm.

"What's that on my plate?" she said.

"It's the daily special, Madame. Beef Bourguignon, stew cooked in red wine."

"It doesn't have any bacon in it, does it?"

"No, Madame."

"Well, take it away, please. It's not what I expected. I'm not eating that muck."

Ichiro burst out laughing and I did too at her chutzpah. In Japan, no little old lady was going to say boo about her meal—unless she was airing her displeasure on a big screen in a movie theatre.

"You over 90. You can saying any what you want. Right, Grandma Betty?"

"Come again, I can't understand what you're saying, Ichiro."

My grandfather, silent till now and seemingly content sucking on a lemon rind, snapped out of his dementia. He looked up from his batter-baked fish and chips and said: "The reason you can't understand him, Betty, is because you're bloody deaf."

"Bloody deaf!" he echoed. We roared with laughter. My grandmother grabbed my elbow and whispered in my ear. "Come with." So I got up, and we made our way to the ladies room, where a single fluorescent tube turned our faces blue.

"My word, Liane," my grandmother continued. "Ichiro's English is dreadful. Lordy, I can't understand a word he is saying. What do you do for communication? Sign language?"

She chuckled, but I did not. The way Ichiro spoke presented

communication challenges, but still he managed to string sentences together in ways that made me think.

Back at our hotel, I told Ichiro what my grandmother had said in the ladies' room. "What a nerve she has!"

He just laughed with a toothbrush in his hand. "I never bothering by what your grandmother say. Why should I? I'm marrying you, not her! Anyway, she say her truth. I admiring her for that."

"Really? You think age gives her license to be hurtful? It doesn't bother you? She's forever insulting people with put-downs. I've got a drawer full of her letters to prove it." But Ichiro had his own take. "Maybe she saying truth from her point of view, and she wanting to help you. This is best she can do. What's wrong with that?"

"Because there's a nice way of saying things and a mean way. That's what I respect about you and your family. Your English might not be the greatest in the world, but you never use words as weapons."

"We Japanese never wanting to offend another human being, so we just smiling and saying nice words, even we holding one hand on a dagger," Ichiro said as he slipped under the covers.

"Well, what do you think we should do about it? Should I switch to speaking Japanese?"

"*Itsudemo ii desu yo*. Anytime. I never stopping you."

My grandmother's words hit a raw nerve because there was truth at the core of her harshness. Ichiro and I couldn't communicate fluently. Jokes and their punchlines were often missed between us. Nods of acknowledgment didn't necessarily mean he or I understood what the other was saying. I had to ignore Ichiro's bizarre English or let it drive me crazy. But on the other hand, his words originated from a waterfall of refreshing ideas that often made sense. I was finding out that English wasn't everything in a relationship.

"I wonder whether my grandmother paid for the muck on the plate in the end," I asked Ichiro.

"She paying for our fish and chips. When she not looking, I paying for her muck." Ichiro smiled a true mensch's smile. Under the radar of my own awareness, his generosity spoke volumes.

HOME IN TOKYO, Okaasan was determined to speak to me in *nihongo*, Japanese, coaxing the words out while teaching me Buddhist traditions. She knelt on a cushion to light a stick of sweet cedar incense. She hit a brass bowl strong enough to trigger vibrations in the farthest walls of the apartment, and then the echoes melodically returned, genie-like, into the bowl.

The impulse to correct Ichiro's English came automatically. But I learned to tone it down by following my mother-in-law's example. When I spoke to her in Japanese, she wouldn't correct me, leaving me to think that I was actually speaking her language. Better to speak in broken Japanese, than to not speak at all. I marveled at her approach because it was actually working.

Okaasan handed me a cigarette lighter. "*Dozo*. Go ahead. Your turn. Japanese could be so economical in words. This incense, she explained, was being lit for Ichiro's grandparents.

"Someday, you will be lighting incense for my husband and me," she said, peering at me through rose-tinted glasses. This ritual meant a lot to her. But I was torn. She had welcomed me into this home with kindness and generosity. Was I to show no gratitude, to deny her the measly comfort of following her Buddhist custom? I hesitated before I copied. But I didn't feel great about doing so.

Obon was around the corner, the important Buddhist holiday when ancestors are believed to return to their home for a visit. It's why families tend to stay put from generation to generation in the "bones" house, as Okaasan put it, the place where one was born. Obon was so important to Ichiro that he took the afternoon off from the White Crane Clinic to light incense in the family altar.

"It's not like you worshipping an idol," Ichiro said, as he knelt by the mahogany altar, the *butsudan*, which fit into an alcove in his parents' bedroom. I moved aside so he could light the incense. He kneeled on the tatami floor, bowed his head, and brought his hands together, eyes shut.

"Your turn," he said.

But when I noticed a little golden Buddha statue in the *butsudan*, I couldn't bring myself to copy his way. "I can't do this. Judaism forbids idol worship."

"Not idol worship, just a tiny Buddha. Please understanding that my father and mother opening their hearts in front of this altar. Prayer at the *butsudan* bringing good fortune to our family."

"Jews have their own way—they open the *Siddur*, the Jewish prayer book, and read from King David's psalms. This is where a Jew finds God," I said, though it hurt to admit that I wasn't practicing what I was preaching. My visits to the Jewish Community Center had dwindled to the High Holidays of Rosh Hashanah and Yom Kippur ever since my closest friends had left Japan—Sue for Bali, Guillaume for Singapore, Marshall and Nobuko for Switzerland, and Matt for Canada. To be Jewish in Japan meant many sad goodbyes.

"I don't pray in my own house, so how can I pray in yours?" I asked.

"You can starting do both!" Ichiro said enthusiastically as he crouched to light a stick of incense.

"Not really."

"Why not?"

"Because it's not allowed."

"Your refuse is a temporary condition, part of culture shock of enter my family. Praying in front of Buddha maybe forbidden, but you're clever and so you won't getting caught. This is the secret: you making a grey zone that going undetected by anyone but you. And besides, nobody looking!"

. "God's looking," I said, quietly noting that the black-and-white differences between us were complicated by another factor I had never suspected—Ichiro's grey zone.

Chapter Seven

A DESTROYED GARDEN BRINGS LUCK

You have given to those who fear You
a test by which to be proven,
For the sake of Your truth, Selah.
—Psalm 60

I had grown close to Mrs. Shima through those surprise pots of curry awaiting me in my fridge and her spontaneous appearance in the garden on a ladder, holding a basket to gather persimmons. She gave me a fresh perspective on aging elegantly. She was a widow who left behind no children, and yet Mrs. Shima was one of the happiest people I'd ever met. At 90 years old, she was still climbing ladders, plucking fruit from the trees with her bare hands, and feeding the carp in her pond. I would have loved staying on in her house. But Mrs. Shima's heart failed, and she passed away alone, discovered by her nieces on her tatami mat floor on the other side of the thin wall that separated us. I wish I could have been in the habit of looking in on her daily, stocking her fridge with food too, but I was her young tenant, new to Japan, and thought it was my place to maintain respectful boundaries. With Mrs. Shima gone, I learn the hard lesson that the flip side of maintaining boundaries is regretting. It was time to move.

My mother-in-law took me around to look at dozens of rentals, but we found nothing nearly as romantic or impractical as the drafty house we were about to leave. With her coaxing, I opted for a reinforced concrete apartment with a little garden in the back.

The apartment was a short bicycle ride away from the White Crane Clinic, and that was a perk too. Ichiro could now cycle to work with no need for the train. The house had three small bedrooms to fill. I thought about trying to have a baby. I wanted nothing more than to be a mother. But my hormones were not cooperating, and Ichiro was so against infertility treatments that I dropped the subject. I was still writing for *The Japan Times* and had met many interesting foreigners while interviewing them and knew that they would love to teach what they themselves had come to Japan to learn. Overnight my home became a small learning center, which I called The House Experiment. Teachers offered their skills in Iyengar yoga, photography, drawing, macrobiotic, Indian and Chinese cooking, shiatsu massage, and creative writing classes. Two small rooms, one with a carpet and the other with tatami, would be transformed into a unified space, by simply opening the sliding open paper doors between them.

These rooms faced a little garden anchored by a single birch tree and rimmed in boxy shrubs. We were on the ground floor and had almost no sunlight, except at high noon. The little garden became the one feature of the apartment I could love. I would stand by the window, softening my gaze while admiring the abundance of leaves. Greenery is something you don't take for granted in Tokyo. One day, two men with electric hedge clippers climbed over the hedge I shared with my neighbor. I thought they had come to do a bit of pruning. In split seconds, they reduced the green hedge to stubs. Leaves were littered on the earth. I put my hand up to my mouth in shock and reached for the phone. Ichiro was working on a patient and couldn't take my call. But Okaasan, my rock, picked up the phone. She chose her words carefully after I told her about the garden massacre.

"There's not a single leaf left!" I cried as if it was the end of the world.

"It could have been a mistake," she said. Drama was not my mother-in-law's thing, and I appreciated her for it.

"Take a walk, calm down and then knock on the landlady's door. Ask her to take a look at what the gardeners did. Let her see and be the judge."

Easily fixed? I couldn't imagine how. Yet, I followed her instructions. I walked down to the end of the street and up the highway to Doutour's coffee shop, soothing myself with a cup of Royal Milk Tea. When I returned home, I took the elevator to the top floor, knocked on the landlady's door, and to my surprise she greeted me in English. This bilingual woman accompanied me back to my apartment, and when she swept open the sliding glass doors to take a look at the stripped branches and shrubs, she, too, was at a loss for words. "I'm very sorry," she said. "The gardeners made a ruinous mistake. We will find a propitious solution."

"Oh, my goodness," I told Ichiro later, "Our landlady's close friend, her neighbor, is about to tear down her old house and uproot her garden, and she offered us anything we want. We can take small trees, shrubs, rocks and replant them in our garden. Now, who would ever think of offering their own shrubs from the rolling lawns of Great Neck?"

Ichiro took the next Sunday off from the clinic. We dug into the neighbor's soil and removed young red maple, plum, and two pines. With help from the greenest of thumbs at the White

Crane Clinic, Tamiyo, the acupuncturist, replanted the trees and shrubs. By the end of the day, it was as if the garden we had left behind at Mrs. Shima's house had followed us to our new home. It was as beautiful as the one we had left behind. I felt awe. I felt as if we'd witnessed a miracle.

There was an invisible hand stirring things up. Out of a loss had come an inconceivable gain. I hadn't been much into prayer until now, but I wanted to show my thanks to the only God I knew. I trekked over to the Jewish Community Center to buy mezuzahs for every room. Inside the mezuzah, the small parchment scroll contained the *Shema* prayer, and I learned that these words straight out of the Torah were not just for protection. They were for thanking God, too. Ichiro showed his thanks in his own way. He vowed to undertake a *shugyo*, spiritual training. In the Taoist sense, you put positive intention into whatever you do. Elevate the task through intention—that's *shugyo*, no matter how routine, or even pointless, the task seems to be.

"A garden comforting for the soul," Ichiro explained. "Cleaning toilets even better for the soul because not comforter."

Entering Yotsuya train station just before sunrise, he would clean train station toilets with his master, then return home to flop back into bed for a few more hours, as if toilet *shugyo* had been all a dream.

"But isn't it pointless to clean public train toilets that nobody asked you to clean?" I asked one morning.

"Nobody say toilet clean cause enlightenment, but it right direction," Ichiro replied. "You should trying."

I wouldn't have been caught dead cleaning the toilets at Great Neck train station. Then again, I wouldn't have recognized the "me" I had left behind if I had passed her with a toilet brush hanging out of her backpack on Middleneck Road. In Tokyo, I could be anyone I wanted to be, even a predawn volunteer toilet cleaner.

I decided to join Ichiro and expand a new ring of possibility outside my comfort zone. We headed out the door at 3:30 a.m. in a gust of black wind and a fast-approaching typhoon. A loose garbage pail lid flew by and could have struck me. This was scary. Rain splashed me in the eyes and pounded at my back. My jeans clung to me. This was unpleasant. My sopping wet sneakers bore down on the pedals to keep up with Ichiro's fast pace of cycling. When Yotsuya train station came into view, a lone white Mercedes-Benz idled outside. Incho, a lone figure in a howling storm, exited from the passenger side. He was garbed as always in a *samue*, a short tan kimono jacket over matching tan pantaloons, greeting us with a quick nod and a wave.

Incho could have remained under the covers of a warm futon, but recently a television crew had been filming him everywhere he went. He could have brought along the television camera crew to this toilet-cleaning expedition. The crew had driven out to Incho's home to film his daily *misogi* water meditation rites in his garden, filming him as he poured ice-cold water over his head while reciting sutras and his German shepherd barked her head off. Compared with the bone-chilling rite of *misogi*, cleaning toilets had to be easy—for him.

"Why is he doing this?" I asked Ichiro.

"Incho worried that if he famous, it go into his head."

Incho opened the trunk of his car, reached in to pull out a long-handled mop and a blue bucket full of cleaning supplies—disinfectants, sponges, a mop, and a *tawashi* scrubber, like a true professional. He waved to the driver's seat, where his wife sent him off with a lipsticked smile. At 4:30 a.m. on the button, the train station shutter rolled up. A new day had begun for Japan Railways. We followed Incho in, men to the right, woman to the left.

Through the partition, I heard Incho rustle out of the bucket the cleaning supplies. All I had with me was a measly sponge. I burst into a stall, sponge in hand, ready to take the plunge. I looked into the depths, but there was nothing for me to do! I ran the sponge over a bowl that had been cleaned already. I had worried for nothing! That's when it dawned on me how not pointless was this *shugyo* training. It was as if there were two of me in that stall. One was going through the motions, and the other was taking notes.

I heard laughter coming from the other side of the wall. The two men certainly knew how to laugh. I had nobody on my side of the wall to joke with, and I couldn't help wondering what it would have been like if Incho's wife had joined me. Could wives of Taoists bond naturally over pink bathroom tiles? I wouldn't know. Incho's wife had children and a long drive home to suburbia to contend with. She would return to a house full of young kids waiting for breakfast and needing to be organized before school. That was her *shugyo* training. All I had to do when I got home was go back to sleep with no concern for anyone but myself.

I reached up to flush the toilet and felt a pang of sadness over the real issue here. It wasn't the cleaning toilets that bothered me. It was that I had no diapers to change, no baby handprints on walls, and no cereal bowls in the sink to clean except my own. I had no child waiting for me.

"I think you doing well," Ichiro said as we cycled home in the dawn under clearing skies. A golden globe spread its rays above the office towers of Shinjuku, which rose like kings and queens on a chessboard. "Look at that blue sky, Ichiro!"

If I had been in bed, I would have missed seeing with my own eyes the colors and beauty that follow in a typhoon's wake.

"Thank you for coming with me today," Ichiro said. "I feel that you're supporting me, and I wanting to support you, too." We paused at a traffic light. Ichiro reached across the handlebars and kissed me.

"Thank you," I replied, returning the kiss.

We rounded the corner to our narrow side street of dilapi-

dated wooden houses jockeying for sunlight with taller buildings that hoarded the sun on their balconies. A thought crossed
my mind. I was blessed. I had a roof over my head, and hardships in my life were few. *Shugyo* was rough and masculine, not
to mention potentially dirty. Cycling in a typhoon was dangerous. I didn't really know whether cleaning public toilets were
allowed by Jewish law. I couldn't think of an equivalent word
for *shugyo* in Judaism. But there must have been one.

With each turn of the pedal, I thought about the overwhelming restrictions spelled out in the Torah, the 613 *mitzvot*,
commandments covering every aspect of life. Ichiro had his *Shu
Han Run*. Jews had their *Shulhan Aruch*, spelling out what to do
and what not to in exacting detail. Maybe too exact. Orthodox
women followed a modest dress code—long skirts, covered
elbows—and kept their hair covered after marriage. They puri-
fied themselves monthly in the *mikvah*, a ritual bath, before
resuming sexual relations. Not that I was following most of
these commandments—but it dawned on me, through
this *shugyo* training, that spiritual growth took not just belief,
but daring to ask reasons why.

"I thought it would be good to do a Taoist rite and understand more about you and your ways, but I came back realizing
this isn't for me—and more shocking, I don't have the understanding why Jews do what they do."

"Why you not consulting a rabbi to sort out your
confusion?"

"What? Tell a rabbi what? That there are two voices inside
me vying to be heard? One that loves the crazy adventures with
you and wants to continue. And the other voice that tells me,
not in words, but in here," I say, pointing to my heart, "that I'm
living so far out of my zone, I'm disconnecting from my faith.
Maybe it's to do with our different backgrounds, our different
religions."

Ichiro sighed in thought. "You just need finding the right

rabbi. I didn't know much about your religion, but it sounding like you ready your relationship with God."

"Yes," I nodded. "After crossing over into your world, I'm ready to return to my own."

A visit to a fertility clinic confirmed that my hormones were not in balance. I came home with a prescription for Clomid, a drug that not only increased the chances of having one child but having twins, triplets, or more at one go.

"A high-yield pregnancy! Let's go for it," I said, finding it very hard to fathom that there was a chance to have many when having even one was out of reach.

"No, I not wanting you have many babies like that. We not rabbits."

Ichiro consulted with Sei-san, a doctor from Shanghai who taught chi-qong at the White Crane Clinic. Chi-qong exercises bring the body back into harmony through gentle movements and breathing. That I could appreciate and was ready to follow. But additionally, Ichiro came home with a baby-making strategy, unlike anything I had heard of before.

"Sei-san saying I lose too much *chi* through ejaculation. For baby-making energy, we better stopping sex for a while."

"Abstain from sex? Are you kidding me?"

tried to recall a single woman I knew who got pregnant through abstinence. I went through the Rolodex of memory, flashing back to women who seemed to reproduce by immaculate conception. What popped into mind was a noisy cafeteria with cracked, mint-green walls, full of young Chassidic women from the Satmar sect, who were my age or younger—and we all were close to twenty-three. Parked baby strollers were crammed between small tables. Their Coca-Cola-laced laughter came with one, two, sometimes three hungry little ones. As I sat there alone, chomping on my blintzes, I couldn't help but observe that these women seemed not at all unhappy with their lot.

In Brooklyn, I had been living a bike ride away from the Williamsburg neighborhood. I would cycle along the East River waterfront from my apartment in Brooklyn Heights, passing the derelict factories, and crossing into Williamsburg to take a break from writing up magazine articles. The change of scenery helped me come back with new insights to ruminate over later. These young mothers were on a mission of their own, conceiving one gorgeous, curly-locked baby after another.

They practiced kosher sex, following the purity laws of *niddah*, inscribed in the Torah, which warns against sexual relations during and following the week after menstruation. Sexual prohibition ends with a trip to the *mikvah* for purification, ritual dunking, and prayer in the presence of a *mikva* bathhouse matron. The couple can then resume sex to their heart's content during the peak days of fertility in the menstrual cycle. A good romp in the hay for the next two weeks—or whenever the next period begins—leads to many blessed children. Literally blessed.

To my surprise, Ichiro agreed to build up good baby-making *chi* energy by following the Jewish *niddah* laws. One night, after our sexual moratorium had begun, Ichiro came home late into the night, slid open the *fusuma* paper doors, and swept me into his arms for a hug that startled me out of a deep sleep.

"Changed your mind?" I said groggily.

"Liane, it's serious," Ichiro replied.

I sat up straight and rubbed my eyes. I checked the clock. It was two in the morning.

"I working on a patient with a bad headache. She coming with a migraine. I giving her a small needle in the neck to relieving her pain, but she go home and vomiting. Maybe I hurt her with the acupuncture needles."

Ichiro found out the next day that the patient's symptoms came from a bad case of the flu, not his needles. But it was a warning sign for sure.

"What more do you need? You are overworking and if you don't hurt a patient, maybe you'll just hurt yourself and end up a *karoshi* statistic—dead from overwork."

"I'm not overworking. I'm betting my life."

Betting his life. Ichiro made this relentless life sound so noble.

"Why don't you quit while you're still alive?"

I heard the fridge door open and the sound of beer being poured into a glass. "I never quitting the White Crane Clinic," Ichiro hollered that night from the kitchen. He had recently been promoted to *fuku-incho*, sub-chief, with responsibility for the junior staff's education and their mistakes. One staff member had left a case of oolong tea precariously on the ledge of the clinic balcony. The case had fallen right below into Icho's parked Benz. It wasn't Ichiro who set the case of oolong tea there, but it was he who paid the price, deducting the repair of the hole in the Benz roof from his own salary. Ichiro whacked the fellow on the side of the head, just as he had been roughed up by Incho.

As Ichiro put it, he was living "on the knife's edge." While Ichiro had built up a tolerance for physical punishment—a way of life at the White Crane Clinic, most of the therapists built up resistance to it as a matter of survival. They learned to accept it as a tradeoff for the exceptional treatment skills they developed by training, or they quit. Albeit, spiritually speaking, hitting has for centuries been ingrained in the Zen psyche as tough love. Without a good strong wooden paddle from time to time, Ichiro would tell me, the White Crane staff would be spiritually asleep to this day. Although it bothered me, I continued to go for my weekly treatments from staff members whose gentle and peaceful souls remained intact.

One day I'd be deeply grateful to Incho for training his staff so well that they could alleviate excruciating pains and help us all make healthy lifestyle changes. The next day I would feel like a hypocrite when my married life was less than ideal.

"It's not my tiredness causing by White Crane Clinic. It's my overconfidence," Ichiro sighed one night as he finished a glass of beer and poured himself the next.

My body knew what my heart didn't want to admit, that infertility wasn't a biological problem alone. I was torn by the White Crane Clinic lifestyle that I observed as Ichiro's wife, wrote about in articles for *The Japan Times*, and experienced as a patient. I was in my mid-thirties now and had talked myself into believing this marriage could be my only chance at motherhood.

Okaasan, was aware of these feelings. She worked discreetly to try to set things right. She proposed that I accompany her with Ichiro's father to the family cemetery on Ichiro's grand-mother's death anniversary. And I agreed. Standing between my in-laws, grey marble rising in front of us, my father-in-law buffed his parents' granite tomb with car wax until his parents' gravestone took the first position as the shiniest in its row. My mother-in-law set two bouquets of chrysanthemums in holders while I poured water over them. My father-in-law lit a cluster of cypress incense sticks wafting a pleasing smoke, closed his eyes, and brought his hands together in prayer. His wife followed, and when it was my turn, I kept my eyes closed. Under the gravestone marked with the Buddhist cross's bent arms, a swastika in reverse, grandma's ashes were stored in a funerary urn. I felt damned if I prayed and damned if I didn't. *Oye vey*. Walking back slowly along a gravel path to my father-in-law's car, parked outside the temple gates, my mother-in-law turned to me with serious news. "*Otoosan* received bad news from his doctor. He has throat cancer. He's so stubborn not to quit smoking."

I bit my lips. I couldn't believe what I was hearing. The semblance of a stable life, calm and with security, came from

Ichiro's parents. They were the other two wheels to my marriage, and I couldn't imagine living without my in-laws there to offer a sense of family normalcy, a feeling of forward motion toward having children of our own. I loved these in-laws and wanted so much to give them grandchildren. Ichiro's relationship with his parents was so easy and relaxed that I knew he would make a great father.

MAY of 1995 came and went with headline news that Aum Shinrikyo, a cult of home-grown terrorists, had sprayed sarin gas inside the busiest subway stations in Tokyo at peak morning rush hour, in a killing spree that left many injured and thousands of lives disrupted. Overnight, any spiritual master who professed supernatural powers became—quite rightly—suspect.

Incho had recently offered a young Chinese psychic with unusual powers to heal the sick with her brain waves—kind of the way dolphins work through echolocation—her own treatment room next door to the White Crane Clinic. Yang Sensei came with an unusual pedigree. She had been on call to treat the highest echelons of Communist government and arrived in Tokyo to treat a seriously ill politician, a renowned Diet member who had cancer. At half Incho's age, amongst her abilities was to make wheelchair victims stand up and walk again.

My father-in-law enrolled for a nine-month course of treatment twice a week and signed me up as well. He told me that he wanted to enjoy his remaining years with his grandchildren. Ichiro's brother and sister didn't seem in any hurry to have children, and so the duty—I got the feeling of creating the next generation—fell on me. I accepted his offer gratefully, open to receiving this seemingly effortless shortcut to fertility and conception—if it worked. Effortless—until I recalled a George Ohsawa macrobiotic truism: the bigger the front, the bigger the back. In other words, the easier things look, the harder they are in reality.

On the first day of treatment with Yang Sensei, I entered a room filled with massage tables. I lay down, swathed in soft pink towels. Yang Sensei was dressed in a white lab coat and wore a girlish ponytail. But her no-nonsense voice commanded instant respect. We were to keep our feet rotating in synchronized arches, like windshield wipers.

Yang Sensei went around the room, slapping feet, and when it was my turn, she massaged my stomach like a baker kneading dough. Pleasant sensations lingered after she had moved on to the next patient. I fell into a doze, half-sleeping, half-daydreaming, as light entered me—not as if I were sunbathing on a beach but as if the rays had somehow made me transparent or even invisible. I could see a ring around me, like entering a CT scan machine standing up, except this was noiseless and pleasant. I felt spaciousness as the light in the tunnel scanned me with loving-kindness. Time stopped, and I stayed in this state for I don't know how long. Seconds? Minutes? All I know is that I have never remembered anything as blissful or divine as this in my entire life.

It wasn't as if Moses, garbed in robes and carrying the Ten Commandments, had appeared in the tunnel. The experience had occurred while I was lying on a treatment bed in Tokyo. I had been transported beyond the reality I knew to a place where I could grasp why the spiritual world was more important to Ichiro than the comforts of his immediate surroundings. Finally, I got it… I was quite literally blown away by this realization: if our souls were attached to a Soul of All Souls, a profound source of intelligence and love, then couldn't that mean that every one of us could be a soulmate to each other? Or did this Soul of All Souls act as some sort of mission control, deciding our fates through random meetings, unlikely coincidences, and working through an artist like Lalenya?

Ichiro was not what I imagined a soulmate to be. Perhaps we had come together to learn how to give unconditional love in the hardest of circumstances by being in a relationship with our polar opposite. Neither of us had come prepared with a manual to bridge the extreme differences in our backgrounds, not to mention our own personality quirks. But perhaps there was hope because Ichiro was open to conversation. He sighed with envy later that night, after listening to what I had experienced in the tunnel.

"I searching for enlightenment my entire life, and you getting there first."

It wasn't enlightenment, alas. I wanted to preserve these feelings of love, inner radiance, and deep peace so strong in the moment. I would use it to make a better marriage. I felt as if my ribcage had been torn open; my heart exposed for all to see, and yet I didn't feel undressed—quite the opposite. My ribcage had been literally a cage of restriction, and I felt giddily in love with my life. I was tempted to bring up this mystical experience with my father-in-law. After all, he had paid for this experience and lay on an adjacent bed in the same room. But since he didn't mention anything unusual, neither did I. Over time, alas, those feelings of euphoria began to fade.

When Ichiro was promoted to the White Crane Clinic sub-chief, he had become responsible for training a staff of ten, and his late nights in the treatment room got even later. I returned to the daily struggle to accept that I had to cultivate happiness from within me. I also was being called upon to develop a fair degree of tolerance for Ichiro's newest *shtick*. He was calling himself "the Messiah."

"One of the thirteen main principles of the Jewish faith is to pray for the Messiah to come and bring salvation to the world, and I just can't understand why you have chosen to call yourself the Messiah. It's egotistical. Anyway, you have here in Japan an Emperor, not a Messiah."

"I'm very exciting because lately I treating two difficult patients with cancer and they both recovering now. I never saying Messiah at work, but at home I trying speak your language."

"Because I'm Jewish, you call yourself the Messiah?"

"Right. I know you like to kidding around." He poured himself a drink.

"The Messiah is going to be a descendent of the House of David, so either check your ancestry or start converting."

Ichiro looked at me quizzically. "Converting? I never converting to Jew."

"Being Jewish," I corrected with a wince.

I knew that Jewish conversion can't be cajoled out of a partner. It has to come from within. I just had to accept that this marriage was my fate.

"You need to finding your own spiritual teacher," he continued. "Then you can start take my joke."

Just like that the subject of conversion was dismissed, and I remembered my mother's caveat: "Dear, just remember, you're marrying into his culture, not the other way around."

A NEW PATIENT started coming for regular treatments at the White Crane Clinic. Edythe Frese van Rhoon had read about Incho's water meditation rites that I wrote for *The Japan Times*. When we met in the clinic's waiting room, we took an instant liking to each other. She was a blonde and blue-eyed Nordic beauty, an introvert who I was to find out rarely left her large and stately residence on the bluff in Yokohama. She wore a brilliant turquoise silk blouse, the shade of a resort holiday sea, accessorized in gold jewelry, a queen's ransom, as if she really could, sartorially speaking, be mistaken for an extrovert. Edythe told me she had been born to Dutch parents in Shanghai in the shipbuilding industry. She was raised in Indonesia, Hong Kong, and Japan and referred to herself, jokingly, as "an Asian woman in a Dutch body."

What an interesting woman, I thought. I would never dream of calling myself a Japanese woman in a Jewish body. Japan was softening my edges but could never define me. We sat opposite each other in Babille, a cellar cafe below the White Crane Clinic, where burnished antique oak tables and fine bone china teacups were enhanced by pretty green lamplight. I mentioned my ongoing struggle to get pregnant. Edythe was dead set against motherhood for herself, yet she thought for me to have children was a great thing. I placed my chin in one hand and the other around a hot cup of Earl Grey tea.

"Why don't you want children?" I asked.

"It's because I'd make a terrible mother."

She had done it all in the past, so this time around, she had come here to work on herself. Okay, I had done my homework in the Chinese psychic's treatment room. We were talking about reincarnation.

"Why can't you work on yourself and have children at the same time?"

"Of course you can!" she said. "But I have graduated from having children."

Graduated! Here I thought that motherhood was a privilege and not to be taken for granted. Edythe was attuning me to the subtler meanings of being *wagamama*—which was not selfish in the way I formerly understood selfish—like hoarding cookies. That definition was easy enough to reform. She was talking about being selfish in the sense of putting my needs first for all to see. I wanted a husband home in time for dinner and reap the joys of raising his own children with me. I needed reassurance that someday he would.

Those young Williamsburg mothers crowding together long

ago with their strollers in a noisy restaurant flashed before me. Edythe may have graduated from not wanting children, but I certainly had not.

"How many years has Ichiro been at the White Crane?"

I counted on my fingers slowly. "Nearly ten."

"You don't want him to be at the White Crane Clinic forever, do you?"

Edythe's question bothered me. "It's fine for you to be *wagamama*," she said.

There it was again—the *wagamama* label. "He's bringing home the larger paycheck now. It would be selfish, maybe even financially reckless, to demand that Ichiro quit for my sake," I said.

"Wanting Ichiro to balance his work life with home life is not being selfish. He's perfectly capable of earning a living, whether it's at the White Crane, Black Crane, or any other Crane," Edythe said, humoring me like a younger sister. She took my hand in hers. Her words were from the heart, but her fingers were terribly cold.

After this *tête-à-tête* with Edythe, I walked down the quiet back streets and counted more vending machines on my way back home than children. Where was the next generation? I saw few mothers pushing strollers on a weekday afternoon. College students had taken over the playground equipment in a pocket park as their smoking hangout. Tokyo had morphed into a playground for adults, with every possible game and distraction to soothe the lost inner child: pachinko parlors for petty gambling, video game arcades, all-night comic book cafes, and a sex industry that announced its depraved and imaginative services in graphic newspaper ads.

It's not that children don't have their place in Tokyo. You just need to know where to look. The *Haru Matsuri*, the May street festival in downtown Tokyo, brings children and grandchildren visiting from other parts of Tokyo, below my in-laws' apartment building. A miniature version of a *mikoshi*, a gold portable shrine, was hoisted onto teeny shoulders. I had never seen an object like this, except in illustrations from the Torah—the ark that God had ordered Moses and the Israelites to build to carry the Ten Commandments across the desert. Carried on poles, the ark never touched the ground. The strange thing was that this *mikoshi* bore an uncanny resemblance to that ark.

Ichiro took the day off to attend the *Haru Matsui*. He wouldn't miss this street festival for the world. He wore a short brown kimono, a *happi* coat, the kanji character for *matsuri*, festival, emblazoned on the fabric. I wore a *yukata*, a cotton kimono designed with forest-green leaves and pink peonies. It had been a beautiful gift from Ichiro's master to welcome me into the community, where I could look as if I belonged.

Okaasan stood under an open tent wearing a crisp, white apron over her sweater and slacks. She handed out free *onigiri*, rice balls with pickled red plums hidden inside. Other women from the neighborhood handed out grilled corn on paper plates to the revelers. I was in a quandary. I wasn't sure where to position myself. I could join the other women under the white tent, stand behind the drinks table, and hand out chilled bottles of tea and snacks straight off the grill. Or I could join Ichiro and be the only woman—in a *yukata* no less—imitating light-footed prance, shouting an exuberant *washoi* as the golden *mikoshi* bounced on our shoulders. I chose the dance. The *mikoshi* rose and fell, like an elevator without a shaft.

"What are we doing this for?" I asked Ichiro.

"We shake the *mikoshi* to awaken God."

I thought this was some sort of spring harvest rite. Awakening God? Or awakening ourselves? In downtown Tokyo, I was doing a dance that hinted at Israelite origins in the Sinai desert. I felt stirrings of my Jewishness alongside these shiny, shimmering golden portable shrines. When the *mikoshi* came to a rest in front of the garage to my in-laws' building, another thought hit me.

"The Israelites carried the Ten Commandments across the Sinai desert, but the Japanese are actually carrying the ark on poles right now in this day and age," I told Ichiro when it was all over.

"You think there's a Jewish connection? You think we carrying Ten Commandments inside? It's just a vehicle for transport God around the neighborhood. You having a good imagination," Ichiro chuckled, pausing to massage the tip of his nose. "I'm not saying there not a connection between the Japanese and the Jewish. Like we ancestors, there might be."

Soon after the festival, Okaasan and her *Fujinkai*, the local women's group who had organized the *Haru Matsuri*, all made the joint decision to learn English. I was chosen to be their teacher. These were the same ladies in white aprons who had handed me cold tea and hot grilled corn. Okaasan told me that they were curious to know about me. To them, I was the blue-eyed daughter-in-law who they noticed barreling through the neighborhood on a *mama-charin* bicycle, just as they did. They had noticed groceries spilling over the front basket of my *charin*, just like theirs.

We gathered for an English lesson at the black-lacquer table in Okaasan's *kyakuma*, the formal tatami guest room. Green tea loosened tongues. Okaasan and her friends were a generation older than I. Through learning English, they pushed me to open up. Foremost, they were dying to know what I thought of Japanese men.

"I only know one! He's easier to talk to than an American man," I said, surprising myself by speaking of Ichiro's communication merits for a change.

I had crossed an invisible barrier into their world by marrying Ichiro. I tried to imagine myself so comfortable with a housewife's downtown Tokyo life that a trip overseas would strike me as an extravagant waste of time and money. With my wrinkly-skinned girlfriends, we would indulge in the Romance Car, a luxury train ride to Hakone's rejuvenating mountain hot springs. We would soak overnight while Ichiro would be off lecturing in a far-flung city on the topic we didn't practice—how to lead a healthy, balanced family life. I couldn't imagine being so content that everything I needed could be massaged and soaked away.

Being a chronic foreigner was something I was genetically equipped to do. I felt I'd spent the last 2,000 years moving from country to country, give an incarnation or two. Jewish adaptability depends on other Jews to share life with and creating families to pass Judaism down to. But now that I was Ichiro's wife, I could go from one Jewish new year to the next—from Yom Kippur to the following Rosh Hashanah nearly a year later —without seeing another Jew. This troubled me when I asked myself who am I at the core of my being. This question wouldn't go away. It wasn't only playing with my mind, but with my hormones. Infertility continued. Late nights at the White Crane Clinic continued. "He's Japanese. She's Jewish" became a habit of thought.

"Go eating ahead," he said over the phone. He didn't mean to be curt and heartless, I told myself. This order to eat alone came from a deficit in language skills. I asked myself what I wished Ichiro had said. *My love, I'm sorry. Something came up at the clinic, and I have to stay. If you're hungry, please eat ahead, and I'll join you for dessert.* Oh, what a difference the heart feels when validated.

What would I have said? "But I ordered in your favorite dinner—takeout Indian curries with naan bread."

"Late again," I said, when Ichiro came home in high spirits, to be met with my scowl. "You're drinking—that is not work. I'm here alone, waiting for you like a fool." It was a bit of an exaggeration. I had a deadline for a *Japan Times* article, and Ichiro's arrival had wrenched me off the computer, which wasn't a bad thing, as midnight approached. I struggled to figure out whether disagreements with Ichiro belonged to the realm of cultural differences or to quirks of temperament.

One night, I finally told my mother about all of this.

"He doesn't have a modicum of common sense. He's insensitive."

"Maybe you hurt his feelings."

"Mom, I feel rejected." I had been reluctant to tell her. I didn't want to hear her recriminating *I told you so.*

"Liane, darling, you must at least entertain the thought that your problems are also due to your very different personalities. Have you got a pen?"

"Yes, Mom."

"Write it down, then: Might there not be another way of doing things differently for the sake of a happy marriage?"

"Mom, that's the way you speak! That's not me!"

"All right, dear. You get the point."

"Thank you."

"Your appreciation is graciously received, but my dear, it would be nice once in a while if you asked after your poor Mum. Your problems aren't the only thing that occupies my thoughts."

Ouch, that hurt. A slap on the wrist is painful at any age. "If so, Mom, then I'm truly sorry. I know I've been distracted, but I didn't realize how self-absorbed I'd become."

"Well, I had an unusually taxing day today. I took Leon to Sloan Kettering, where he had a procedure to examine his colon. The surgeon found a polyp but is 90 percent sure it is benign."

"Thank God," I replied.

"Yes, thank God all is well. They'll do a biopsy pro forma. But I always find a visit there very draining, as you see such tragic things."

Later that night, Ichiro brought home a package of

fried *senbei* rice crackers and a can of Guinness Black, a peace offering and the only beer I occasionally sipped.

I paraphrased my mother as best I could. "Why don't we try things differently?"

"Of course," Ichiro said gently as he took out two small glasses. "What about we taking a day trip so we can talk?"

On Ichiro's rare day off, we took the train up to visit Nikko, a World Heritage Site of sacred shrines and temples set on a forested hillside. Home to sixteenth century Ieyasu Tokugawa's Shinto-Buddhist kingdom, Nikko was the shogun's spiritual campus during his life and his mausoleum upon his death. We wandered down a gravel path flanked with tall and ancient cedar trees.

I had with me a book about Mussar, nineteenth-century Lithuanian Torah wisdom. In Mussar, the two voices inside vying for dominance had Torah-given names: an inclination to think and do good, *yetzer tov*, and its formidable challenger, *yetzer hara*—a tendency toward evil, self-sabotage, and downright unattractive behavior.

Ichiro had demonstrated how our choice of words could impact health in his consciousness training seminar at the White Crane Clinic. By lifting an arm and saying first "good," then "bad," I witnessed with my own eyes how a negative thought could impact the body. Uttering "good" gave strength to an unbending arm. Saying "bad" would instantly deplete the arm of strength. And still, the habit of thinking positive was something I couldn't just switch on overnight. I had become mindful of my thoughts, but like all unpracticed wisdom, I needed constant reminding. Mussar jogged my memory, inspiring me to make uplifting thoughts an act of habit.

It helped me see and appreciate in simple terms a concept I had originally learned from Fred Flintstone—the patriarch of the modern stone-age cartoon family and maybe even the Grand Poobah of Mussar. When Fred Flintstone needed to make a big decision, two little beings would appear on both sides of his head. One was an angel, and one carried a pitchfork telling him to go ahead and do the wrong thing.

"I'm learning in Mussar that there is a Jewish name for these two opposites—*yetzer hara*, the inclination toward doing evil, and *yetzer tov*, the inclination to do good."

"Who is your constant companion?" Ichiro asked.

"Sadly, I feel that the voice inside is mostly critical. It has to be the *yetzer hara*. And it's dark."

"What's dark about it?" he asked.

"I'm full of doubts. I'm not at peace."

Ichiro picked up a stone and threw it as far as he could. It rolled into a ditch.

"Don't you ever get depressed?" I asked.

"What's the good we both being depressed?"

"It's lonely at the bottom. We have been married for six years, and I still haven't conceived."

"Just leave it natural—you'll having a baby when it's the time!"

"Could you spend more time with me?" I said, just as my cell phone rang. My friend Donna was on the other end. Her cat, Brownie, had escaped over the walls of her Tokyo garden. I had stayed at Donna's home to cat-sit and had come to adore Brownie too. I went into advice mode: put up signs on lamp-posts, inform the next-door neighbors, and visit the park nearest her home. Maybe the cat had turned up there. Only after I had hung up the phone did it hit me. I had just done to Donna what I didn't like Ichiro doing—which was fact gathering, informing, and advising, rather than feel my friend's pain and loss. If I couldn't do that myself, how could I expect Ichiro to do better?

We turned a forested corner and climbed up a flight of stairs to reach the cadmium orange *torii* gate. Beyond was a wooden shrine with rich carvings above open doors. Nikko Toshogu

Shrine's famous three monkeys looked down upon us, accompanied by a sign: See no evil, hear no evil, and speak no evil.

"If we don't hear, see, or speak evil, we ourselves will be spared evil," Ichiro read from his guidebook, adding that Nikko held a *Koshin* festival in the spring and autumn, where worshippers came to ask heaven for forgiveness for their sins. This sounded like Yom Kippur, the Day of Atonement when Jews ask God to forgive their sins and blessings to be inscribed in the Creator's annually updated Book of Life.

We walked on in silence. Ichiro plunged deep into his own thoughts. His silence continued until we returned to the shrine's parking lot. We sat on separate rocks, facing buses that filled with foreign tourists.

"Tokugawa Shogun, he building Nikko, and he doing something amazing. He mixing Shintoism and Buddhism, putting shrines and temples together. Why don't we trying the same with our Jewish and Japanese ways?"

I gave him a nod as I watched the passengers alight on the tour buses and depart. To imagine myself belonging to a tour bus was unthinkable. I wanted to make our marriage work because I couldn't imagine any other life than the one I had created.

"Now we agreeing let's making marriage happy. How we are doing this?" he asked.

"Just quit the White Crane Clinic!" I said.

The sun was setting, and the stone I was sitting on had grown cold. Ichiro took off his jacket and put it over my shoulders. Then he stroked his beard. "When Incho telling me it's time, then I can leave."

"Stop being so weak! You must be the one to decide when to leave the White Crane Clinic!"

"But Incho depending on me. I never abandon my responsibilities."

We descended the long, sloping shopping street toward

Nikko train station. Wearing his traditional workman's outfit, a *samue*—kimono and pantaloons in matching blue denim— Ichiro looked as if he had just walked out of an old samurai movie set with me as his modern-day stagehand.

"Well, dear," my mother said when I called her from home. "I like Ichiro. I like his parents. But just remember, you needn't walk three steps behind him."

I put the receiver back in its cradle, half-wishing she had said, "Darling, you know that you have a home to come back to any time."

But she didn't say that. She didn't encourage my doubts.

I want to believe her restraint took courage. My mother wanted this marriage to work out as much as part of me did, and her straight talk—although maddening at times—gave me the strength to continue.

❀

Chapter Eight

TWO VOICES INSIDE

Your wife is a fruitful vine
in the innermost parts of your home,
your children are like olive plants
around your table.
—Psalm 128

When Ichiro introduced a series of consciousness training seminars, he asked me to join as a student. The training was to program thoughts in a positive direction. I liked his premise: that positive thinking could be approached as a force of habit. I had no idea that this positivity bias was straight out of Torah too.

This is how the seminar worked: two people would face each other, each taking a few minutes to make eye contact in silence with hands joined. Direct eye contact is considered rude in society, Ichiro had more than once told me, so this exercise was a stretch for most of us. I think until this point I liked the fact that the Japanese are not touchy-feely. I had grown up with skepticism toward affection, thinking that parental hugs and kisses were emotional gateways, only permitted when one parent or another was in a good enough mood to receive them. I was ready to do away with that terrible misconception.

"The basic point is when you saying thank you to a problem, or your illness, or a difficult relationship, your conscious mind automatically shifting in a harmonious direction," Ichiro said while reading from a clipboard.

"Positivity and enthusiasm making good result for patient," Ichiro said as he glanced down at his notes, then looked up into the eyes of his audience. This was his first attempt to deliver a talk in both Japanese and English and he was doing just fine.

"Liane understanding this—because she's Jewish."

I chuckled nervously.

"Rabbi Akiva, the greatest Torah scholar, leaving this world after he getting torture by the Romans, but until the moment he dying he always saying to his 24,000 disciples that everything happening for the best. Even he in his dying moment, Rabbi Akiva reciting the prayer that saying 'The Lord is One.' Then his soul leaving his body."

I had no idea that Ichiro knew about Rabbi Akiva.

A man stood up: "You say everything is for the best? But do you really believe it?"

"Yes! I believing every trouble in life giving opportunity for growth."

The man frowned. "What suffering do you know? You're young. You haven't experienced the half of life yet."

The man introduced himself. Mr. Matsumoto was his name. He used to own a construction company, but when Japan's long growth spurt came to a halt in the late 1980s, the first industry hit was construction. Mr. Matsumoto went bankrupt. "I tried working for someone else, but that didn't work out. I'm in ruins. I drive a taxi to make ends meet. I was going to end my suffering. I was planning to jump off a bridge this morning, but then I remembered that your Consciousness Training workshop was today. So, here I am." Mr. Matsumoto burst into tears.

"You are a courageous man," Ichiro answered in Japanese. "Maybe it seemed easier to jump, but you know it would cause tremendous pain for your family for the rest of their lives. Your intuition told you to do the right thing, and you listened."

Ichiro's years of training late into the night at the White Crane Clinic had led to deep empathy for his patients' hardships, and today he was saving a life. At that moment, my heart melted. Ichiro asked Mr. Matsumoto to join him at the front of the room. He wrapped his arms around the man and silently, without prompting, one person after another stepped forward to embrace them both until they were enveloped in everyone's arms.

At another seminar, Ichiro had us all draw. He had been sneaking out of the White Crane Clinic early to take a Jungian art therapy course taught by a foreign psychotherapist in Tokyo, Dr. David Tharp. Ichiro told us to set clear intentions and then draw a simple illustration of a personal goal. "Change yourself is very hard, but Carl Jung *Sensei* proving that if you changing how you seeing yourself in a drawing, your future changing automatically." I drew myself very pregnant on a beach, and it felt like a glorious snapshot from the future. When it was my turn to stand and speak, I said: "I can see a baby girl, a calm delivery—a birth by the ocean." And I meant it.

"I am happy to helping you realizing your dream. Anytime!" Ichiro laughed.

We both blushed, and when we returned home, Ichiro uncorked a bottle of wine, we made love and when we finished, Ichiro got up. He inserted a video into the player and watched his teacher, Ikuro Adachi, stand by a whiteboard and give a lesson—something to do with raising one's vibration. I left him to his devices, made myself a cup of tea, and sat at the dining table with a new box of Rembrandt pastels. I drew one picture, then another from my imagination. Maybe Ichiro was right. The more I drew my heart's desire, the more I could feel I was drawing my baby toward me.

Ichiro's workshops had turned on a creative switch and I began to draw daily. It became a joy and a surprise to see what would come out of a box of pastels when I jotted a positive word on the back of sketch paper. I could see that this intuitive approach, creative visualization through drawing, worked for me. The following August, on my 36th birthday, Ichiro agreed to take a rare day off and accompany me to the farmhouse of a Welsh artist, Pam Honda. She lived near Lake Kawaguchi, famous for its stunning reflection of Mount Fuji in its tranquil waters. Pam welcomed us to a workshop for just the two of us, introducing her intuitive approach to painting. I had been drawing only with pastels and this felt like a leap into the unknown. It was just what I was seeking.

Sliding doors opened to a garden of meowing cats, chirping cicadas, and the whooshing sound of wind blowing through tall shoots of late summer *susuki* grass. The veranda wrapped around a rustic farmhouse with thick wood beams that held up a thatched roof. A small hill covered in bamboo behind her property obscured the view of Mount Fuji.

Pam's handmade quilts were piled in one corner of the room. She had us lie down on the soft sunbaked tatami and guided us on a meditation of which I remember nothing, except falling into a peaceful sleep. I awoke to find a table laid out with pots of paints in every color of the rainbow. Pam had clipped butcher paper to two easels. Brushes stood ready for action in a coffee can. I couldn't wait to begin. I felt like a kid again, ready to play and get messy with no expectations for the outcome. We had arrived in this wonderful, creative and nature-filled space. That was enough. I had no inkling this was going to be a defining moment in my life, that this painting experience was going to pivot me toward becoming an artist—which is probably why it happened.

Pam explained that when the hand and the heart worked together the paint brush would move on its own accord. This intuitive way of painting meant that each brush stroke led to the next without a clear image. I covered my butcher paper with pastel blues, pinks, and yellows, and when I stood back I was surprised. Mount Fuji stared at me from the easel even though I couldn't see it. I had no idea how this happened. How could I have drawn the likeness and proportions of a volcanic mountain that I couldn't see? In intuitive art, Pam explained, we were tapping into the world behind your eyes.

Ichiro was being playful and intuitive too. He went back and forth between his easel and the garden, collecting *susuki* grass and gluing it stalk by stalk onto his paper. His process revealed a side of himself that I had never seen before—he was completely immersed in getting his creative inspiration from nature.

I wished I could carry back to Tokyo a new habit of doing art together and to uncork it as our special shared activity. In the countryside, without the pressures of city life, Ichiro seemed so content, taking his orders from no one but his creative self. It was almost as exciting as encountering my own creativity to discover that the impulse to create art was well within him, too.

On the train ride back to Tokyo, I proposed to him a radical idea.

"Why don't we get ourselves a rustic old farmhouse and live simply off the land? They're cheap! They're standing empty all over the countryside. Why not reinvent ourselves? You could give treatments from home and I could continue to write and paint. Our baby would surely appear without city stresses."

"Baby not come because of locating." Ichiro shook his head. "I'm not quit White Crane Clinic."

We got home and I hung our art side by side on the living room wall. I passed the pictures every day hopeful that Ichiro would join me in painting together. But he didn't give it much thought and it wasn't long before our grey cat Griffin had teased and torn off the *susuki* on Ichiro's work of art, one reed at a time.

"Maybe you should be married to him, not me," I said one night, as Ichiro popped the video of Adachi Sensei into the player.

"This is my relaxation way. I working all day, so what? I getting rid of my stress by hearing wisdom of my teacher."

I wanted to return to Pam's for more painting classes. But money was tight so I continued to put dabs of color on paper the way she had taught me. Sometimes recognizable things emerged to make me smile. I continued, while Ichiro went on a spending spree that caught me quite off guard.

"This plate takes away the bad effects of microwaves," Ichiro explained.

But I never used the microwave function on the oven and didn't plan to start using it now.

When he brought home a large and expensive ornamental titanium flower mounted on a base, I admired its artistry—not that it was my taste.

"What's this for?"

"This take away disharmonious vibrations at home. Ichiro named a price that made me see red.

This energy normalizer could have bought us two plane tickets to New York to see my family. Now that to me would have brought family harmony.

Ichiro would hear none of it. We could have been eating off of Limoges for the same price we were eating off dinnerware printed with patterns resembling atomic particles. Ichiro believed that these patterns were good for us and good for our marriage. In his mind, they came with an energetic warrantee.

He thought they could help us change our consciousness, raise our vibration, and this would make for a more pleasant destiny together. There was no way to argue with his noble intentions.

Ichiro pointed toward the front door, where I had affixed a mezuzah—the miniature scroll to protect the home and family, which is as old as Torah itself. The mezuzah's hand-crafted cover made of brightly colored stained glass had been a gift from my mother.

"You believing mezuzah having spiritual power. Adachi Sensei making objects that doing the same. I accepting your mezuzah. Why can't you accepting my way of protection? Look, you not having to believe it works," he added.

I continued to draw pictures before bedtime while Ichiro watched his videos. I drew scenes of a healthy pregnancy, children and a happy family. But it wasn't enough to only visualize these things. Something had to change and I didn't know what. I fell into a depression thinking that I'd grow old and childless with Ichiro. We would end our lives sitting on opposite ends of a small apartment, he, watching his teacher's instructional videos for a family that never materialized, and me, drawing pictures of children who never were born to us. How pathetic. When I voiced these thoughts, he wrote me a letter:

Dear Liane,

I had a lot of thought about our relation. The biggest thing which I aware "every phenomenon is happen from self-vibration." Nothing is wrong another person. I always communicate with you from position that "I do right thing and you doing wrong." It was my first mistake.

But something more big mistake exist which I never aware till now. That is "trouble is happen because deeper level of yourself giving you a problem to try to make you grow.

Every problem is happen because you can clear it 100

percent so please not run away. You should receive everything
that happen.

We came to the earth through using body and emotion.
Through that we can taste what is joy and what is sadness, what
is suffering, so we should taste deeply.

If it something make you pleased, we taste deeply but if it
something make you not pleased, we put responsibility
somebody else and run away.

I put the letter down and turned the kettle on. I ran my
fingers over my scalp and pulled a few hairs out. Then I pulled
some more. I felt confused. Ichiro cared deeply for me, enough
to labor over these sentences in English and translate his
teacher Adachi Sensei's ideology for me. He wanted me to think
well, and it would be well. I wish I could have taken a deep
breath and said to him, "Goodness! All this inner turmoil is here
to be experienced because I have what it takes to clear it."

But something inside me wasn't buying into it. He was
lecturing me from *his* comfort zone. Maybe if he had proposed
another day out to Pam's farmhouse and put me back in *my*
comfort zone—a nature-filled oasis where I could see clearly
past the stresses, I'd have been more inclined to embrace his
point of view. But Ichiro's life didn't allow for breaks. His was a
nonstop world of striving and I was mirroring that. A holiday?
How indulgent. A day of rest? Nobody else at the clinic took a
day off every week. Why should he?

I asked Ichiro to give me some time and space while I struggled with my own demons. In truth, I was confused. I didn't
know if Ichiro's lifestyle or his life choices were at odds with
mine. I couldn't blame him. I had entered his house on my own
volition. The last thing I wanted to think was that this had been
a mistake, or that our very different backgrounds and upbring-
ings could be the source of our problems.

Ichiro returned to his parents' house. He left me in the

apartment with our two cats, Griffin and Maillol. He took only his clothes and his cachet of energy-adjustment gadgets and plates. Alone, I wrote articles, read books, drew with my pastels, painted on canvases, and met my friends for tea. The separation went on for two months.

Ichiro had written in his letter something that I couldn't get out of my mind. "If we running away from thing which we having to do for our soul growth, exactly that we having to do coming in the future and next time it should be more hard."

What if this were true? If I left this marriage, would we incarnate again in another life and have to go through this ordeal one more time? It was a terrifying thought. Running away from my problems was not the answer.

Michaela was our angelic friend and helped us reconcile. She lived in the same building as the renowned psychiatrist, Dr. Keiko Ochi. Michaela got us an appointment to get help from the hard-to-see doctor. We were still living apart when Ichiro and I entered a large room fragrant with lavender and patchouli oil and took our seats on a salmon pink leather couch that wrapped around the sunny room. Dr. Ochi took her seat on an ottoman near us. With a clipboard in hand, she wrote down our different versions of the story of our lives, and reading it back, Dr. Ochi brought us to tears. If Ichiro was afraid of leaving the clinic and becoming his own master, then I was just as afraid of believing in the new Ichiro I had yet to meet when he stood up on his own two legs.

"Ichiro, you are your own master. It's time that you own your power," Dr. Ochi said very softly. "I not wanting this marriage to end. I will quit if you won't divorce me," Ichiro sobbed into a tissue. And for me, words of support came too. "Liane, open your heart to Ichiro. He loves you very much." I reached for Ichiro's hand. He took it, then he hugged me. "I'll quit the clinic for you." He paused as the realization hit him. He drew a long inhalation and then he exhaled the truth. "I'll quit for me." Ichiro would give a year's notice and then quit the White Crane Clinic. We would save up money, travel overseas, and come closer than we ever could in Tokyo. Man makes plans and God laughs, as we were to find out.

We packed up our apartment and moved across town to live in Ichiro's parents' apartment building in Nihonbashi. We downsized to a studio with two futons, chests of drawers, and the comfort of knowing that the in-laws were just one floor above us. I would hear their footsteps before sunrise. The front door would close shut with a turn of the key. I became curious where they could be going before dawn. To get out of bed at such an early hour, it had to be time well-spent. One night, I woke up and followed them out the door. Under bright street lamps, my eyes puffy and my mouth dry, I was still in a sleepy fog when we arrived at a narrow three-story building. In front stood a sandwich-style signboard offering a cheerful message: "Come on upstairs. We are waiting for you!"

I was to learn that lives were saved from suicide by that welcoming sign. We climbed the narrow stairs, entered a room with frosted windows and grey metal desks that looked as if they were left over from the General MacArthur occupation years after Japan lost World War II. In 1945, the US had retaliated for the attack on Pearl Harbor with air raids that flattened downtown Tokyo. Firebombs had torched the center of the city, turning the heavily populated district where Ichiro's family lived, worked, and where his father went to school, into a field of ashes and burnt corpses.

Gradually, the room filled with grandmas and grandpas who warmed their hands around a kerosene heater. Bent and wobbly, they were tough war survivors. Here in this small room they made it a daily habit to count their blessings and focus only on the good. A kettle was coming to boil. Okaasan handed me a hot cup of green tea. I took a seat on a folding chair next to her, and since words hadn't yet traveled up to my head at this ungodly hour, I drank the tea in silence, inhaling kerosene fumes.

My father-in-law led this chapter of the nationwide Rinri Morning Meeting Association. He said a few words of greeting and the group joined him in reciting from memory Rinri's core values to honor everyone's story—and for the storytellers themselves to frame their version of the truth in the most uplifting way possible. Now I understood where Ichiro's world view came from. The apple didn't roll far from the tree.

Each octogenarian took a turn speaking. We found out that one mother had a breakthrough phone conversation with a son whom she hadn't spoken with in years. A grandfather described a trip to the ice cream shop to celebrate the recovery of a hospitalized grandchild. Their big hearts gave me the courage to talk about my struggle to conceive. But my voice froze when it was my turn to speak. Nothing I had to say could hold a match to their sacrifice or suffering. "Is there something you would like to tell us?" my father-in-law prodded softly. I looked past the wrinkles and into a room full of gentle eyes and said: "I'm scared. You all don't have to think twice about being an outsider. But me?"

One by one, these wizened Rinri members told me of their own experiences and how feeling like an outsider was not limited to foreigners. One had an autistic daughter and met with the disapproval of a harsh mother-in-law who insisted on keeping the grown child at home out of a sense of shame. One widow's husband had died in World War II, and she'd been told that she was too old to remarry. At 22 years old, she followed what she was told, and spent the rest of her life alone.

"We're still here!" Ichiro's father exclaimed, changing the mood, as his hands reached for the comfort of his warm tea cup. "We're old and we've learned to enjoy our lives!" The stories had happy endings because Rinri meetings gave members a daily opportunity to revise sad personal histories in a more positive direction. Still, I couldn't help but feel their pain. Ichiro's father had suffered severe food deprivations which probably explains why he stood a head shorter than Ichiro. He had been forced to flee during the Tokyo carpet bombings that destroyed his child-hood home at the end of World War II. He had lost three sisters to diphtheria when he was old enough to remember each adorable one of them.

A granny with gold front teeth nodded. She held a cane and patted her wool-skirted knees. I laughed to see her prove she was still in body and thanked the group. She tugged my sleeve and smiled. "Keep yourself busy. That's the secret to happiness in old age." Busy. Yes, even the oldest of the old seemed to thrive on being in perpetual motion.

Unwittingly, the pace of life was what had drawn me to Tokyo in the first place. Busy people attract each other. Keeping busy twenty-four-seven was seen as a national virtue. To ask after someone's health, came the automatic answer: *isogashi.* I'm busy. It meant that you are to be respected. You are a somebody. To be busy still is a badge of honor.

I returned home to the in-law's apartment, slid closed the gold paper doors, sat down, and rested my head on my arms on a low black lacquer table. Within reach of a lace-covered tissue box, I bawled my eyes out.

Okaasan must have heard me from the kitchen. She slipped into the guest-room and took a seat next to me. "Don't worry. I'm praying for your happiness," she said. Okaasan rubbed my back and I became calm. Her words of encouragement were from the heart. "I'm blessing you to have children," she contin-ued. This is how my mother-in-law calmed me down so I could get back up and believe that having children together would bring us closer.

Weeks passed and then the miracle happened. My tempera-ture elevated and stayed up. I was pregnant! Okaasan immedi-ately took me to Suitengu, a Shinto fertility shrine, where women pray for an easy pregnancy, a safe childbirth, and a healthy baby. Okaasan clapped her hands, pulled a rope, and tossed coins into a giant charity box. I stood waiting outside, wishing I knew the equivalent way to welcome my baby to the Jewish faith.

Chapter Nine

ROSH HASHANAH BABY

✤

Kindness and truth are met together,
righteousness and peace have kissed.
—Psalm 85

Kohno Sensei, my midwife, escorted me to a birthing pool, the kind you might inflate for your kids in your backyard. I sat up to my neck cocooned in turquoise plastic, a container filled with body-temperature water to help reduce the pain. But this agony was like nothing I had experienced before.

"This is definitely not relaxing. I'm out of here," I said, as I climbed out of the pool and grabbed a towel. I was ready for dry land with gravity on my side.

Contractions are a misnomer. They suggest localized pain, at the worst a big squeeze, whereas I was being struck by lightning. I was ready to ask for an ambulance. "Let the paramedics take me. I'm ready to surrender to epidurals, a C-section, whatever it takes, but not this!"

Ichiro took my hand. He reassured me in a sympathetic

voice, "You can't changing the pain, but you can changing reaction to it. How about try to say 'thank you' every time contraction coming?"

"I don't feel like saying thank you," I said, my eyes scrunched, and I grimaced.

"You don't have to believing it. Just you say," Ichiro coached.

"Thank you," I said in a tiny voice. I knew he was right.

"Thank you," Ichiro repeated. "Louder, again."

"Thank you."

"Louder! Louder!" he repeated.

"Thank you!"

That third thank you did it. Shoshana crowned. The midwife guided our baby girl into this world, and she came into my arms sheathed in a waxy coating. Thank you, I cooed to her as I held her, in awe of her presence. She had a full head of dark, spiky hair, a lovely round face like my mother-in-law's, with rosebud lips.

Ichiro called Shoshana perfect. Call it a mother's intuition, a glimpse of things to come—my daughter had announced her Jewish presence. By Torah law, a child born of a Jewish mother is Jewish, no matter what. But Shoshana was born six days before the due date, on the holy day of Rosh Hashanah. Her soul seemed to be telling me to pay attention. Born in Japan, she too was a soul tracing back to Mount Sinai and the witnessing of God's thunderous voice calling out the Ten Commandments.

When Shoshana was one month old, we drove to Shitaya Jinja, the family's go-to Shinto shrine on a tree-lined street. I had dressed Shoshana in a beautiful, frilly white gown that trailed to Okaasan's knees. She was carried by her grandmother up the steps to the front porch of the small, weather-beaten, wooden shrine sheltered under tall keyaki trees. We got back in the car, drove to the family's Buddhist graveyard behind Jo-onji Temple. Here came more prayers before the graves of Ichiro's grandparents. This baby had been given the full Shinto and

Buddhist welcome by her traditional Japanese family. But when it was time to take Shoshana to the Jewish Community Center for a baby-naming ceremony and blessing, I was on my own. Ichiro and his parents thought it unnecessary to come. They had done what was expected according to their faith. And, as Ichiro put it, he wasn't against Shoshana's Jewish ceremony. It was a Saturday, a workday, and they were all just too *busy* to attend. The words my mother had spoken echoed back: This is the life you have chosen. You're entering a proud family that follows the traditions of *their* ancestors. You have married into Ichiro's family and not the other way around.

Okaasan worried about exposing Shoshana to germs, coughs, sniffles, smoke, and drunkards—they were all to be avoided. Since we lived in one of the most densely populated areas of Tokyo, stepping out the door would surely lead to unwelcome exposure. I was essentially under house arrest. You never knew who was going to contaminate the newborn. But staying indoors was tough during autumn's finest days of sunshine. A postpartum view across the street onto other micro-dwellings was getting me down. I needed a botanical surge, leafy oxygen, and most of all, the sense that I was a grownup who could jolly well make my own decisions. So telling nobody, I tucked Shoshana into her carrier strapped over my shoulders and around my waist and I snuck. We headed to Shinobazu Pond, a sanctuary of green lily pads that float at the center of Ueno Park. While Shoshana slept, I pulled out my crayons and drew the lovely scene, and gradually I returned to myself.

At home, during Shoshana's naptime, I let my imagination go wild on a canvas. This quiet time to create was the unspoken gift of living on the floor below my in-laws. My maternal role was to rest. It was oddly short of duties. Okaasan cooked for us, did the laundry; I hung it and she folded it. She prayed for us, she shopped, and we cooked together. My mother-in-law did the day shift and I did the night shift, breast-feeding Shoshana to her heart's content. Here, in my in-laws' home, sliding paper doors created fragile boundaries. Ichiro bathed Shoshana nightly in a blue plastic tub that fit into the kitchen sink. My father-in-law took Shoshana for walks, puffing away on his cigarettes as he pushed the stroller past the utility poles where I wished there were trees.

Ichiro had turned his grandfather's office into a treatment room. We passed each other in the elevator, and much as before, we went about our separate lives. He cultivated a new circle of friends who also studied with Ichiro's teacher, Adachi Sensei. Okaasan talked on the phone to her sisters about Shoshana's every milestone. Her sisters were the first to know when the baby sat up, turned her head, smiled, rolled off the dining room love seat, began crawling and standing by herself. I thought it was sweet that she wanted to share the news. But when Okaasan added my doctor appointments to her daily phone broadcasts, I snapped.

"It's none of her business!" I cried to Ichiro, when we were back downstairs within our own four walls.

"Please thinking my mother's point of view. Her spirit sacrificing to send you a message."

"Sacrificing what?"

"She doing her best. She wanting us all to living together as happy, peaceful family."

"Then why did she talk about my gynecological visit, as if she were the one stepping up on the exam table?"

"Because maybe she not seeing you as outside her boundaries," Ichiro said.

He had a point. With all that Okaasan was doing for me, washing and ironing Shoshana's pretty outfits, many of which were gifts from Okaasan in the first place, I had no choice but to tolerate being the headline news item in her phone calls.

"What I'm resenting is not Okaasan, but feeling split in two,"

I said. The minute I went upstairs, I realized I'd forgotten something in our room below—like extra diapers. I would spend the day going up and coming down the building's exterior staircase.

When Shoshana turned one, I threw a party up on the in-law's rooftop. She pushed her bright new red wagon and let it go to take her first independent steps. My girlfriends—Andrea, Felice, and Zohara—had come with their kids. Felice was pregnant with her second child, Andrea and I had met at the birth house, and Zohara had been the Rabbi at my Jewish basement wedding. Our husbands, most noticeably, were not with us.

"Companionship—what were we thinking?"

My girlfriends nodded as I offered squares from a platter of carrot cake. We lived scattered across Tokyo and had met quite by chance, developing close bonds when we found out we were Jewish. We could discuss ways of bringing modest signs of our heritage into our Tokyo homes, like the Shabbat candlesticks, a Hanukah menorah and mezuzah on the doors. Shoshana toddled over to me. She put her little hand in mine, as if to remind me how long I had waited to become a mother and to have the blessing of minor or perhaps self-invented hardships.

Ichiro and I had slipped into the roles of two overgrown children living with his parents, who were generous to a fault. The in-laws didn't seem bothered by this arrangement, but I took this as a temporary situation at best, the price to pay for Ichiro leaving the White Crane Clinic and starting over as a lecturer. I wanted my own home. Ichiro said that we couldn't afford to move yet.

"When is the right time?" I asked.

Ichiro said that we needed to wait until he got back on his financial feet.

"What about if I work?"

"On, no needing. My mother very busy so she can't watching Shoshana all the time if you to work."

One day, quite unexpectedly, Adachi Sensei called me and

asked if I could edit the English version of his late sister's best-selling book, *To Live as We Are*. I took it as an honor o be asked by the *erai sensei*, the great teacher, and I couldn't say no. When I asked Ichiro about payment, he said: "Just trust the universe." And so, I did.

For the next year, with Shoshana on my lap, I learned to edit with my tiny collaborator. In the end, I wasn't paid for the work but I received remuneration in a more profound way. Sachiko had become a master intuitive, and her book served as a practical guide to using intuition in daily life. Sentence by sentence, I absorbed her lessons like an acolyte, and she primed me for the next phase of my life. I would go on to create the deck of Genesis Cards and teach many others to trust their intuition through art.

WE LIVED in the apartment below Ichiro's parents for two years, lock and step with their daily habits and traditions. Some of them were wonderful. I loved the way my mother-in-law made time to talk at appointed hours of the day she called teatime, right after an early breakfast, and again mid-afternoon. She would clear off the dining table of newspapers correspondence, business documents, calligraphy brushes, Ojiisan's blood pressure machine. He would dutifully zap off the television with the remote control, so that the dining room could become a place to munch on rice crackers, *sembei*, drink green tea, and crane our ears for Shoshana's first little sentences.

"I wanting *sembei* too!"

The in-laws laughed at her cute English. I bet they never imagined having a grandchild who would be speaking the most coveted language in post-war Japan after their own. But something here was not funny. Shoshana was speaking Ichiro's English, not mine. I had become used to his way of speaking, but I hadn't anticipated it would be passed down to the next generation. I cringed to think of the impact it would have on Shoshana.

"I want a *sembei!*" I corrected.

I knew that Ichiro didn't exploit English grammar to spite me. It was a generous combination of self-confidence and laziness that drove him to speak as he did. Communication between us could very easily become a prolonged English battle on the grammar front, now that we had a baby. I tried switching to Japanese, but I spoke haltingly, and my grammar was probably as ridiculous as his. Ichiro grew impatient. He wanted me to spit out thoughts in Japanese faster than I could process. In limited Japanese, our communication stumbled along a band of topics to do with childrearing. Then one day, I had *The Japan Times* spread out across the dining table upstairs at the in-laws dining table. A small classified ad caught my attention. The ad invited foreigners to an English-speaking community on the Boso Peninsula of Chiba. "Live in the middle of a forest at a fraction of the cost of living in Tokyo! Join friendly expanding foreign artists' community!" I later read the ad to Ichiro, which nudged memories of Pam Honda's idyllic setting in the countryside.

"For you maybe it sound good," he said, with furrowed eyebrows. "If it getting rid your stress, why don't you look? But I never moving out of Tokyo." Not long after, I bundled Shoshana into the stroller for the two-hour train ride out to Chiba. We left behind a drab grey boxy world for green lush rice paddies and shimmering grasses on one side of the train tracks. Who wouldn't want to live here? On the other side of the tracks were beaches and the sea. We completed our journey with a taxi ride to a gentle humpback hill covered in cedar trees. I stepped up on the porch of an imported New Zealand vacation house—and as I took in forest in all directions through the big picture windows, I knew I was home.

When I got back to Tokyo, that night I was too excited to sleep.

"Ichiro, you know how much I'm craving fresh air for Shoshana, trees and an art studio."

"But the Boso Peninsula is the dead end of Chiba," he protested. On his map of life, Nihonbashi was the epicenter, and everywhere outside of central Tokyo led to destinations he would never want to live—or subject me to live either.

"Think of it. Long sunset walks on beaches."

"The place you looking at is a battlefield in the 18th century," he said.

"How do you know?"

"I researching and finding that bloody battle took place there. Battlegrounds not lucky places to living," Ichiro said, pointing to a map he had spread out before him.

"Look, the battle happened 300 years ago." I tapped the outer reaches of the map. "The house is all sunshine and cedar, and it's a short bike ride to the ocean."

"Eight kilometers not bike ride. You better driving," Ichiro said, as his finger rat-a-tat tapped the map.

"You know I don't drive."

"So you learn. I can't stopping you, but I stay here," Ichiro said, as he folded the map and turned to his pressing matters. He had a talk to prepare—something to do with how to achieve harmony in the family. I walked over to the sliding glass doors and stepped onto our tiny Tokyo balcony. A row of buildings stared back at me. "You missing the convenience!" Ichiro called from inside. "An hour to the nearest grocery store?"

"Don't worry," I replied. "I'll bring my bicycle."

❀

Chapter Ten

AN APPLE AND HONEY IN THE FOREST

In lush pastures, He makes me lie,
besides tranquil waters, He leads me.
—Psalm 23

Ichiro loaded his father's Toyota Crown and buckled Shoshana into her baby car seat. Maybe this could work. I would move to the Boso Peninsula first. I hoped that Ichiro would eventually warm up to country life and join me. In the meantime, we would go back and forth between city and country living. I trusted the intuitive voice that said: take a risk, give it a try, you'll make it work—though my mother thought it was madness.

"Crikey! But you're married! What in God's name are you thinking? Is that the way for a couple with a young child to live?" cried my mother into the phone.

We lurched out of Nihonbashi, weighed down with cardboard boxes, suitcases, the pet carrier with meowing Griffin and

Maillol inside. There were just some things that a mother didn't need to know.

We drove out to Nakadaki Heights to begin life in a story-book pine house with flower boxes and a high-pitched roof. The veranda faced a vegetable patch, camellia bushes with waxy pink flowers in full bloom and evergreens hat grew in neat rows. The native forest had been chopped down during World War II to provide firewood for Tokyo, and fast-growing cedars were replanted where a rich ecosystem once existed. But coming from Nihonbashi, who was I to complain? Green was green. To look out onto nothing but cedars and a blue sky above, unhindered by power lines, I was overjoyed.

Ichiro unloaded the car, drove me to the local farmer's market, and later waded in the pond with Shoshana. Then he kissed his baby goodbye, patted her on the back, got back into his father's car, and drove off into the sunset back to Tokyo. I was on my own, with our eighteen-month-old toddler, and ready to make a go of it.

Each week Ichiro borrowed the Crown and drove out for a night or two and I'd spend two nights back in Nihonbashi. Soon Shoshana was old enough to enter the country *hoikuen*, an idyllic daycare center for toddlers with sunny classrooms and a sweet potato patch. We would take the train into Tokyo midweek and return to Chiba with Ichiro on the weekend. This was our compromise—not quite living apart, but not quite together.

In the house in the forest, I stopped lighting the Shabbat candles altogether. It was too dangerous, I thought. The house was made of pine, and sudden earthquakes would occur without notice, rattling the foundations to the rooftops in terri-fying jolts.

With not a single Jew anywhere near us, it was painfully easy to forget I even was one. The small Jewish community I had left behind in Tokyo was now hours away, and more out of reach than ever. Without a prayer book or a Jewish calendar, I put Jewish life behind me—or so I thought. But God had other plans. I had vivid dreams in the forest. One morning, I awoke from a dream in which Shoshana spoke to me. It was not her usual toddler prattle: cookies, kitties, and cake, cake, cake. In the dream, she offered me the precocious word *instead*.

What was my toddler trying to tell me?

Instead of Tokyo, we were in the Boso Peninsula of Chiba. Instead of living in downtown Tokyo, in her grandparent's splendid penthouse apartment, we were living humbly in our fairytale cottage. Instead of her grandparents and Ichiro being there for her, Shoshana had only me. In the dream, Shoshana wanted me to know what she knew: that instead of her parents living together, they were living apart, and she didn't like it one bit.

I told Ichiro about Shoshana's *instead* dream while we were driving over to the local farmers' market to pick up red juicy tomatoes and cucumbers straight out of the fields. He looked up from the steering wheel, staring unblinking out the windshield. "Perhaps Shoshana sending you a message. You could moving back to Tokyo."

"Could move," I corrected.

"Okay, you could moving back," Ichiro plowed on.

In the forest house, I didn't have to lock horns with Ichiro over grammar. I sighed as I asked myself: Am I to deny my daughter time with her father because of his disastrous English? Or am I going to take responsibility for my own shortcomings? Living in the countryside I was becoming fluent in Japanese, or at least I liked to think so. My vocabulary had grown but my Japanese grammar was still as horrendous, if not worse than Ichiro's English.

The big fall festival was coming up in the nearby town of Chojamachi, and I asked Ichiro to join us. I had hoped he would enjoy the revelry, but he had a lecture to deliver in Shizuoka. I went with Shoshana to partake of a spectacle straight out of an Akira Kurosawa movie. The junior high school soccer field had been taken over by a cavalry of glittering golden portable shrines, *mikoshi*.

Shoshana and I sat on a pink picnic sheet decorated with Hello Kitty, the red-bowed, wide-eyed, button-nosed, and mouthless mascot of girlhood. Hello Kitty offers a not very subtle message that cats, and perhaps females, should be seen but not heard. On a grassy slope, facing the soccer field, bare-chested men, their privates covered in white loincloths, formed teams to carry each of the *mikoshi*. Men of all ages shouted archaic battle cries, while wives, grannies, grandpas, and grand-children cheered them.

Shoshana's little classmates from her nursery school, *hoikuen*, noticed us. One little girl patted Shoshana's straight brown hair and hugged her tight enough to lift her off the ground. This was what it could feel like to belong—you're spot-ted, welcomed, and hugged. I wished somebody would lift me off the ground, too.

When we returned home, Shoshana decided that she, too, like the revelers, should run around without her clothes on.

"No, Shoshana. It's October."

She ignored me. The emotions rose as we faced off on oppo-site ends of a queen-size bed. She screamed at the top of her lungs. I played the role of a ridiculous and helpless ogre, gnashing my teeth and getting nowhere with my demands that she put her clothes back on. Shoshana burst into tears. I wanted a shoulder to cry on. When I called Ichiro, he didn't know what to do either, so he put his mother on the phone.

"It's mid-October and Shoshana is running around without clothes on."

"Maybe she isn't cold," said Okaasan.

Interesting observation.

I passed the phone to Shoshana, and she switched to

Japanese: "*Zen zen samukunai.*" She said to her grandmother. Then she turned to me and repeated in English: "I am not cold!" I had been so swept up in my imagined duty to prevent Shoshana from catching a cold—at any cost—that I lost sight of her feelings.

Okaasan began to sing the *Itomaki* lullaby that Shoshana had learned at nursery school. She calmed down upon hearing her grandmother's warble, and then joined her. The only part of the *Itomaki* song I knew was the refrain: "*Don, don, don.*" Shoshana pressed the speaker phone button, filling the bedroom, right up to the pitched cathedral ceiling, with her grandmother's voice. I'm not sure whether she did this intentionally. I don't think I had ever before turned on the speaker phone.

Okaasan praised Shoshana over the amplified phone: "What a clever girl you are, a wonderful, sweet girl!" Shoshana opened up to her grandmother in a way that she couldn't do with me. She told Okaasan how she missed Tokyo. Life in a forest in the Boso Peninsula wasn't—in my toddler's opinion—worth the tradeoff.

Winter brought snow to the fields, and we spent more time in Tokyo warming up with the family on the sixth floor. March brought back the birds and the ponds thawed. With Spring in the air, our little community at Nakadaki was growing with the arrival of a family from Tokyo who took on the management of an outdoor conference center. Not long after they had settled in Talia, my sister, had from called New York to say that our father had suffered a massive stroke and was hospitalized in intensive care at Mount Sinai hospital in New York.

I took the first available plane to be with him in his final days. As soon as I arrived, Ichiro called me to report more bad news. Our neighbor's four-year-old son had slipped into a pond and drowned. Shoshana had loved that little boy. I returned to Japan, leaving my father on a respirator, with no chance of recovery.

When I returned to the cottage in the forest, Shoshana fell into my arms and I was overjoyed to see her. Far away from New York, I could hardly believe that I was a daughter in mourning. I felt incredibly ill-equipped to mourn. Besides lighting a memorial *yahrzeit* candle, I had no idea what other Jewish customs to follow, and I had no idea how to comfort my toddler in the loss of her friend. Her grandparents had decided to take her to the little boy's funeral and had her view the child in his open casket before cremation.

This was not what I would have done. What could I say after the fact? That we Jews don't do such things? That it would have been decent and mensch-like to call me in New York and give me a say in the matter? I wondered to myself, is this it? Have I signed away my parental rights to belong to this family? Have I cut the last cord to my Jewish roots altogether? I felt lost inside, like one of the cranes I had spotted, perched on a farmhouse rooftop in the rice paddies. When you're in migration, you know it's only a matter of time before you must move on.

"Goodness, it's hard," I confessed to my mother one night.

"Darling, I know it is. Remember I had to fly over to London when your grandmother passed away—on my birthday, no less! Talk about timing. Lordy!"

"What do you think I ought to do, Mom?"

"Chin up, darling. Simply carry on."

I was reciting Kaddish for my father, the prayer of mourning when a package arrived unexpectedly. It was addressed from Chabad, the very same Brooklyn-based Chassidic Lubavitch movement that Didi, so long ago, had tried to lure me to after a friendly game of tennis. I tore open the wrapping to find a crisp, red Fuji apple and a small packet of honey to usher in a *Shana Tova*, a sweet new year.

Inside the envelope was a brief message: "You are more than welcome to join us for the High Holidays in Tokyo." The note was signed, "The Rabbi and the Rebbetzin."

From what I recalled Didi telling me on the Central Park tennis courts, Chabad welcomed Jews like me. They weren't judgmental. They didn't care if I was married to a non-Jew or married at all. Chabad was a franchise of home-based Jewish centers scattered across American cities and college campuses, run by rabbis and the indispensable brains and backbone of Chabad, the wives, the *rebbetzin*. Chabad couples often established their centers from next to nothing when they were newlyweds. I remember Didi telling me that they had one mission: to bring Jews back to a Torah-led way of life.

Had Chabad really come to Tokyo, where there were so few of us Jews to bring back? Being alone in the wild and beautiful Boso Peninsula, was wearing me down. If I hadn't been living so far removed from Jewish life, I wonder if the impact of Chabad's arrival in Japan would have been as strong or felt this miraculous. It was just a package containing an apple, a pack of honey, and a Tokyo return address. Maybe I was blowing this out of proportion.

Chabad had included a phone number. It was only polite to thank them for the apple and honey. But with the receiver in my hand, I felt nervous and I hesitated. I had certain ideas about religious people. My parents had successfully instilled both awe and repulsion for ultra-Orthodox Jews. Their line of reasoning went that they had attained spiritual heights to which we couldn't aspire, and shouldn't aspire, and that they were judging as we were judging them. This was not only because we were born in modern times that called for full enjoyment of our right to go to the matinee movies on Saturday, but because the Orthodox made us feel guilty for doing so if we happened to pass them on the streets in their best Shabbat clothes. I'd heard that their approval of working women was low. Their appreciation of college diplomas was even lower. Everything that I had worked for would be nullified in their world. It was no wonder I had been terrified of meeting ultra-Orthodox Chassids on their own turf in Brook-lyn. But in Tokyo, they were curiously enough on my turf now.

As for a Chassidic Rabbi, I had never even spoken to one. Not that I sought the opportunity. I had this notion that they would frown upon someone that had once worn cutoff jeans and a Rolling Stones tongue ironed onto a tank top. They would have judged me as a *Yid* who had fallen off the *derech*—one more child of the God of Moses who had lost her way.

But curiosity got the better of me. If a Chabad Rabbi was actually going to set up a house for Jews to gather in Japan, I ought to visit just once. I was ready to put suppositions aside and find out what on earth they were doing in Japan with so few Jews here. There weren't a thousand of us in all of Japan—and that included Jews coming and going—travelers, teachers, students, and business people.

I called the phone number. A cheerful voice picked up the phone, *"Beit Chabad, Yechi HaMelech."*

"Hello. Are you the Rebbetzin?" I said, not recognizing what she had just said. Four words and already I was out of my depth, beyond reach of my puny Hebrew vocabulary. The English came with a funny accent, as if her preferred tongue was Yiddish, the universal language of Ashkenazi Jews in pre-Holo-caust Eastern Europe.

"Do you speak English?" I asked.

She switched to a familiar Brooklyn accent. "Hullo. This is Chabad House."

"Hi, I just received a packet of honey and the apple you were so kind to send me," I explained. We had a short conversation, enough for me to glean some extraordinary news. The senders of the apple and honey were here in Tokyo to stay. Their Chabad House welcomed all Jews, any time of the day or night. I tried to picture my entrance into their insular, ultra-orthodox world. Who was I kidding? But I heard a voice inside say something else: you may find you have more in common than differences.

The sun was setting between the cedars when I hung up the phone with Chabad's address jotted down. I turned on the kitchen lights and phoned my mother. "You are not going to believe this. I just spoke with a Lubavitch Rebbetzin from Brooklyn. Her husband comes from Israel, and they belong to the Chabad movement."

"Chassids in Japan? Go on." She chuckled.

"They've just moved to Tokyo!"

"The black hats?"

"Mom, that's derogatory."

"What on earth are you thinking? The Jews of Tokyo already have the JCC—the Jewish Community Center, for heaven's sake! I won't be berated by my own daughter when I'm simply trying to be helpful, so you won't have aggravation with them in the future. Anyone who follows the Jewish faith with as much devotion as the Lubavitchers would have only one intention in mind when meeting someone like you—and me. That's to turn us into one of them."

"Ha! In Japan? Are you serious?" I burst out laughing.

"Well, yes I am serious, darling! Remember that they are an impossible act to follow."

So what is Chabad? I was to learn that it was a worldwide movement under the leadership of the late Lubavitcher Rebbe, Menachem Mendel Schneerson, who most say passed away in June of 1994. I began my research with a search on the Internet. In a flash, facts and figures about Ultra-Orthodox Judaism originating in Eastern Europe popped up before my eyes. I learned that the Lubavitcher Chassids originated in Russia, flourished in Poland, and fell on hard times in Latvia. My maternal ancestors came from Latvia, ground zero for the Jewish enlightenment movement, the Haskalah, which loudly rejected Hassidism as a barrier to the education of women, assimilation, and social climbing. They thought that shedding their Jewish identity, they would give their good Christian neighbors cause to end their ruthless anti-Semitic attacks. Yet, though these Maskilim might barely have identified outwardly as Jews, they too were indiscriminately murdered during World War II by the Nazis, and by their neighbors in the European countries where they built their homes and businesses. These assimilated Jews were also pushed into crowded cattle cars, marched to the gas chambers, as if by some catastrophic mistake. They weren't supposed to have been murdered. They had been good loyal citizens, high ranking members of society, leaders in the sciences, education, medicine, psychology, music, and the arts.

Rabbi Yosef Yitzhak Schneerson had been imprisoned in Russia for defying the czarist laws that prohibited learning Torah and spreading Jewish practice. He's revered as the *Frierdiker Rebbe*; Yiddish for "previous Rebbe," and was the sixth rabbi in a lineage of Chassids of Russian decent. Rabbi Yitzhak Schneerson brought the Chabad Lubavitcher movement to America in 1940, along with a priceless Chassidic library, more than a 200-year legacy of Lubavitch rabbinical wisdom and Torah scholarship. Putting the trauma of prison torture in Russia behind him, the *Frierdiker Rebbe* began his new life in Crown Heights, Brooklyn with a few Holocaust survivors who had lost everything and everyone during World War II. He spent the last decade of his life, 1940—1950, preparing newly married couples to leave behind their sheltered community in Crown Heights for Jewish outreach work. He inspired young rabbis, especially his son-in-law, his successor, the 7th Rebbe, Menachem Schneerson, to establish Chabad House outreach centers and rebuild Jewish life in America.

Chabad, unlike other Chassidic sects, maintained insular lives in their community, but with a decidedly American and radical twist. Young yeshiva students and newly minted rabbis ventured out of their communities to mingle with those who were estranged from a Jewish life—with no questions asked. Chabad Houses were set up where they were needed most, on college campuses and cities with big Jewish populations. Over the decades Chabad emissaries landed in remote places, where Jewish residents might be few and far between but the Lubavitcher Rebbe intuited a need. These were often places where Jewish life was all but gone or minuscule, but where Jews were settling for business, language learning, or academic opportunities—like Tokyo.

EMERGING from the Omori train station sent me back in time. I had lived in a cozy apartment in Omori with my first *Japan Times* colleagues. Omori had a unique pre-war German history. German concert hall musicians, university professors, businesspeople, and a small number of prominent European Jews fleeing the Holocaust found sanctuary in Japan in the years before European borders were sealed and the concentration camp gas ovens were turned on. A number of Jews owed their lives to the German engineer and industrialist Willy Rudolf Forester, a stateless but vastly wealthy resident of Japan since the 1930s. He cooperated with an organization set up by the Jewish Refugee Committee of Japan to help rescue Holocaust survivors by employing them in his F. and K. Engineering Company in Omori—a stone's throw from where I was heading now.

Omori hadn't changed much since I'd lived there while working for *The Japan Times,* though the German bakery, makers of Tokyo's best sourdough rye bread, had sadly been replaced by a convenience store. A main street arcade still kept pedestrians and cyclists dry from the rains. I had remembered to pack the diapers, wet towels, and an extra change of clothes for Shoshana, but I had forgotten to take the address for Chabad House taped to the refrigerator in the cottage.

I spotted a Western woman hurrying along the busy main

street, *Ikegami dori*, wearing a smart-fitting navy suit and high heels, wheeling a small suitcase. When I asked if she was heading to Chabad House, she shook her head. Her crisp hat was perched over blonde hair lacquered into a perfect bun. No, she was a flight attendant.

Hundreds of people exited through the ticket wicket. It didn't occur to me that any Japanese would be heading to Chabad House. So, we waited and waited. I bought Shoshana an ice cream cone. We waited some more, until a late-afternoon gust of wind signaled that it was time to leave. I carried Shoshana down the steps to the train platform in both arms. We got back on the Keihin Tohoku train, switched at Shinagawa station, and I slumped into a seat for the long train ride back to Chiba. The house in the forest seemed more remote than ever.

We arrived at Chojamachi station as the sun dipped below the farmhouse rooftops. I fetched my bicycle from the station parking lot and hoisted Shoshana into her bicycle seat. She seemed not the least bit gloomy in this failed attempt to find Chabad House. She sang happily from her baby seat, her little hands warming me as she clung to my back. I switched on the bicycle lamp, and it illuminated a thin strip of pavement running through the rice fields. It seemed that God wasn't about to lead me without effort on my part to find Chabad House to meet these pious Chassids. It was as if my ambivalence toward the Jewish faith was being tested. I hadn't realized how much crossing into the Chabad world meant to me until I couldn't find their home address through no fault but my own.

Shoshana brought me to my senses with a pat on the back.

"Mama, where's Papa?" she asked. I felt her squirm in her seat.

"He's in Tokyo," I replied. I pointed to the forested camel-back hill we called home. Our house was hidden behind the cedars and it occurred to me that the house wasn't the only thing hiding. I was hiding from my identity too.

"Why doesn't he live with us?" Shoshana asked.

"He does—sort of," I said cheerfully. "He visits us, and we visit him in Tokyo."

"Then why isn't he with us now?" she said with a sense of rightness that took me aback, the assuredness of knowing what was best for her. Shoshana's intuition exceeded what I imagined a three-year-old could grasp. But I didn't know how to explain my need for breathing space.

With another holiday coming up, I gave Chabad a second try. Pushing Shoshana's stroller up the steep hill in Omori, I stopped to catch my breath. This hill reminded me of climbing Masada, where Jews fleeing their Roman conquerors took refuge twenty centuries ago. After Romans pillaged and destroyed Jerusalem's Holy Temple, they went after the small community of Jews trapped on Masada, an isolated mesa over-looking the Dead Sea. It took the Romans three years to reach the outpost in the sky, and when they invaded, they discovered that the Jews of Masada had opted for mass suicide rather than submit to their antisemitic conquerors.

Climbing Masada is a rite of passage that even my grandad, at eighty years old, undertook with his trusty wooden cane when he visited Israel. I climbed too, under punishing sunshine, on my first trip to Israel a few years after in 1980. Once I had reached the top of Masada and walked among the stone ruins, passing among the rubble of homes, bathhouses, and grain storage houses, I came to the spot marked by stones where the house of prayer had stood. This was where the Torah was learned and followed till the dying collective breath of the community. The sobering thought lingered that a Torah-led way of life takes courage.

A steep road with potted plants garnished a quiet hilltop neighborhood. Big homes fronted narrow streets. Trees were largely absent. As a twenty-year-old, I hadn't been able to imagine sacrificing my life on the day I climbed Masada. It was hard enough to keep myself safe on the darkened streets of Manhattan. Better to disassociate from, then to invite, tests of faith into my life. Or so I thought. By avoiding Jewish life altogether, as I got closer and closer to Chabad House, it occurred to me that I had outsmarted nobody. It was time to face my Masada.

I turned a corner into the neighborhood of Sanno 4-chome, worried that this Chabad House would pry out of me a Jewish version of Sunday church confession. I had rehearsed my response. I would bow my head before the rabbi and confess I had been a bad Jew. Instead of reading Mishnah, I had been reading *The Mutant Message Down Under*. I would tell him that I had not thought through my marriage to Ichiro. My arm brushed by a rose bush, and a thorn wedged into my forearm. Serves me right for wearing a short-sleeved, above the knee shirtdress. They will think I'm vulgar for dressing so immodestly.

I heard the voice inside. It spoke softly and lovingly. *Don't put yourself down. You did the best you could do. Remember those first words when you and Ichiro met: you've come together in this life because there's work to do and a family to create.*

I'd reached a neighborhood where I was ready to be tested. If something in my marriage was to be confronted, here was the place to do it. Except for a smattering of fringe neo-Nazis, whom I had seen once parading around Shibuya's shopping district, making complete imbeciles of themselves in military uniforms, Japan was a country with little appetite for antisemitism. Jews were free to practice their beliefs, so long as we didn't do anything stupid, like sacrifice sheep in the backyard. In Tokyo, the only restrictions to observing a Torah way of life came from my own ignorance.

Strung above a wooden front gate, a yellow banner presented the Lubavitcher Rebbe, with his bushy white beard and a black Borsalino hat that looked as if it had seen better days. He waved a lighthearted welcome from the banner. Below him, a woman smoked a cigarette, slouched with her eyes closed under the eaves of a rambling old wooden house. She wore a spaghetti strap top, to better show off her tattoos, I suppose. Her cutoff blue jeans rode high up her legs. I looked down at my beige safari shirtdress, bulging with pockets filled with crispy rice *sembei*. Maybe I was overdressed.

Shoshana tugged at my hand. She took matters into her own hands, pushing apart the sliding wooden doors. Shoes and sandals littered the *genkan*, the foyer. Shoshana immediately set about tidying up the shoes, lining them up in neat rows. She parked sturdy Hush Puppies next to Nike sneakers and Dr. Scholl's sandals. She paused to try on a pair of stiletto heels while singing could be heard from inside.

I didn't know what to expect, but this certainly wasn't like any Jewish house of worship, or Jewish home, for that matter, that I had stepped barefoot in before. A Tokyo address, come whether you're religious or not, dress as you like, with the Lubavitcher Rebbe waving his approval over the door—what in the world was this place?

The thought of making an about-face did occur to me. What right did I have to celebrate a Torah that I didn't read or follow? Just as I was ready to bolt, the Rebbetzin appeared. I assumed it had to be her—the sender of the apple and honey. She wore a buttoned up black-and-white silk stripe blouse paired with a skirt that brushed her ankles. She was carrying a newborn baby in her arms. The Rebbetzin welcomed me with a brilliant smile. "Welcome to Chabad House. Our home is your home!"

I smiled back with great relief. Being welcomed home, perhaps I wouldn't face an inquisition after all.

"You've come at the perfect time," she continued.

"Perfect? How's that for good luck!"

"Simchat Torah marks the completion of the annual reading

of the Torah. Next Shabbat, we begin reading from the book of Genesis all over again."

New beginnings. How auspicious. I smiled as I reached out to touch the tiny, warm hand of her 5-day-old child. The baby's eyes were tightly shut, off in his own world of bliss.

"Your baby is lovely," I said, trying hard to fathom how this baby, born in Japan of Chassidic parents, could possibly thrive here. I was about to find out that Simchat Torah offered the answer.

"How long are you here for?" I asked, as I followed the Rebbetzin down a short corridor, padding along barefoot on a pinky grey carpet.

"Until Moshiach comes," the Rebbetzin said, turning to me with a straight face.

"Moshiach? You mean the Messiah?" I followed the young Rebbetzin into a tatami-floored room decorated with a huge portrait of the same Rabbi as on the sign outside Chabad House.

"The Rebbe, Rabbi Menachem Mendel Schneerson, gives us the strength to be here."

"Your Rebbe has nice blue eyes." I had no idea what else to say.

What I knew about Simchat Torah was limited to a lithograph that used to hang in the dining room at home in Great Neck. The Chassids, drawn in pen and ink, were dancing in a circle, coat tails flying, heads thrown back, long beards mopping the air. I had thought the artist had a great imagination. But here they were in Tokyo. It was as if that lithograph in my childhood home had come to life. I would find out these young Yeshiva students were visiting from Crown Heights. They had come to help out the Rabbi and cook for the Rebbetzin.

"You've come at the perfect time!" the Rabbi said, appearing before us. He echoed his wife's invitation as he opened his arms, greeting me like a long-lost friend. "Welcome to Torah Island!"

he said effusively, as if Torah Island were a real place. In his mind, maybe it was.

I reached out to accept the Rabbi's hand. He instantly withdrew it. When I frowned, he thought it hilarious. This was how I discovered that in the Orthodox rulebook of life, there could be slapstick moments, too.

"I've never touched another woman's hands in all my life! Except my wife!" The Rabbi exclaimed.

"It looks that way!" I laughed, as I recalled standing outside the Omori train station, just days before, without the Chabad House address, when it was clearly not the perfect time. I followed the Rebbetzin to join her at a long table crowded, like a Fellini movie, with people you wouldn't expect at a Chassidic gathering. It was autumn, and still lots of skin was to be seen. A forearm here, well-pierced earlobes there, a rose tattoo. A bit of cleavage, a lot of cleavage, and that was only one side of the table.

This was not normal, or at least, nothing like the normal I associated with Orthodoxy. Would the Rebbe, staring down from his huge portrait, approve of such revelry? Years later, I would find out that this directive was not only to welcome, but to love every single Jewish soul, and had been passed down since the late 1700s by the Baal Shem Tov, the founder of Chassidism.

The Rabbi and Rebbetzin were young. They radiated warmth and social ease beyond their years. I was old enough to have been their mother—had I been a Chassid myself and begun birthing in my teens. The Rebbetzin wore an attractive wig of real brunette hair that fell straight and flipped stylishly to her shoulders. She complimented my unruly shoulder-length hair without a trace of judgment—even though no Chassidic woman in her right mind would be caught dead without a head covering.

"Tell me, why are you here?"

"We were given a blessing by the Rebbe to start a Chabad House in Tokyo."

"How do you get a blessing from a man who's no longer alive?"

"Never say that! Our Rebbe *is alive!*" the Rabbi practically squealed.

"Well, how do you get a blessing from the grave?"

"It's a Chassidic tradition to correspond by writing letters, inserting them into the Rebbe's many volumes of letters and teachings," the Rebbetzin explained. She passed me a plate of boiled egg crescents sprinkled appetizingly with paprika.

"We received a blessing to become *shluchim.*"

"*Schlu*—what?"

"*SHLUchim*—we're emissaries," the Rebbetzin explained. "We came here to give Jews a place to feel at home—and Japanese, too."

"Why Japanese?" I asked, as I thought of Ichiro, off on the other side of Tokyo, in a world steeped in Taoist, Shinto and Buddhist beliefs and traditions.

"The Rebbe instructed all his *shluchim* to teach the Seven Noahide Laws, which are the basic code of morality for non-Jews."

The Rebbetzin handed me a card printed with the seven Noahide Laws spelled out: 1. Do not worship idols. 2. Marry to have children. 3. Do not commit adultery. 4. Do not consume blood. 5. Do not steal. 6. Do not murder. 7. Do not bear false witness. So this Chabad House was here for the Japanese as much as the Jews. The list looked reasonable. No bending over backwards was required to follow these seven laws. In fact, it looked to me like a code of basic decency, until my eye circled back to that first law: Do not worship idols.

"Idols are everywhere in this country! Just down the street from here, there's a small shrine with a row of stone-chiseled babies wearing red bibs. They're there for families who lost their infants. Mothers feel great comfort by praying in front of these idols. How will you manage here?" I asked.

"Hashem will provide!" The Rabbi's hands reached up toward a fluorescent circle of light.

"It doesn't make one bit of sense," I told Ichiro later, when I got back to his parents' home. "These people are in a different league from any Rabbi or Rebbetzin I've met."

"A different league? Are they dangerous?" Ichiro asked with a worried expression, as if flashing back on Aum Shinrikyo, the renegade spiritual group that had brought homegrown murder and pandemonium to Tokyo's rush-hour train platforms, and beyond.

"No, they're not dangerous! To be in a different league is an idiom! They come from a place called Crown Heights in Brooklyn, the center of the Lubavitcher Chassidic movement."

Ichiro listened, deep in thought, as he snacked on a shrimp rice cracker. I explained that this young couple were among many who followed their Rebbe's inspiration.

"You ought to come with me to meet them," I said.

Ichiro offered me a cracker.

"Thanks," I said. "But today I'll pass on the shrimp."

The next Shabbat, I was so excited I could barely sleep. Ichiro agreed to push Shoshana in her stroller up the great hill in Sanno and accompany me to Chabad House. We were going together to meet this enigmatic young couple, the prankster Orthodox Rabbi and his gracious wife. We arrived just as the Rabbi began his lunchtime *D'var Torah*, a Shabbat talk that relates the weekly Torah chapter to the here and now.

"This week a visitor asked me why Chabad House guests remove shoes at the door. I explained that it's very important to

follow the customs of Japan. Local customs must be followed—
if they are not prohibited by Torah."

Ichiro nodded approvingly. "You see, Rabbi, I telling Liane
this all the time. Do in Rome as the Romans doing. It good for
her to following local customs."

"Ichiro! The Romans destroyed our Beit Hamikdash! Our
Holy of Holies! They sent us to live in the diaspora!"

The Rabbi reached for Ichiro's plastic cup and filled it with
wine.

"*Diaspora?* What's that?" Ichiro's brow furrowed as he
scanned the great internal rolodex containing his English
vocabulary, searching for the unfamiliar word. But he couldn't,
because nobody he knew had ever been forced to uproot from
they're birthplace to a foreign land while running for their lives.

"Ichiro, have you ever heard of the Beit Hamikdash, the
ancient Holy Temple that was destroyed?" the Rabbi asked.

"I recalling smash glass under chuppah."

"*Beduke*–exactly. The Beit Hamikdash, the Holy Temple, was
where God rested among us. It was the meeting place of the
Twelve Tribes of Israel, where we came three times a year to
offer sacrifices to Hashem. The Beit Hamikdash was destroyed
by the Romans. It was our catastrophe—but you know the miracle, Ichiro? The Western Wall remains standing in Jerusalem.

"Where Jews next went?"

"They were forced to leave Jerusalem. Many settled in
Lebanon, Syria, Afghanistan, Iraq, and Persia. Others followed
the Silk Road into India and China. Some crossed the Mediter-
ranean by boat to North Africa or they went to Europe and
followed the idol-worshipping ways—God forbid!—of the
Roman Empire."

The Rabbi pointed to the framed photograph above him.
"The Rebbe, of Blessed Memory, spoke about the Lost Tribes of
Israel and said that the Jews reached Japan, too. You know what
that means, Ichiro? You could be Jewish!"

Ichiro laughed wholeheartedly, as if this was a most prepos-
terous notion. I laughed, too, but for a different reason. I
thought how nice if this were true. This Rabbi and Rebbetzin
were firing me up to learn about and own my Jewish story. It
didn't feel daunting, even if it could take a lifetime to know only
a drop of what there was to learn in Torah. The inquisition that
I feared upon arriving at Chabad House never happened.

"It's great you learning about your Jewish roots," Ichiro said
after we arrived home. I stepped into our *genkan*, a tiny foyer,
removed my shoes, and placed them back in the shoebox.

"Look how you adapting to Shintoism, Buddhism, and
Taoism. Now you blending it with Jew-dism."

Tears welled in my eyes. "Judaism."

What's the matter?" Ichiro said.

"It doesn't feel right."

"What doesn't feel right?"

"Trying to adapt to your world is tiring me out. It's time that
I learn about my own customs, and beliefs."

"But Japan is your home, now!" Ichiro insisted. "I never stopping you. See—you wanting to live in Chiba, so you doing that."

The Rabbi said that foreigners like us follow the customs out
of respect. But that doesn't mean you have to lose your soul
along the way. I'd like to think I can take my shoes off in the
house and keep my Jewish backbone at the same time. If we can
do that, then there's hope.

I was ready to move back to Tokyo. I flipped on the
computer to research houses for rent within an easy commute
of Chabad House. I had hope now that we could rechart our
family's destiny in a Jewish direction. We found an apartment in
the Meguro Ward of Tokyo, an easy train ride to Chabad House
and to Ichiro's parents, too.

I started to help out the Rebbetzin on Fridays, participating
in the behind-the-scenes activity that led to beautiful Shabbat
meals for those who reserved and those who walked in. I

learned to douse traditional Israeli salads made from tomatoes, onions, mashed eggplant, and hummus with olive oil, garlic, fresh lemon, za'atar and paprika. This way of preparing salads was so tasty that I started preparing Chabad-style salads at home.

Some things that the Rebbetzin did were less easy to fathom. I noticed that whenever I visited Chabad House, the hands on the wall clock weren't moving. The time was perpetually 2:00 p.m. "Is there some special meaning in keeping it up there?" I asked the Rebbetzin one day. I knew so little about Chassidic ways that everything seemed open to scrutiny, including the Rebbetzin's relationship to time.

"No, not at all," she burst out laughing. "The clock keeps breaking, so I've learned to live with it."

This was kind of crazy. Or maybe the truth of the matter was that the little money they had went to putting food on the table for their guests. This Chabad House never charged for their beautiful homemade meals. They survived on donations. My strong reaction to the broken clock came from another ingrained idea instilled in me by my mother. No clock—in fact, not even a hairpin—would be found in my childhood home if it was not in service and performing its job.

I walked to the nearby shopping arcade in front of Omori station and returned with a new clock. It would sit in its box for weeks before it was swapped for the broken clock. I didn't know how to take it, whether it was a mitzvah to live in utmost simplicity and shun unessential gifts, or whether it was just an interesting quirk of the Rebbetzin to do so.

"Of course, time is important, especially birthdays," she clarified, when I decided to bring up the clock issue again on a different Shabbat. She could deftly maneuver a conversation by aligning its subject with Torah. "People notice time around their birthdays. In my family, the day my parents discovered the Lubavitcher world became like a birthday."

"That's interesting. So, your own parents discovered Chabad as adults."

"Yes, that was in the 1960s, when the Chabad movement was just beginning to organize on college campuses under the Rebbe's leadership." This Tokyo Chabad House wasn't just the Rebbetzin's home address. In a profound way, she wanted me to feel that this Chabad House belonged to me too.

"The Rebbetzin is in that kitchen day and night preparing for guests," I told my mother on the phone. She cooks all those meals without expecting anything in return."

"Much as I admire her generosity, Liane, I beg of you. Be careful. There's a catch."

She was serious. My mother used my name when she wanted to emphasize *her* point.

"Stop being so naïve, darling! They want you to become like them."

"What would be so bad about that? You would rather me become a Buddhist?"

"You? A Buddhist? Oh, you do make me laugh. I adore Ichiro and his parents, but enough is enough!" my mother chortled. "I am delighted that you're interested in the mitzvot in the Torah. Forging a closer relationship with God certainly can't do any harm. But maybe there's another issue here. If you and Ichiro had regular date nights, you might cure yourself. For in truth, the prospect of spending twenty-five hours in Shabbat obser-vance, to me, is very ambitious. But I'm afraid it's your life, now."

On Shabbat afternoon, after the hot pot of cholent was cleared from the table and platters of imported nuts and dried fruit appeared, the Rebbetzin and I got into a routine of opening the Gutnick edition of the Torah. All my daily worries would disappear within its brown-and-gold embossed cover, as I came to not just know more about the journey of the Israelites crossing the miraculously split sea, but feel I had been there too, receiving the Ten Commandments from Moses on Sinai, collecting in my hands manna from heaven, and fearing the reprise of fierce giants who stalked the land of Israel. One Shabbat at a time, Torah lessons helped me acquire more strength to own my beliefs. I had no idea how essential this would be in the years to come.

Whether it was learning Torah or helping prepare for Shabbat at Chabad House, the Rebbetzin's kitchen was her mission control. We would stand side by side, preparing the challah dough. The Rebbetzin would measure out flour from a huge sack. When the dough had risen, we rolled out logs and braided them, talking about family, friends, and Torah while waiting for the bread to rise. She talked about how every child was a blessing, and I loved her positive scan for the good in everyone. We also spoke about mundane things that weren't so trivial to the young Rabbi and Rebbetzin with little working knowledge of the Japanese language. Where do you buy ripe, but not too ripe avocados? Where do you stand—by the door or crouch under the table—if a big earthquake hits? We spoke about topics I'd never considered before, like where to go to get a wig washed and blow-dried. In the Rebbetzin's kitchen, conversation meandered this way and that, while trays of challah baked in the oven. The Rebbetzin handed me a roll to taste.

"Perfect," I said.

The Rebbetzin made herself available to me despite having not a free second for herself. I wanted to learn, and I wanted to give back, and yet my insecurities persisted about where I was heading with this growing connection to Chabad House.

Shoshana, too, had her doubts and her questions. They were a child's questions and just as valid and Torah-based as mine. She wanted to know why she couldn't share her chocolate with the Rebbetzin's growing brood of children. The chocolate had been stamped with a K for kosher, but also a D for dairy. It meant that the milk put in the chocolate hadn't been under enough Rabbinical supervision to be certified kosher.

"Then I never want to be like them," she pouted, with a preschooler's precocious convictions. On another occasion, Shoshana brought her favorite orange plush monkey, a soft, velvety toy to Chabad House. She wanted to present the monkey to the Rebbetzin's son. I had to gently steer her from that sweet gesture, after the Rebbetzin pulled me aside to explain the problem with stuffed animals of a certain type.

"But why, Mama?"

"The monkey is not a kosher animal."

"The baby isn't going to eat the toy, is he?"

The Rebbetzin was gentle in declining the gifts of non-kosher animals and other things that I had no idea were forbidden. Shoshana didn't like the rejection, and the growing gap between how she was being raised at home and what she saw at Chabad House bothered her a lot.

It would have been different, if she had cousins to play with, but Ichiro's brother and sister didn't have children. Ichiro's cousins with children of the same age were seen under the most solemn of occasions—dressed in party dresses and little suits for weddings and funerals. So, sadly, Shoshana had little chance to know her cousins in a relaxed way. She had few friends in the neighborhood, although her classmates' mothers weren't shy to ask me to teach their children English lessons. Spending Shabbat at Chabad House intensified her feeling different from the Rebbetzin's own growing brood of children. The heroes of Shoshana's favorite fairytales—lions, tigers, horses, bears, and pigs—were non-kosher animals and thus off-limits to the Rebbetzin's children. I told Shoshana that we could respect Chabad's ways and follow our own at home.

I kept returning because there was more to respect than not. The Rebbetzin had been incredibly courageous to leave behind a familiar world, where her entire life could have been scripted by marriage within her community back in Brooklyn. Instead, here she was adjusting to the unfathomable, birthing and raising Chassidic children and educating them on tatami-mat floors. She would role-play with Shoshana and her own toddlers. Shoshana loved when the Rebbetzin stooped over, grabbed an umbrella, and behaved like a very old lady in order to get the children to care for the weak. Shoshana became her happiest self when given the chance to run and bring the old lady a chair or a glass of water. The Rebbetzin made the children laugh, got their undivided attention, and with a scarf over her wig, a tremble in her voice, the great actress could barely conceal she was pregnant with another baby.

"I'm over forty," I sighed, interrupting the fun when it was time to take Shoshana home. "I guess one child is it for me, though I would love to have a second."

"Of course you can!" she said. I stood in the small foyer after picking up Shoshana, and, as often happened, talk was so meaningful that I found it hard to pull myself away—until it came to Torah. At first, I wanted to understand their way of life, but not necessarily follow it. But I came to realize that becoming an observant Jew was not just about observing. It did mean following too. As long as I resisted, a plexiglass wall existed between me and the Chabad way of life, with the Rebbe, Menachem Mendel Schneerson, guiding a mission that I was the beneficiary of, but couldn't quite bring myself to follow. This family practiced selflessness, kindness, and inclusiveness like nothing I had ever witnessed before. The Rebbetzin listened to my self-doubts and offered a surprising take of her own. "We are all on the same journey. As more light comes into us, we have more light to give, to serve, to be available to help other people," she said encouragingly.

❀

Chapter Eleven

A MOHEL FOR AKIVA

Because of you
I'm able to run through a troop;
and with your help,
I scale a wall.
—Psalm 18

To become Orthodox would mean committing to a way of life so different from the one I knew from childhood. It would affect my marriage in drastic ways. Practicing the Chabad Lubavitcher brand of Orthodoxy felt like a vast undertaking. But I was drawn to this Rebbetzin's many kindnesses to strangers, the Rabbi's generosity, and their childrens' comfortable and respectful way of speaking to their parents. If anyone of these *middos*, Yiddish for virtues, rubbed off on me, could there really be any harm?

One afternoon, on my way home from Shabbat lunch I stood waiting at the bus stop with a bag of groceries. Shopping on Shabbat was a no-no for the Orthodox, but who was I? A

Shabbat celebrant? A conservative Jew who could bend the rules as required? Just as I was thinking these thoughts, I looked up to see the Rabbi passing me with a wave and a smile. He was on his way to the mikvah, for his Saturday afternoon bathhouse dunk and he had caught me red-handed with my groceries smack in the middle of Shabbat. But incredibly, his facial expression didn't change. He didn't show a hint of disapproval. Any thoughts he had about my violation of the Sabbath, he kept to himself. Regardless, I was shaken up. My conscience voiced what the Rabbi didn't say: that I didn't want to go on this way, partaking of the Shabbat meal but not putting in the effort to experience a full day of rest. Who knows? Maybe I'd like it. Change is scary. If it I did find Shabbat pleasant and relaxing, I instinctively knew that there would be no turning back.

"A *Baal Teshuva* is not expected to dive in to observe all the *mitzvah*, the commandments of the Torah. The mitzvah will only stay with you when you take them on very gradually," the Rebbetzin reassured me when I called her after Shabbat to discuss my hesitations.

"Which mitzvah do I begin with?" I asked.

"How about lighting Shabbat candles on time?"

"Okay, that's easy enough." But in fact, it wasn't.

I started arriving at Chabad House with Shoshana eighteen minutes before Shabbat, to light candles. *Not* twenty minutes. This was not simple for someone who timed her life, as Ichiro would put it, on the knife's edge. The Friday afternoon traffic could make a twenty-minute bus ride take double the time.

I learned that the rabbinical sages had instituted this practice of adding a few minutes to Shabbat before and after it starts to make sure that work was not accidentally performed. I discovered, too, that the peaceful, gentle energy that comes with lighting the candles actually had a gender. Shabbat is female, a queen, and a bride.

"If the Sabbath is compared to a bride, shouldn't there be a groom?" I asked the Rebbetzin one Friday night while we ladled soup for a long table of guests.

"It goes back to Mount Sinai. When Israelites stood before God in the desert, they were told to remember Shabbat and keep it holy. But God also made it clear that Shabbat was the mate of the Jewish people. We need Shabbat to complete ourselves."

The mate to the Jewish people was a day of rest.

The Rebbetzin explained that two extra souls descend on us. One is automatic. It will come down, no matter what. The other is dependent on happiness. This Soul comes down in the spirit of rejoicing.

By arriving on time, I could join in singing *Lecha Dodi*, the beautiful, melodic, 500-year-old prayer to welcome the Sabbath Bride, the peaceful energy of the seventh day of the week. *Lecha Dodi* offers eight catchy stanzas and a refrain that rises to the crescendo: *"Bou-ii-Kala. Bou-ii-Kala,"* "Enter, O Bride! Enter, O Bride!" I had been practicing *Lecha Dodi* at home, reviewing the Hebrew alphabet, with its complexity of dots and dashes for vowels, so that I could more easily read along. With growing confidence, I belted out the tongue-twisting lyrics and alliteration, as if the Soul of all Souls, God himself, were to walk in the door at any moment. Just then, I felt a tug at my sleeve. I looked down to see Shoshana wagging a disapproving finger.

"Not now, I'm singing *Lecha Dodi*," I hushed. I was on a roll, and nothing was going to stop me.

"But Mama, you're the only girl singing."

I looked around. By golly, my four-year-old was right. Only the men were singing.

At the dinner table, I brought up the singing matter with the Rebbetzin.

"Yes, Shoshana is so observant! Women don't sing because it could arouse men."

"Where does it say in the Torah that women can't join in the singing?" I asked after we had all sat down for chicken soup.

"The Talmudic interpretation is that a woman's voice is *ervah*, immodest, like exposing her nakedness," the Rebbetzin said.

"Believe me, no man is going to be aroused by my singing. Perfect pitch? Not even close," I laughed.

Shoshana leaned over to whisper in my ear. ""Mama, just stop singing. You don't want to be naked, do you?"

The Rabbi's sharp ears had picked up our conversation. He also had a brilliant smile, well-aligned teeth, and an impressive black beard. He radiated joy like heat from a furnace. You would have thought that coming to Tokyo to repair this Torah-forsaken corner was for the Rabbi the greatest privilege in the world.

At Chabad House, I learned to tap my foot, never bothering to ask if that's allowed either. In my own home, I sang my heart out.

"There has to be a catch," my mother said into the phone. "They'll never cross into *our* world."

Our world? I was torn. Was my mother telepathic? That evening, the Rabbi dropped by to put up mezuzahs on the door frames of our home. To Shoshana's delight, he brought his little boy. But when Shoshana invited him in, he bashfully waited in the hallway for his father.

"Come on in! Our house is your house!" I said.

But the little boy wouldn't budge. We had been to Chabad House so many times that it was only natural to want to welcome the Rabbi's son into our home, too. I don't know whether it was our two cats, Griffin and Maillol, that he feared, or the Harrod's Teddy Bear guarding a pair of slippers. The Rebbetzin later explained that it was because the Rabbi had been in a great hurry to get on to his next appointment.

"Please have him come another time when our little ones can play together," I said.

She smiled, and it never happened.

This relationship was going to be unlike any I had had with a woman before. The Rebbetzin was wise beyond her years, and yet I was practically old enough to be her mother. She reigned in her kitchen with a sense of purpose and joy that I found astonishing: she could multitask like nobody's business. I learned from her while peeling vegetables hours on Thursdays, a comfortable day before the arrival of Shabbat guests—those who made reservations and those who just showed up in the way family members do when they feel at home.

I started to get a wonderful feeling that the Shabbat table was as much theirs as mine. When the last guest had gone home for the well-deserved *shluff*, when it's utterly okay to take a Shabbat nap in the middle of the afternoon, we would, more times than not, open the Gutnick edition of the Torah. With nearly every page offering differing insights from the Rebbe, Rashi, and other rabbinic luminaries, we would work on solving one perplexing issue after the other—except the Rebbetzin never called this work. She called it learning, and I found this sweet and inviting. To "learn Torah" sounded pleasant and from the heart, with no pressure "to study." Nobody was going to test me. The tests would come from how I now interacted with the world around me, and learning about the subtleties of self-control by waiting until Shabbat had ended to do some shopping.

The chapter we were reading was Chayei Sarah, *Sarah Lived*, which starts paradoxically with Sarah's death. News of her one and only son Isaac's imminent sacrifice at the hands of her husband, Avraham, caused a heart attack, and she passed away instantly. She didn't live to hear the end of a sentence. It was one more lesson in choosing words and the timing of their delivery with the utmost care. Sarah never heard the part about the ram—which was sacrificed instead of her beloved son.

At Chabad House, I was learning, week by week, how ancient Torah can provide striking comparisons to daily life choices today, and the raw material for rich conversation and a blossoming friendship. I became closer to the Rebbetzin through Torah learning. The intimacy of sharing the Torah with a study partner means that I could leave behind my troubles, which paled in comparison to Avraham and Sarah.

As we got deeper into the story of the near sacrifice of Isaac, the plot thickened when the ram appeared through Divine intervention. Here was a lesson for the toolbox of life: to act out of faith and let God choose the sacrifice. I could accept Avraham's act of faith. But what bothered me was how Isaac, a 37-year-old grown man, would compliantly lie down, allow his father to bind his hands, and raise a knife to his neck. What sort of a son does that? There's not a word here to hint at Isaac's reaction.

The Rebbetzin read each sentence slowly, absorbing *Sarah Lived* as if for the first time, even though she had been learning Torah all her life.

"There's no hint of Isaac's reaction," I said. The Rebbetzin explained how Mishnah and the Talmud, which is rabbinical commentary written down after the destruction of the second Temple, have filled in Torah for the past 2,000 years. Not that she was suggesting I take up swapping Talmud for the daily newspaper. Her words were more nuanced than that. She explained that the learner and life circumstances shape one's understanding of the Torah. Since each chapter shows up once a year, she explained, we read the text differently each year.

Gradually, I could come to accept the Rebbetzin's viewpoint: Isaac didn't surrender like a sheep. Talmudic commentary on every word of Torah, she explained, illuminates the unfathomable. "Isaac was so eager to do what God had commanded his father that he begged his father to tie his wrists to his feet extra tight, to prevent him from jerking suddenly under the knife."

Whew, that's intense.

"Let's read on," she said. "Along came a ram which appeared after Avraham heard God's angel. The ram trapped in a nearby thicket so Avraham could easily slaughter it instead."

When Avraham reached the end of the road, not even challenging God to a debate—when there was nothing more for Avraham to do, except following God's orders—that ram's appearance showed divine intervention. It also required quick thinking on Avraham's part to put aside an intention he was poised to act upon at the very last moment.

"How do you know whether your actions are ever correct?" I asked. "You can't always expect a ram to be waiting in the bush."

The Rebbetzin laughed. "Why not? That's what it means to have faith in *Hashem*."

My faith in the God of Avraham didn't happen overnight. But week by week, it gained traction, as I absorbed Torah word by word. I may obsess over Isaac's mysterious complacency this year, and next year, maybe I'll get into a tizzy over the ram's sudden appearance on a rocky, desert mountaintop. Sarah had become a mother at ninety. Miracles could happen.

Learning Torah on Shabbat was one thing. Having the faith that it actually could mean something significant in my life was another. I had to take Sarah, the matriarch, and her extraordinary birth in old age out for a test drive. In other words, I had to apply lessons of faith to my own life. I thought to myself, what can I do that would be a stretch of faith? Having a child at 42 was something I never believed possible.

"I feel lucky to have one child. It took six years of trying to conceive Shoshana," I told the Rebbetzin. And here, I hesitated to admit the truth. "I would love to have a second child. But can I?"

"Of course, you can!" the Rebbetzin said.

"Tell me, what is the secret? Why is it that Orthodox women seem to have an easy time of conceiving one child after the other?"

"The mikvah," she said.

Now, this was going to be a stretch. It just wasn't the thing to do in my family.

"The ritual bath for purification where women go after their menstruation ends? But there is no mikvah in Tokyo, is there?" I asked.

"You can do it in the sea." The Rebbetzin made it sound like no big deal. Naked.

"Well, there are hordes of people on the beaches."

"We know of a secluded beach."

And just like that, my faith would be tested. I would do a mikvah, a ritual dunking in sea water timed to my fertility cycle. On the appointed evening, the Rebbetzin turned up at my front door, with the Rabbi in the driver's seat.

"He's coming?" I asked in surprise. This private women's affair was about to morph into a Chabad House project.

The Rabbi adjusted his black hat with a taxi driver's smile. "This is my job, too."

I stepped into a van with a giant menorah fixed to the roof. He might as well have driven with a banner saying: "Off to Purify the Menstruator!" We zoomed off for a fast drive to the Miura Peninsula coast. The beach was empty when we got there, well past dark. The sea was tranquil, and bright stars were our only Peeping Toms.

The Rabbi stayed in the car, far from where we were heading. The Rebbetzin swapped her wig for a scarf; then, she accompanied me waist-deep into the sea. She held a prayer book up to the moonlight, and I recited a short prayer. I dunked for an instant, then reached for the towel in the Rebbetzin's hands.

We drove to the Miura peninsula a month later to do my second mikvah in the sea. I didn't need to do a third. I became pregnant just like that. But at week 22 I was admitted to Red Cross Hospital to prevent premature delivery.

I had never in my life been hospitalized before—as my mother reminded me when I called her with the news. "Don't go for the short end of the stick. You're going to have a marvelous baby, for heaven sakes. Morbid thoughts have no place in a hospital." None of us on the New York side of my family had been hospitalized much. The preferred way to exit this world in my family was to drop dead of a stroke, or better yet, drift off in an old age sleep.

With my art supplies and sketchpad scattered over the bed, I drew pictures of my children, the one I could hold and the one inside me. These drawings kept my spirits up, especially the ones I made of the baby boy inside. Together we were reassuring each other, in drawing after drawing, that everything was going to be alright.

After a month, I was allowed to go outside in a wheelchair. Okaasan pushed me through the parting glass-front doors into a garden shaded by lush blossoming pink yaezakura, the double cherry blossoms, that come out in mid-April. I sent up a prayer in thanks for the powers that be that placed this garden here for patients and families to bring much needed joy during hard times. We came to a stop by a park bench. A black crow sat on a limb overhead, cawing so loudly Okaasan had to wheel me to another bench.

"The baby will be fine," she told me. "I've been praying for you both."

"I've been praying for all of us too," I said, with no trace of spiritual rivalry.

Being in the hospital wasn't just tough on me. It was very

hard on Ichiro, as he juggled work, picking up Shoshana from preschool, and taking her by bus to see me. He sat by my bedside and would disappear into his notebook, writing about the experience of being a house husband—as he called it. With his nose in his book, Shoshana and I had much needed time together. But when the dinner tray arrived, Shoshana tugged on my arm, although I was hooked to a drip. "Mama, come home."

"I can't right now. But I will very soon and bring home a baby for us all to love."

Shoshana had brought Eric Carle's *The Very Hungry Caterpillar* and slapped the caterpillar on the cover hard to get my attention. When I slapped the caterpillar back, she didn't like that one bit, so she hit me. Shocked, I broke down. My tears became unstoppable. Ichiro looked up from his notebook. He didn't know what to say or do. He put his hand on my back instead to send me energy. He pulled out a container with wands of carrot sticks he had cut for me at home.

"I'm sorry. I'm tired. I'm worried. It's a lot of work take care of a child."

"I know." I looked over at him.

He reached into his briefcase to pull out a notebook. "I keeping a journal. Can I reading it to you?"

I looked at Shoshana. She snuggled into my lap, perhaps happy to see us talking to each other—no matter what her parents were feeling inside. Shoshana re-opened *The Very Hungry Caterpillar* and looked at the pictures on her own.

"Everything that happens is for soul growth," Ichiro began reading. "I may not liking it, but God providing me with the best. I understanding why John Lennon say it's a good lesson be house husband. Now I hanging laundry in the morning, then I folding it at bedtime. I making school lunch boxes before I dropping Shoshana off at school. I picking her up for visit her mama in the hospital. Then I repeating the same thing the next day."

Ichiro's written words reached my heart. I guided his hand to my belly, our baby kicked back at him, and Shoshana squeezed in between us.

"You not staying here forever," Ichiro said.

"But the doctors want me here till I deliver."

On the tray was a traditional dinner of miso soup, grilled mackerel, little side dishes of vegetables, and a bowl of rice. Shoshana ate the chocolate pudding for dessert, while Ichiro called the White Crane Clinic to see what Incho thought about getting me home sooner.

"Incho saying 99 percent chance you delivering not early if you getting treatment at the White Crane Clinic."

I was ready to return to go home, to get treatments at the White Crane Clinic, and stay positive. The drawings I made in hospital were training me to see what was ahead in the best possible light, and that's all one can do—to believe in the best possible outcome. It took negotiating with Red Cross Hospital, but after five weeks of hospitalization, Incho at the White Crane Clinic put me on a blood-cleansing, uterus-space-making, vegetarian diet and daily treatments to gradually regain my strength. Two weeks before my due date, on the evening of July 24th, I gave birth to my son. Akiva arrived in this world with Ichiro's round Buddha-like face and my Ashkenazi blue eyes—just as I had drawn him. As the Torah affirmation goes: *Think good and it will be good.* Visualizing the desired outcome with love in my heart, right down to the last detail in a drawing, seemed like an act of the imagination. But I learned at Red Cross Hospital the power of a drawing to literally "draw toward me" the good.

RABBI MOISHE LEIDER, a towering father of eleven, arrived in Tokyo with an overnight bag packed with his surgical tools. The Rabbi had found this *mohel* to do the circumcision. He had tracked down the director of UC San Diego Chabad House, a rabbi with a long, dark straggly beard streaked with white who wore the Lubavitcher uniform: a dark suit, white shirt and a black hat. Ichiro and Okaasan poured hot tea for my dear friends, the early risers who crossed town to be with our family for Akiva's *Brit Milah*, his circumcision ceremony.

"This must be hard for you to see. Thank you for going along with it," I whispered to Ichiro. "It's very hard for me to see, too." My father-in-law had stayed home because he couldn't stand the sight of blood—not that any of us except the Mohel saw it.

"Circumcision is hygienic. Less chances of infections down there," Ichiro said, having put up no resistance to Akiva's circumcision.

"Thank you. You understood how much this means to me."

When it was time to begin, I handed our baby to the Rabbi. He cooed happily with his eyes closed. I almost detected a wink. Sunshine filtered through the blinds, landing on the Mohel's surgical instruments. Akiva looked angelic in his flowing white gown, seated on the Rabbi's lap. The mohel took up the knife. I held my breath. In the silence, I felt the generations of men in my family filter into my imagination. There was my father, holding a paintbrush in one hand and a civil engineer's three-sided ruler in the other. My uncle Max showed up carrying a colorful stained-glass lamp he had made in the psychedelic sixties. My Romanian grandparents were there, standing in front of the tall oak doors to their stately house in Braila. I saw my English grandparents standing on opposite sides of a London tennis court, where they first laid eyes on each other. These were the Jews of my ancestry and the memories I carried that brought them to Japan. This is also the beauty of religion and carrying traditions forward. As my father liked to say, "I got out of Romania to continue the *chainya*."

All eyes turned toward Akiva, resting peacefully on the Rabbi's lap. I bit my lip. It was hard to witness my newborn's pain. When his cry came, I cried too while Rabbi Leider took a napkin, dipped it in red wine, and placed it between Akiva's lips. He patted the baby's little back with big hands, and Akiva calmed down, falling asleep on the *mohel's* shoulder.

The Rabbi grabbed Ichiro's shoulders, planted kisses on left and right cheeks, and got us all singing: *"B'Simon tov u'mazel tov! B'Simon tov u'mazel tov!"* It was a happy moment, as only heaven knows. My Jewish family made in Japan was complete.

OVER THE EARLY WEEKS, when Akiva still had the scent of sweet milk, I threaded his chubby arms through white kimono sleeves. He slept peacefully, and when Shoshana wanted his attention, his big blue eyes sought her out. Shoshana loved gazing at her calm baby brother. We all did.

Along the gravel path framed by forest at Meiji Shrine, our shoes crunched over small stones. My mother had come for a visit to meet her grandchild, and no matter how many times she came to Tokyo, she marveled over the gardens.

"Simply marvelous! Japanese gardens are wonders of the world."

"Yeh.

"Yeh? Just yeh? Darling, a penny for your thoughts."

I admitted to my mother the truth—that even though I was blessed with two beautiful children, a loving husband, in-laws above reproach, good health, few financial worries, I was feeling depressed.

I let her put her arm around my stiff shoulders. We continued walking with Shoshana running ahead and Akiva in his baby carrier, close to my heart. "You have nothing to fear. Just open up to Ichiro directly when you're feeling this way."

"Well—the problem is that I know what I have to do. I just haven't acted on it."

"Which is?" my mother asked, her voice rising in response to mine lowering.

"To raise Shoshana and Akiva with Jewish identity in Japan. My conscience won't allow me to think otherwise."

"That's very admirable, but not very practical," my mother said, tutting under her breath. "The children are Ichiro's as well as yours."

"Sometimes I wonder whose side you're on," I shot back.

"Of course, I'm on your side, darling. You're my daughter, my own flesh and blood. But I do have my concerns. You're not thinking of becoming a Chabadnik, are you?"

I broke into a smile. "Come on, Mom. Who me?"

We had come to the end of the path leading to Meiji Jingu, Tokyo's most sacred Shinto shrine, a sprawling compound composed of grand one-story wooden buildings built around a vast courtyard, their soaring rooftops surrounded by trees. Worshippers stood outside the shrine, said a prayer, pulled a rope, and tossed coins into a charity box that ran the length of the main building's porch.

Leaving the tranquility of Meiji Shrine, one among Japan's three Imperial sacred sites of worship. I was in a quandary. I could imagine myself going in the Orthodox direction but I couldn't imagine *not* going anymore to Meiji Shrine, a sanctuary in Tokyo of forests and peaceful gravel strolling paths.

We headed to Omotesando, the splendid tree-lined shopping street modeled after Paris's Champs Elysees. My mother wasn't interested in the luxury brand stores—Christian Dior, Louis Vuitton, or Ralph Lauren. She wanted to go see *kabuki*, so we boarded the subway to the Ginza, got our discount tickets, and took our seats in the upper mezzanine of the Kabukiza Theatre. Lighthearted dancers in brightly patterned kimonos pranced in front of pine trees in an era when Tokyoites could see Mount Fuji from their sliding paper doors. My mother whispered how lucky to be able to see kabuki whenever I wished, but I told her that this outing was not the norm. The last time I'd been to this theatre was on my mother's previous trip to Tokyo.

"You see? You've become so involved with Chabad that you have denied yourself going to the theatre."

"Mom, Ichiro and I never went to the theatre before Chabad."

"Why not?"

"Theatre tickets are expensive."

"Come, now," she said, as she bit into salmon sushi, thinking this was nonsense. "Certainly, there's always the upper mezzanine seats like we're sitting in now. But you go on dates with Ichiro once in a while, don't you?"

"Not really."

"Why on earth not?"

"I guess I just gave up after a while. You don't go on dates once you've had children. It's not the done thing here."

I pointed out to my mother that the Rabbi and the Rebbetzin never went on date nights either. "They don't have time to waste, and they see no necessity because they work together in every aspect of running Chabad House."

"Well, you're not running a Chabad House."

It wasn't that Ichiro was avoiding me. But he needed to feed his family—he told me. If that meant late night and weekend meetings with Adachi Sensei and his followers gathered in different cities around Japan, then I had to accept it now that Ichiro had become one in this inner circle.

On my mother's last Shabbat in Tokyo, I took her to Chabad House to meet the Rabbi and Rebbetzin, whom she'd heard so much about. She chose a pale-green lightweight tank top shell and matching cardigan, which she coordinated with white Capri pants, a straw hat, and sunglasses. The Rebbetzin greeted us warmly. She kissed my mother as if she were a long-lost relative.

"Make yourself at home, Adrianne. Consider this your

home," she said. The air conditioning wasn't working in the dining room, so my mother cooled herself with the fan advertising low-interest loans that she had been handed at the train station.

"If you would be more comfortable, please feel free to take off your cardigan."

My mother breathed a sigh of relief. She took off the cardigan and gave me a wink. I smiled back. Too much skin, but never mind. She grasped in that instant what I had found so inspirational about the Rebbetzin. She had an empathetic heart. The Rebbetzin could accept anyone who walked through the door into Chabad House, even if it meant putting herself into another's shell.

A CHILDHOOD RITE of passage is the *Shichi, Go, San* ceremony. On Shoshana's seventh birthday, we drove to Shitaya Shrine near her grandparents' home. Shoshana followed the elders' lead, clapping her hands, pulling a rope to ring a bell, and looking herself like a doll in a red floral kimono, her shiny brown hair piled high for the camera. I'd become used to these Shinto occasions and saw no reason to be a hypocrite and object, especially when my own wedding had been consecrated by the Shinto priest at the Imperial Hotel. They were doing their best to accommodate the changes I was going through toward embracing Jewish mitzvot. I was doing my best to respect their traditions too. And every step of the way, our children were growing up between these fragile balancing acts.

The kimono-clad waitresses greeted us with a knowing look in their eyes, as if to say: Ah, that's the foreign daughter-in-law, the one who requests that the seafood specialty of the house be swapped for tofu. I thought it was too much to explain to the restaurant that the *oyomesan*—me, the daughter-in-law—was Jewish, followed special dietary laws, and had a long list of things she couldn't eat. But they knew because Ichiro had called ahead, and the restaurant went to great lengths to present exquisite morsels made from *tofu* and just plain *fu*, made from the gluten of wheat.

THE IN-LAWS WOULD COME to our house to tutor Shoshana in Japanese. Grandma had her day. Grandpa had his. I was attempting to teach Shoshana to read in English too, but we were struggling with auditory processing causing her dyslexia. The one family member she felt understood by was her grandmother, given that I was often the subject of her frustration.

"Why did I have to be born to not only an American but a Jewish mother?"

"You're Japanese and that's what matters," her grandmother consoled her with a message I would have worded differently. It's no wonder Shoshana was confused.

"You have to believe in your strength. Don't be afraid of your child. All children want to be loved and accepted," the Rebbetzin advised me on a Shabbat afternoon when she sent out one of her boys from the dining room for a timeout. At Chabad House, a timeout involved learning a hefty *pasuk*, a verse of the Torah. In my house, a timeout meant quiet time, incarcerated with books, stuffed animals, puzzles and Lego.

"It looks like punishment, but when the children get older, they can appreciate that the punishment was a gift," she explained. The Rebbetzin had turned her thinking around for me to see, but there was no way I could follow it.

"I can't order my kids to memorize the Torah! I can barely control their TV-watching habits."

Akiva was now growing up fast with priorities of his own, especially on Saturday mornings. He sat glued to the latest TV episode of *Transformers* when I had other plans. I wanted to spend Shabbat with both kids at Chabad House.

"Mom, what am I going to talk about with my friends if I miss my show? They all watch *Transformers*."

Akiva's admission was a sobering reminder that he was different in so many ways from his friends, that he had to try harder, to be as up to date, if not more, on the latest Japanese television shows. His bionic superheroes were the talk of the classroom, and he was right. Being half-Japanese, with a foreign mother, he couldn't afford to be left out of the conversation.

"I have an idea. How about we save up money to buy a videocassette recorder? Then we can go to Chabad, and you can watch *Transformers* after Shabbat ends?"

He gave me a suspicious stare.

"I'm good for my word."

"But Mom, sitting through prayers is so boring. Why does Shabbat have to be a whole day?"

I knew the complaints all too well—from my own child-hood. I had rebelled against attending synagogue after I had my bat mitzvah. Until then, my parents would not compromise. European parents believed children should be seen but not heard, I was told. In other words, parents decided on the agenda, and children followed.

Faith by force was not what I wanted to repeat with my kids. Yet here I was in Tokyo, ready to cut a deal to get them through the Chabad House door. They would sit through Saturday morning prayers. I would save up to buy a videocassette recorder as their reward. This is how I got Akiva and Shoshana to board the Saturday bus to Chabad House. On weekdays, we watched coins pile up in a glass jar, and in the span of a few months, we had saved enough to buy the VCR so they could watch their favorite shows after Shabbat had ended.

With coins spread over the round dining table, Shoshana counted out the exact amount, but Akiva changed his mind. "Mom, I kind of got used to having the television off. Maybe we don't need that recorder after all," Akiva said.

"But what about conversations you look forward to with your friends about *Transformers?*" I asked.

"My friend Atsuto is very kind. He tells me what I missed. I think he is used to me being different from them." But just as quickly, his eyes lit up with a new idea. "Mama, Lego Star Wars has a new model coming out. Can I have the Imperial Star Destroyer set instead?"

Shoshana went along with the change of plans, too. She wasn't going to assert herself over an issue that was more Akiva's than hers, and so the Lego set won out.

I WAS A LIGHT SLEEPER, not prone to dreams. But one morning, I awoke with a dream so clear in my memory that I reached for a memo pad and wrote it down. It took place in a superb kitchen, presumably mine, with a dishwasher and other neat appliances I would find in a Western-style house. I said to Ichiro, I wish we could live this way. Then a woman entered the kitchen, someone I didn't recognize. She went into the living room and rearranged the furniture. I was shocked while she was doing it, but afterward, I could see that tall cabinets had been blocking a window with a magnificent view. Outside was a night sky. Our house was perched up high with twinkling lights far into the distance. I wondered how it could be that I never noticed the view before.

What was the dream telling me? Was it that I was missing the bigger picture, focusing too much on being tied by the apron strings to a cramped Tokyo kitchen? I was constantly knocking things off shelves while rustling up meals.

I observed close-up the way the Rebbetzin conducted herself in her kitchen. It was her power spot. She took phone calls by the refrigerator, attended to her children's needs by the stove, prepared glasses of hot tea for guests while never drinking it herself. I observed how she wrote shopping lists with focus and speed, while her kids had grown into mother's helpers. One threw a load of laundry into the washing machine, another took the shopping list and headed off to the supermarket, and a third changed the diaper of the youngest baby. With an apron around her ever-expanding-and-contracting waist, one pregnancy after the other, this was the life she welcomed and, with God's help, created. I wanted to think this way too and take full responsibility for the life I had made in Japan. But my dream was a red flag and I phoned my mother to discuss it.

"Hi, dear. What's cooking?" I could hear the car radio tuned to opera.

"Where are you?"

"I'm driving. I have an appointment at the hair dresser's, and she hates when I'm late. Just give me a minute while I put you on speakerphone."

I told my mother about the dream with the beautiful kitchen and how some random woman had stepped in to rearrange the furniture and reveal a beautiful night sky outside the window. I asked her what she made of it.

"Lordy, you've got me on this one. It may have something to do with change. A little bit of upheaval is good for us mortals, darling. Routine can be so dull."

My mother ended the conversation with an invitation to spend two weeks in the Berkshires. That was her sweetness, to change my worries with a change of scenery and to make plans far in advance so we could enjoy seasons of planning together. The next summer, we had our reunion in Great Barrington. I took Shoshana and Akiva to free children's concerts on the rolling lawn of the Village Green. David Grover and his band brought us to our feet with "Caterpillar, Butterfly," and other G-rated ditties. Everything I wanted or thought I wanted for my children, seemed tantalizingly close under sunny skies in Western Massachusetts.

The storybook Berkshires had its tests, too. My stepfather,

Leon, drove his brand new Lexus without seeing any need for signaling left or right, whether he turned a corner or changed lanes. My New York driver's license had long expired, but thanks to Leon I spent the holiday taking driving lessons and getting my license halfway through the vacation. It felt monumental. One of the barriers for me to return to the United States—I thought—had been over the issue of driving. By the time Ichiro arrived to join us for a week in the Berkshires, it felt mighty good to be in the driver's seat.

Heading down busy Route 7, I slowed the car and pulled into a driveway, when I noticed the "For Rent" sign in the window of a Cape Cod-style house. The property had its own parking lot, as if somebody had used it for a business rather than a private home. With its green lawn and shady trees, this house sure looked welcoming. The front door was smack in the center of the house, where a front door ought to be, not hidden away on the side as in Tokyo, as if thieves wouldn't think to look there for a front door. The steep roof was inset between dormer windows and a chimney. I pulled in and came to a stop under an old oak tree. Ichiro and the children waited in the car.

"Want to join me?" I asked Ichiro.

He shook his head.

For as long as I'd been in Tokyo, I'd had a fixation with looking in real estate windows for a home we could buy. Apartment rentals cost us a fortune, but Ichiro and his family were dead-set against us being property owners. I thought this was peculiar and I couldn't help but wonder if they viewed this foreign daughter-in-law as a high-risk investment. If they did, they hid their true feelings masterfully.

I peered through windows, letting my imagination go wild. The front room would be the café, the back rooms would hold a massage table for Ichiro, an art studio for me and a playroom for the kids.

"What do you think? Would you ever consider moving to

America?" I said to Ichiro as I coaxed him out of the car to take a look.

"If we moved to the Berkshires, Shoshana, and, in a few years, Akiva, too, would not feel so alone. They could go to school with children of mixed heritage and feel a sense of belonging," I said.

"But then why you leaving Great Neck? It was all there, where you coming from!"

"It's true. I didn't feel I belonged there."

"What's that expression? The grass is always green on the other side? You remembering you moved to the house in the forest, too, looking for nirvana?"

"Greener is not necessarily better, I'm ready to admit." Ichiro had brought me back to my senses by making me laugh. But nagging questions remained: Where is home? What is home? Will I ever feel at home in Japan?

In the Berkshires, Akiva's third birthday was approaching. His hair was falling in his eyes and onto his shoulders because I wanted to wait until his birthday to cut his hair. The *Upsherin* is a beautiful Chassidic tradition, where family and guests each take a turn cutting a snippet of hair in preparation for the birthday boy's first day at school. With my mother and Leon, Ichiro too, I wished to do something that connected us as a family to our Jewishness.

"He looks a mess. Take him to the haircutter's, and he'll come back a little mensch," my mother said. We were sitting by a pretty lake, the water lapping the white sandy beach as we watched Shoshana and Akiva busy at work digging holes.

Shoshana overheard this conversation and once we got back home, she took matters into her own hands. She found a pair of kitchen scissors, and while I was out of range, she gave Akiva bangs, leaving the rest of his wispy hair wild to his shoulders.

I was shocked when I saw her handiwork. What Shoshana

began, my mother completed by taking Akiva to the barber's to tidy him up.

"Mom!" I protested. "I was waiting for the *Upsherin.*"

"And then what?" she tutted. "Are you going to next put Akiva in a kippah and wear *tzitzit?*

I laughed. She had me. I wasn't going to have my son stand out in society any more than a blue-eyed Japanese boy already did. My mother did have a point beyond the haircut itself. Even if we were to move back to America, I couldn't imagine embracing Jewish Orthodoxy by joining a sheltered community where Torah values ruled every aspect of life, right down to the kippah. No, I wasn't there yet. Not by a long shot. Chabad had shown me the path into Jewish life that was fascinating and doable, small step by step, precisely because it was happening in Japan.

WHILE THE REBBETZIN and the Rabbi in Omori were growing their community, another Chabad House was flourishing not far away. They had set up a preschool program that I enrolled Akiva in right after returning from America. This other Chabad House had established itself in a townhouse in central Tokyo for the small, permanent Jewish community, and out of town travelers. This Tokyo Rabbi's Torah talks contained inspirational teachings and gave me plenty to contemplate for days afterward.

"This week's *parsha* is *Chukat,*" the Rabbi began one Shabbat, "the Lubavitcher Rebbe, Menachem Mendel Schneerson, of Righteous Memory, compared the spiritual root of existence to a man's lungs. We must always inhale and exhale, just as the universe's spiritual life also fluctuates in a rhythmic, constant cycle of vibration, emanation, and withdrawal."

This Torah teaching was in total alignment with the Tao— the teachings of Lao Tsu. And come to think of it, this was

Adachi Sensei's central theme at the whiteboard—that everything in life can be seen as a rhythmic, constant cycle of vibration.

When I got home, fired up by the Rabbi's talk, I couldn't wait to tell Ichiro. To discover that his beliefs were corroborated by the Torah was exciting beyond my wildest imaginings. There must be a bigger frame to God's plan than I could possibly see.

"Today the Rabbi discussed the Torah from a vibrational point of view—it's what you've been telling me all along!" I told Ichiro when I got home.

I opened the Chumash, to the *Chukat* chapter the Rabbi had just spoken about.

"That's great you finding this out for yourself," Ichiro said flatly.

"What?" All the air went out of me. He wasn't excited by the news. He was downright defensive.

"I know you desiring that I come into your Torah world, but I still don't feeling it in my heart. You having your way. I having mine. Why we can't respecting our differences?"

"Well, we could if it was just two of us, but we brought two children into the world. You assume I belong in your world. Maybe what's worrying you are the sacrifices you would have to make by becoming Jewish."

"Become Jewish? Who, me?"

I fell silent. Maybe he was right, and I was being selfish to think that Ichiro, a man who lived his life in Tokyo had any need for Judaism other than to please his wife. He had his religions—Taoism, Buddhism and Shintoism. Why should he go through the arduous process of conversion? For the sake of the kids? For peace in the home? Yet nothing I said could move him.

THE RABBI AND REBBETZIN, and most *shluchim* in the Chabad movement, follow the tradition of writing down their problems in the form of a letter addressed to the Lubavitcher Rebbe which is then slipped into one of the Rebbe, Menachem Mendel Schneerson's many volumes of collected letters. There are about 80 of these volumes addressing an encyclopedic range of personal issues by religious and non-religious Jews. By putting a letter into a randomly selected page, the Rebbe's response written fifty years ago could be surprisingly relevant even now.

I chose a volume with a gold spine, among many identical such books holding the letters that the Rebbe replied to the countless who sought out his blessings and his advice. I wrote the following:

B"H (Blessed be God—a reminder that all comes from God)

Dear Rebbe,

I'm writing to you about my struggle to give my children a Jewish education. I live in Tokyo. I'm married to Ichiro. He's a good man, but has strong beliefs of his own. It seems he will not cross the line to becoming Jewish himself and wants very much to give the children a strong Japanese identity. I'm at a loss to find balance here. I don't know whether to keep the peace and accept the life I find myself in or put myself in a new situation. Your wisdom is my comfort.

I inserted my letter into it and flipped the volume open to this page. The Rebbetzin read silently in Yiddish before translating the passage into English for me.

"You asked how to give your children Jewish identity, and the answer the Rebbe gives is *Ahavat Yisrael*—a love of Israel. Here is what the Rebbe answers: know that in Israel you will find the support needed to give the children a Jewish education."

"Israel? That's impractical! No, it's impossible!"

I couldn't imagine by what means I could uproot and take

the children to Israel, when Ichiro wouldn't even consider moving to the USA—a country that I knew.

The two voices inside of me were at odds again. One voice sounded a lot like Ichiro's. It was telling me to be happy with life as a stay-at-home mother. I was becoming a bore—and not happy about it. That other voice kept getting louder. It told me to take a risk and try something new.

We had moved to a small two-story house in the Setagaya area of Tokyo in order to be closer to the children's elementary school. The house was chock-full of kids' toys and my canvases. We had more stuff than we had closets to put it in. I would scout the nearby recycle shop, and a truck would pull up with tall cabinets and bookshelves to alleviate the mess. With each piece of furniture, the house's floor space shrank, till the only place we had to get from room to room were narrow trails between the upright furniture.

Doing art together became a family affair in the new house. I had begun teaching art classes using my homemade deck of Genesis Cards that I printed off my computer. If I was reasonably alert, the 44 cards would come out fine. If I was tired, more often than not, one side of the paper would spew out of the printer in reverse. These images would prompt art exercises and conversations, and for Ichiro, Shoshana and I, could open up sensitive topics that we would find hard to voice otherwise. Drawing a picture and talking about it felt safe when looking at a drawing alongside one of the 44 randomly chosen Genesis Cards and seeking connections between the two.

Art supplies spilled out of drawers and closets too, and soon I dreamed of having an art studio and taking that homemade deck of Genesis Cards and having them professionally printed with a guidebook. Our new home in Kyodo, an area of Tokyo once dotted with small farms was now a busy college town where all roads led to Tokyo Agricultural University. I spotted a "For Rent" sign in a second-floor window above a dress shop along Nodai Dori, the main shopping street. Upstairs I peeked inside a glass door. A long room had nothing inside it except for track lighting on the ceiling and a parquet wood floor that fit together like a jigsaw puzzle. That Cape Cod cottage on Route 7 in the Berkshires flashed into my mind. A phone call later, I discovered that the owner had used this space for an art gallery. It was perfect—a much-needed anchor in the city I called home.

After I'd put the children to bed, I told Ichiro about the space. We were sitting facing each other at the dining table, me with my tea, Ichiro with his beer, and the floor plan from the realtor between us.

"It's a miracle! The room would make a great art studio and workshop space."

"You? Going into business?" Ichiro went into the kitchen to fetch himself another beer. He could have just stretched his arm for the fridge, but a tall dish cabinet now stood in the way.

"Why not?".

"You don't know anything about business."

"Well, then, I'll learn." A pioneering yoga teacher from California had only a few years earlier opened her yoga studio in Tokyo. It was thriving. If Leza Lowitz, my passionate and gutsy new friend could do it, then I wanted to believe that I could, too.

Ichito saw that I wasn't going to take no for an answer.

Before going ahead with this leap into the unknown, I asked my mother-in-law to see the space for rent. Okaasan would speak to me straight. She was a clever businesswoman, steering the family fortune from rice polishing machines to real estate. Okaasan turned her umbrella sideways to see which was wider —the staircase or the umbrella. The staircase won by a hair's breadth.

"A staircase this narrow will be hard for business," she pronounced, to my chagrin. "It will be difficult for strollers." My heart sunk. This was not what I wanted to hear. "But this studio is for people of all ages!" The bull-headed daughter-in-law who had recently come into a modest inheritance from her Great Aunt Vicky prevailed.

I signed a two-year lease, plonked down six months' rent for starters, and thanked my Great Aunt Vicky up in heaven for leaving me the means as well to print that homemade deck into a beautiful set of Genesis Cards and guidebook, called the Genesis Way. The name of this studio would be Genesis art Lounge—with a small "a" in the middle. I wanted the world to know that "art" was for everyone. The problem was that I didn't have a clue who that world might be. I thought that marketing was unnecessary for a business on a busy shopping street that had a lot of passing pedestrian traffic. The other problem was that the studio was on the second floor, out of sight and mind. But as I learned from the intuitive artist Sachiko Adachi when I had edited her book, growth happens outside of one's comfort zone, not in it. So, I trusted my first impression and just to make things more challenging, I vowed that I wouldn't work on Shabbat.

Soon after I opened Genesis art Lounge, Adachi Sensei, Ichiro's esteemed teacher stopped in for a visit. He greeted me warmly, studying my paintings on the wall with genuine interest. The solitary man I'd known mostly from his whiteboard presentations on a video became approachable in an art studio full of plants and sunlight. He had soft charisma, a quiet self-confidence. Adachi Sensei had brought with him six of his disciples, who joined him around the studio's long oval table. When he took a seat, the disciples followed. They closed their eyes as if on cue, when their teacher addressed me. Adachi Sensei hadn't come for a Genesis art lesson—not by a long shot. He had come to teach me a lesson.

"You have a mission to teach art. What's important is not just making art, but taking action. Every work of art contains a message to help raise an artist's vibration." Adachi Sensei scanned the deck of Genesis Cards, pausing over a figure of a king standing in the arched stone doorway of a place lodged in the memory of Old Jerusalem when I had backpacked through in my college years. He nodded and smiled with approval while his six disciples continued to sit there like statues with eyes closed. Adachi Sensei's validation meant a great deal to me. Before he got up to leave, he turned to me like a friend who's not afraid to speak the truth.

"You complain about Ichiro because you don't understand that you're studying from him through his behavior. It's important to show thanks."

He sensed the rivalry between us. I thought it was a low-grade bickering fever that kept us up a night, but the tension was clearly noticeable to Adachi Sensei, too. When I opened the art studio, not long after Ichiro had decided that he would not become Jewish, he announced that he would be writing a book about the Chabad Rabbi and Rebbetzin. He would take a sabbatical and, he said with assurance, we could depend on the generosity of his parents to bail us out if we came up short on the rent.

I was appalled. "That's sabotage. How could you stop working just as I'm trying to launch Genesis art Lounge?"

"Not sabotage," Ichiro said. "Adachi Sensei saying everything is a message. We having a great chance to studying each other through our behavior."

Ichiro wanted to write a book about his frequent visits to Chabad House and how we as a family were being transformed one Shabbat at a time. Maybe, just maybe, Ichiro's book about the Chabad House Rabbi and Rebbetzin would bring Ichiro and me closer together. *Think well, and it will be well.* These Torah words of wisdom came back to me.

Along with the pressures of paying the rent and utility bills came panic over the all-important weekend opening hours.

Saturdays and Sundays were essential days to be open. Even though I had vowed not to work on Shabbat, I became desperate when I failed to make even the rent. I talked myself into forgetting about Shabbat, that God didn't mind if we needed the income. While Ichiro was out in cafes writing his book, I spent late nights at Genesis art Lounge cramming as much as I could into six days of the week. This was when Akiva took matters into his own hands to show us that things were just not right at home. One night, Akiva slammed his finger in a sliding fusuma door with such force that it took a surgeon and general anesthesia to put parts of his finger back together again.

Ichiro and I were in shock. We waited outside the hospital operating room alone and silent. While he paced with worry, I opened the Book of Tehillim, King David's psalms, and prayed like never before. I begged for divine intervention and vowed to make *teshuva*, to change my ways, and seal the vow with a pledge to charity. I would make Saturday a full day of rest—for the children and me, and I prayed that Ichiro would join us. Akiva's accident had happened Saturday evening, right after a Shabbat when I had been working at my art studio.

"You practicing Shabbat out of guilt, never making a good result." The operating room doors opened. The nurses wheeled out our son, groggy but thank God, the surgeon pronounced that Akiva's finger would be fine.

How could I reach Ichiro? He was right to believe that guilt never makes a good result. But feeling regrets is a first step toward admitting a mistake and opening up to change. I decided right then and there in the hospital corridor that I would follow the Jewish faith, whether I understood why or not. Didi had said long ago on the tennis court that practicing faith builds faith. First, you follow, then you believe.

❀

Chapter Twelve

AN ART STUDIO CLOSED FOR SHABBAT

Have we forgotten the name of our God,
and stretched out our hands to a strange god?
Would God not have searched this out,
for he knows the secrets of the heart.
—Psalm 44

On Shabbat at Chabad House, the afternoon routine of opening the *Chumash* deepened. The Rebbetzin would help me understand the grey boxes along the Gutnik edition's margins. These "Last Words" and "Sparks of Torah" were replete with practical wisdom straight from the Lubavitcher Rebbe, Rashi and other Torah luminaries.

As I came to understand more about the journey of the Israelites crossing the Sinai desert, their forty-years of circuitous wandering and existential tests before entering the land of Israel, I wanted to visualize this better, so I began drawing scenes of the weekly Torah portion. It wasn't enough to believe the formula for our survival: faith in God, patience, self-restraint, and trust in the words and wisdom of the Prophet

Moses. I had to visualize it in drawings with my own eyes, even if it meant putting a Borsalino hat on a rabbi carrying a lamb through the streets of Pharaoh's Egypt. I had committed to keeping Genesis art Lounge closed on Shabbat and other Jewish holidays, and I stopped worrying about making ends meet through my art studio. Somehow, it was going to flourish, or, in God's infinite wisdom, it was going to fail. This was not my desire, but I was ready to trust that closing a weekend-based business so that I could observe Shabbat was the right thing to do. It would be a test of faith.

Ichiro would offer to help me update my website by translating the pages into Japanese. By the time he had his bath and his beer, it was often close to midnight before we got to work. I was crabby, unappreciative, and sitting in front of the computer with him doing his best to help me after I'd put the kids to sleep was more than I could handle. I started to feel heart palpitations. It's hard to get a good night's sleep when you're constantly worried about money.

"You think I'm ungrateful."

"No, I just doing my best, and you doing your best."

I blinked back dry eyes in front of the glaring computer screen.

Clients were coming to Genesis art Lounge from Hokkaido and Okinawa, traveling by the bullet train the length of the country. Some brought their friends, their children, their husbands, and wives. Students would leave with a work of art, and on the best of days, with a passion to continue. Genesis art Lounge became a hangout for Shoshana's and Akiva's classmates too, and when parents asked me to teach English through art, I did so through Akiva's much-loved stable of puppets. The future looked rosy, if only I could stick out the rough beginning. But those late nights of office work on the computer were wreaking havoc on my body. One night I awoke with chest pains so strong, I thought somebody was sitting on my chest.

This couldn't continue. I took a rest. For weeks Genesis art Lounge remained shuttered. During this time, I asked myself whether there was another way to teach art without the stresses. I reasoned that it wasn't God's wish for my art studio to fail, but rather for me to stay whole and alive.

On a rainy Sunday in July, I peeled off the contact paper letters spelling out Genesis art Lounge in the front window, packed up the art supplies, the paintings, the children's play carpet, the puppets and the Ikea shelving units that I had jubilantly assembled. Ichiro hired a van to help me move the studio back home again. I continued my art classes in parks and garden settings, and when the cold weather set in, Ichiro offered to share his office in downtown Tokyo with me, where Genesis art Lounge would become Genesis Art Workshops, with the more self-confident capital "A."

On Shabbat, Ichiro would join me as part of what he called research into writing his book about the Chabad House philosophy of the Rabbi. But those words of Lalenya, so long ago, echoed back to me. What is the root of all research? It's to research yourself. What if Ichiro's months of trailing the black hat and coattails of an unconventional Rabbi were not about publicizing his selfless activities of helping Jews and Japanese— what if Ichiro had a deep desire to emulate him?

I wished I could reach him. My writer friend Cherryl had recently left Japan to marry in San Francisco and give her late-blooming marriage the best shot she could to make it solid and enduring. She and her husband attended a workshop based on the pioneering relationship work of Imago Therapy founder Harville Hendrix, PhD. The workshop Cherryl attended was actually facilitated by one of Hendrix's star students, Hedy Schleifer, and her husband Yumi, a Holocaust-survivor. The Schleifers had been through their own ordeals over a very long marriage. Maybe it could help Ichiro and me.

The workshop used a wonderful metaphor for deep,

nonjudgmental listening to partners, called *Crossing the Bridge*, and entering each other's "neighborhoods of concern." Hedy and Yumi had spent decades working through old traumas that stemmed from the guilt of Yumi having survived the Holocaust after the Nazis had gassed his siblings. With a past like that, our problems seemed, by comparison, eminently solvable.

Ichiro agreed to fly to Miami for the weekend workshop. As it happened, Ichiro's flight was delayed due to a blizzard in DC, where he changed planes, and his three-day weekend was shaved to two. I'd arrived separately to make a holiday out of the trip and sink my toes in the sand with my dear friend Keni, who had packed up his vintage couture business in New York City, opened a fashion museum in the trendy Wynwood district of Miami, and understood me as only a friend from teenage years could. We had once both been outcasts from our own religions. I didn't know how he was going to take my spiritual overhaul, but thankfully he did so true to form, with a great sense of humor.

"I love the hat. It's so elegant. Are you shaving your head too?" Keni asked.

"Not every Orthodox woman shaves her head!" I laughed, as a gust of wind lifted the hat off my head and sent it flying over the sand.

Keni's family was Sicilian and Catholic, but he had been around Jews all his life. In New York City, he had started out as a fashion designer who reinvented himself as the king of vintage couture owing to his knack for attending estate sales and finding treasures in the closets of socialites, not a few of whom were Jewish. We both knew that fashion was an identifier, a way of being instantly recognizable as a member of whatever tribe you chose.

"You're coming closer to God," he observed without a trace of judgment.

"Because of the hat?" I grinned.

Keni had an uncanny way of seeing beyond the clothes to the person inside.

Ichiro arrived on a balmy February night at a hotel near Miami International Airport, just before sundown on Shabbat. More than fifty couples had flown in from all over the globe to make their relationships work. We took our seats in a circle. Ichiro and I exchanged glances. Hedy entered, a striking woman and cancer survivor with white hair shorn fearlessly within a breath of her scalp. She had clear eyes and ageless features and wore pajama-like silk pants and a matching hoodie. Her big earrings jangled as she spoke. Yumi, much older and dressed more conservatively, held her hand when she sat down. They inspired hope in me that with deep listening, respect and commitment, a relationship could be healed at any age. Yet, I couldn't help noticing the obvious: that they were both negotiating their differences from a shared Jewish heritage.

Yumi wore a kippah. "It's Shabbat today," he declared, "and so I want to welcome you to our congregation." Their congregation! I sighed in relief and laughed. I had been worried about breaking Shabbat for this retreat. Yumi had found the loophole.

Hedy introduced us to the idea of conversations taking place in emotionally charged neighborhoods. She spoke about entering these neighborhoods as if they were sacred places, where one speaks with an open heart to a partner whose role is to listen. The speaker feels safe to express what she or he may not have had the courage to admit before. It was time to face our partners.

"What neighborhood would you like me to cross into today?" I asked Ichiro, following Hedy's instructions.

"I'm Japanese. You're Jewish. How about the neighborhood of our different expectations?"

"Okay," I said as Hedy suddenly pulled up a chair to listen closely. She coached me from the sidelines with four words: "I hear you say…"

"I hear you say you are Japanese, and I'm Jewish, and we have different expectations."

"Yes. In your culture, you say whatever you wish. Your religion always right."

I flashed back to a walk the day before on the beach with Keni. Yes, it was true. I said whatever I wished and I loved my friends for speaking their truth too. Truth can be hard, but my friends cared enough about me to be honest. With Ichiro, his impeccable behavior was driven by a sense of honor, almost a vow not to say what was on his mind.

"I hear you say that in my culture, I say whatever I wish. My religion is always right," I repeat.

"Yes, you have no trouble saying what's on your mind, even though it hurting me," Ichiro said.

"If I see our relationship through Shoshana's and Akiva's eyes, they might think, heaven forbid, that they have to choose between our different beliefs to win our love," I said when it was my turn to speak.

"I hear you saying that you are seeing our relationship through our children's eyes. Then he interjected: "You nothing find good?"

"Of course! You are a gentleman. You are kind and faithful, and you are a good father. I ignored Torah when I met you. But my life comes with this manual that I can no longer ignore."

"I hear you say you ignored Torah," he repeated.

"I know it's hard for you to accept who I am now. Maybe you think I'll go back to the way I was, but I won't. I can't! I discovered that crossing into your family's world of Shintoism and Buddhism, watching you follow the ways of Adachi Sensei and your Taoist master at the White Crane Clinic—none of this brought us closer. Ichiro, you have said to me that the only person you can change is yourself. Now I'm doing that. I'm changing myself by returning to my Jewish faith."

"Japanese, we accepting all religions! Why can't you doing the same?"

Hedy sat between us for the main exercise we had come to learn, called *Crossing the Bridge,* a way of listening compassion-ately without reacting. By the end of the session, we agreed to continue "crossing the bridge" when we returned to Tokyo. Well, we had the best of intentions, but the Tokyo that we returned to was not the same that we had left.

Ichiro's father had been diagnosed with third-stage pancre-atic cancer, a death sentence that gave him less than a year to live. For all his background in oriental medicine, Ichiro decided that the best way he could help his father was psychologically, by keeping a journal of his miraculous recovery that he would publish as a book. Yukiko, Ichiro's younger sister, a boutique owner, did the research that led to immunotherapy and other life-prolonging treatments. Ichiro's younger brother, Masahide, a French chef, made frequent visits to prepare nouvelle cuisine with a twist: healthy traditional Japanese meals with an emphasis on presentation.

If harmony alone among family members could have caused *Otoosan* to recover then the miracle would have happened. Ichiro and his siblings helped their mother so she never for a second felt alone. I couldn't imagine what life would be like when my father-in-law passed. I didn't want to consider it. But, in fact, I didn't have time to consider it. Shoshana was having trouble at school and this led to sleeplessness, and days of intense energy, mania it was called, culminating in acute psychosis. While the three siblings supported their sick father and distraught mother, Shoshana and I were on our own when she was admitted to an old-school psychiatric hospital, where unapologetic solitary confinement was the first line of treat-ment. It was a terrible, frightening environment for any young woman, but especially for fourteen-year-old Shoshana.

I begged Ichiro to let her come home. The Rabbi urged the

same, telling him that all we had to do was chain Shoshana to my ankle until she returned to normal. But Ichiro was convinced that Shoshana's breakdown was a result of the disharmony between us.

Seeing Shoshana in such conditions broke my heart. The amount of pharmaceuticals she was being pumped up with was enormous. She lost control of her jaw muscles. She drooled uncontrollably, and her beautiful smile vanished. It became hard for her to bite into an apple. Through slurred speech, Shoshana asked: "Mama, did I do something wrong?"

But every night, when I got home drained, Ichiro met me at the dining table with his beer and a different mindset. He wanted me to trust the doctors.

"We can't keep Shoshana in such conditions."

"But she not well. We bringing her to hospital meaning we trust treatment to doctors."

"She's never going to forgive us for abandoning her."

Ichiro handed me the tissue box, but the tears wouldn't stop.

"First, we having to fix our marriage. That our work. Hospital taking care of Shoshana. We should being gratitude for that." I could have wrung his neck. "How about we making family life more peaceful. Couldn't we accepting each other just as we are—for Shoshana's sake?" Ichiro was asking for my sympathy. It wasn't just Shoshana. He was overwhelmed by his father's pancreatic cancer. The chemotherapy was affecting *Otoosan's* muscles. He had grown too weak to walk on his own. Visiting Shoshana on Sunday was all that Ichiro could mentally handle. I sighed and shook my head. Ichiro didn't understand that I was doing everything I could not to fall apart inside too.

Ever since Akiva's thumb slamming incident, I'd never let a day go by without reading Tehillim, the psalms. To me, they were not just a lifeline, but a kind of insurance. Psalms became a discipline to detach me from my daily to-do list of things. This morning routine put God front and center in my life. I could allow myself to feel devastated, but not hopeless. The miracle I was asking for could present itself in a form I might not even recognize at first.

The Chabad Rabbi and Rebbetzin never for a moment questioned that the miracle would happen. They suggested that a radical shift in my life and my thinking could be in order. At this point, becoming wholly observant, a Baal Teshuva, wasn't some leap into the unknown. It was as obvious as moving one foot in front of the next and carrying on.

The Rabbi drove to the hospital to meet me there one day. He had been raised by parents who had taken in traumatized Israeli war veterans, and his parents had nursed generations of these young men back to health. The Rabbi wasn't afraid of their behavior. He taught me that even mental illness has a rhythm and a godly prescription.

The Rabbi sat with me in a courtyard with straggly bushes that needed a good pruning. Even the shrubs looked manic. Nothing looked normal anymore. He told me of his own childhood experience, sitting at the dinner table each night with these war veterans. Some were bipolar or schizophrenic, others depressed. They lived in his parents' home until they could return to an unlocked world. Many married, worked for a living, and were blessed with children. Some live with the Edery family in Kfar Chabad, Chabad Village, to this day.

Progress could feel like slow motion—if not reverse. Over the weeks, the hospital moved Shoshana to a room that shared a wall with an upright piano and gifted pianists deep in their own mental crises played the scores by heart. A new milestone came when the nurses gave Shoshana permission to use the public phone to call home. "I know it's hard. It's really hard. I know you want to come home badly, and all I can say is that I'm working on it."

Shoshana asked me if anyone from school had called her. Here was another heartbreak. It was too hard for me to say no.

Even good people don't know how to handle mental illness. I knew that the school community was deeply concerned, but they were also scared. To see a teenage girl you think you know so well transform before your eyes into someone in acute crisis who needs hospitalization is very hard. I was sorry that the schoolchildren had to witness the final days of knowing Shoshana this way and that it happened within a sprawling mock-Tudor home with storybook flowerbeds bordering grassy a lawn.

Shoshana told me that it got noisy along the hallway, especially at night. She heard other women crying and banging on the doors. She couldn't sleep well. She told me that an anorexic woman paced the corridors until she had put in her ten thousand or so steps for the evening. And all I could say is: "I'm so sorry. I'm so sorry. I'm working on getting you home, where you can breathe fresh air."

To recite Psalms and drop coins daily in a charity box brought comfort and made me aware that when you start listening to the voices in your head, you can drive yourself mad. Prayers restored calm and trust in God's great mercy. That's the only way I can explain what transpired. One day, returning from seeing Shoshana at the hospital, I stopped at a Starbucks near home for a tea latte. I happened to sit down on the wood deck in front of Baji horse park facing a tall man, clad head to toe in cycling gear. He smiled. I smiled back. He looked funny in black and yellow, like a skinny bumble bee. Next to him was his bicycle. He told me that his name was Dr. Douglas Eames and that he had just finished his daily 25k bike ride—before his return to work. We got chatting. He told me that he treated psychiatric disorders, that his office was close by, in our neighborhood, and if we wanted, he could see Shoshana as an outpatient. Miracle of miracles. I called Ichiro to tell him the fantastic news. "It's an act of God! I've just met an English-speaking therapist who treats psychiatric disorders! Can you believe it?

We can bring Shoshana home and know she is safe in his hands."

But Ichiro was unmoved by the miracle. "Can you managing by yourself? I having to helping my father, you know. It's dangerous to bringing Shoshana home." His priorities confirmed his loyalties. But taking on Ichiro's fears and doubts was optional. Days later, a second angel showed up. Keiko was my new student at Genesis Art Workshops I continued to do from home throughout Shoshana's hospitalization. As fortune would have it, Keiko was a professional home care nurse, supporting families in exactly our predicament and living five minutes from our home. Ichiro relented. He agreed to Shoshana's discharge, iterating and reiterating that her home care and recovery was my project and responsibility.

Shoshana came home to a world where the doors were unlocked, where she could see flowering cherry trees and daffodils and gradually walk outside accompanied by Keiko and get medical supervision from Douglas. My father-in-law's health had declined drastically during the four months of Shoshana's hospitalization. He was bedridden and almost blind now. A halo of paper shoji screens surrounded his jaundiced, sunken eyes. Shoshana insisted that the first stop after her recovery was a visit to her Ojiisan.

Shoshana approached her grandfather's bed, unperturbed by his condition.

"Can I give you a massage?"

Shoshana drew near and tenderly rubbed his bony shoulders through his pajamas. I reeled to see the love preserved in those hands.

MY FATHER-IN-LAW HAD BEEN an old-style patriarch with a ready smile and eyes on the back of his head, always ready to lend a hand where it was needed. But now he was weak, his eyesight and his appetite diminished. From his bedside, my father-in-law groomed Ichiro to manage the family properties, negotiate leases, and remain on good terms with tenants and realtors. Ichiro psyched himself up by telling us all that he wasn't just going to maintain the property, he was going to heal two middle-aged buildings.

On March 11, the Great Tohoku Earthquake devastated the North of Japan. Six floors above ground, the in-law's apartment swayed like a pendulum. China cabinets and sliding glass doors rattled angrily with each aftershock. Doors jiggled open, and dishes crashed to the floor. Books fell off shelves, and the little Buddha statue in the family altar tumbled onto the tatami. My father-in-law reached for the television remote control. We all happened to be lunching with the in-laws since Akiva's school had cancelled classes because of the flu epidemic.

With aftershocks rattling the building, we watched a live NHK television broadcast record the monstrous tsunami barreling into seaside towns and villages, swallowing cars and the lives of more than fifteen thousand souls who hadn't been able to flee to higher ground. People drowned in their own homes and vehicles. Then, more horrific news was reported. The tsunami had engulfed an aging nuclear power plant in Fukushima, and greater Tokyo, with its 35 million, more than a quarter of the nation's population, was going to be in big trouble if the reactor overheated, melted down, and spewed radiation in the direction of the capital.

Ichiro had a new mantra in those first days after the earthquake, which he repeated over and over: "Tokyo 250 kilometers away; we having nothing to worrying about." The threat of Fukushima's nuclear meltdown was first reported by CNN foreign correspondent Anderson Cooper, followed by the shocking news of the actual meltdown. Some friends and their families headed south, as far away from the Fukushima radiation disaster as they could. Others flew home to stay with their families following the strongly-worded advisories of their governments. Ichiro thought it was all an overreaction.

"You really thinking government holding back the truth? If the government saying Tokyo safe, I believing them."

I pulled away the newspaper shielding Ichiro's eyes. Below the headlines were horrific photographs of destruction, Sendai Airport washed away, and once picturesque coastal towns criss-crossed by rice paddies unrecognizable.

The phone rang. It was my mother. "I've deposited money into your account, dear. It will cover three round-trip plane tickets to Florida—but if you feel that you must stay together as a family, then that's entirely up to you."

I have to give her credit. There was no guilt-tripping or imploring me to come to my senses and get out of a potential nuclear disaster zone. Instead, she gave me the financial means to make the decision either way. Chabad House had remained open and swung into full-on earthquake relief mode. They calmly assisted and eased the nerves of anyone who reached out to them. The Rabbi obtained a permit from the police department to enter the disaster zone. Among the emergency Red Cross vehicles, his van stood out with its oversized menorah on the roof. On his first trip up, he went to the coastal town of Iwanuma, handing out toothbrushes, water, leftover challah from Shabbat, and returning with a long list of survivors' requests.

I was affected by the Rabbi's decision not to flee, although his parents and the Rebbetzin's parents too implored the family to leave Japan until it was safe to return. Following the lead of this fearless Rabbi, it felt unnecessary to panic. I went about life shopping in the half-stocked, semi-lit supermarkets under grey skies, gathering up toys that Shoshana and Akiva had outgrown, and sending them along with the Rabbi's growing convoy of supplies. The Rabbi and the Rebbetzin struck an arrangement with the manager of National Azabu supermarket. He would

drive up to the disaster-hit areas with donations of food, clothing, diapers, daily necessities, and special requests from the
survivors. He began with his van, upgraded to a truck, then a
second and third, adding more drivers daily to handle the swell
of donations. And Ichiro went up too. Trains, the lifelines of
Tokyo, were running erratically. Weeks after the earthquake,
the ground still shook from the aftershocks.

Long before the earthquake, I had planned a Genesis Art
Workshop at a beautiful teahouse in Tokyo. I'd asked my father-
in-law to teach calligraphy, and my mother-in-law flower
arranging. Due to the earthquake and the erratic train sched-
ules, every last person cancelled, so the workshop was down to
just us as a family. Grandpa sat next to Akiva, Grandma next to
Shoshana. I was seated across from Ichiro at a black-lacquer low
table with rice paper, ink, and calligraphy brushes lined up
before us. My father-in-law dabbed his brush in ink, demon-
strating how to write the *kanji* character for love, and we all
followed the stroke order. Akiva turned to me. "Mom, I didn't
know you could write kanji. How many kanji do you know?"

"About 300," I said.

"That's not even enough to read the newspaper!"

"So true," as a shaky version of "love" came from my inky
strokes.

"How can you know so little kanji after being in Japan for so
many years?"

"When you arrive in a foreign country as an adult, the
language doesn't go into your head the same way as a kid.
Besides, if I spoke to you in Japanese, you would never have
learned English."

"Or a little bit of Hebrew," Shoshana added, while Akiva put
the finishing tail on a kanji that looked like a zoo animal.

It was a cloudless March day, and bare branches hung over
evergreen shrubs trimmed into globes. The sun arched across
the southern sky. We could have been practicing the kanji for

the word "love" back at the in-laws' home. But there, the television, the computer, and the phones took over our lives. I could hear my children's rhythmic breathing as their grandfather guided their calligraphy brushes.

THE IMMUNOTHERAPY WORKED until it didn't. Fifty radiation treatments took their toll, leaving my father-in-law bedridden. On a Friday in August, I had found a parking space near Chabad House, put the coins in the parking meter, and grabbed the one-hour ticket. We had a few minutes to go until candle lighting time, after which I generally turned off the phone until sunset the following day. As soon as I had lit the candles, my phone started ringing, persistently. The longer it rang, the shriller it sounded. The Rabbi and Rebbetzin would never answer the phone after Shabbat had begun. I was trying my best to copy their ways. Sometimes I was successful. But this time I couldn't ignore the phone. I did what I had to do.

"Huh-low." It was Ichiro, speaking in a whisper of a voice.

"My father passing away now."

"I'm so sorry," I said, with a lump in my throat.

"Okaasan finally agreed to having round the clock nursing care at home, and while she was signing the application in the dining room, he left."

"He never liked the idea of helpers, did he?"

"No, my mother proud. She wanting to do everything herself."

I told Ichiro how his father's death time was printed on the parking ticket. He knew where to find us.

"Chabad," he said softly.

ICHIRO'S FATHER'S black loafers were parked by the door, tidy and parallel as if the shoes were waiting for their master to return. I felt tempted to call up to heaven: "Wait a minute— Come back! You forgot your things!" Ties, cravats, golfing clothes, Harris tweed jackets, tuxedos, raw silk kimonos, his collection of summery cotton kimonos, a Panama hat, and a trove of department store-bought paintings—all got left behind.

The Torah helped me to grasp what had truly been left behind: this man's acts of kindness, his generosity, and his impeccable preparation for this sad day by putting his finances in good order. Is this not the purpose of life? We would remember him for his good deeds. In death, he was carrying nothing now but his legacy: the comfort of knowing that he had done his best.

Akiva sat facing the *tokonoma*. On this raised alcove, bouquets of white chrysanthemums were everywhere. He clutched close to his chest a formal portrait photograph of his grandfather and thanked him for being his best friend in the world. When he vowed to do something with his life that would make him proud, the tears welled in my eyes.

Akiva asked for a few of his grandfather's clothes.

"Let's pick some out then," I said, as I wiped away his tears.

"Thanks. I want to remember his scent," Akiva sniffled. "In my dreams, Ojiisan will know where to find me." In the morning, I found his grandpa's shirt tied over his pajamas.

My father-in-law rested under a slim veil of cotton for one last night before the hearse came to take him to the crematorium. Ichiro had wanted the children to sleep with his father's body.

"I'm sorry, Ichiro. The Torah forbids the kids and me from sleeping with your father, viewing him, and participating in the cremation ceremony in any way."

The debate was cut short by the doorbell ringing. Standing at the door was the Chabad Rebbetzin Efrat.

"I've come to offer my condolences," the Rebbetzin said. The

Rebbetzin stood by the door of the tatami room where my father-in-law lay, opened a *Siddur,* and read out loud to Ichiro and his mother a passage about purification laws.

"Purification?" her mouth opened in surprise. Sadness turned to a smile. "Did you know that purification in Shinto religion is one of four essential rites?"

"Really? I have no idea about Shinto customs. But in Judaism, we have *tahara*—purification before burial. Members of the community wash and dress the body before it's laid to rest."

My father-in-law's dying request had been that three Buddhist priests officiate at his funeral. Each priest, dressed in fine black silk robes, took turns chanting while a procession of families, friends, neighbors, politicians, doctors, White Crane Clinic and Matsuzakaya department store staff filed by his casket. I'd heard how he had once won a big lottery ticket and given most of the winnings to fill the local community coffers. But what else had he done? I had no idea how loved he was— and how much good he had done outside the family—until this moment. With more than 600 people coming to show their respects, the procession took most of the morning.

Ichiro reflected the sadness in my eyes. I held the children back from seeing the body of their grandfather with the soul no longer there. At the crematorium, we were guided to approach ornate and brassy art deco doors, the kind you see in New York skyscraper elevators. The doors opened, but no elevator was inside. My father-in-law's casket went in on a gurney. The doors shut slowly as my mother-in-law, Ichiro, Shoshana, Akiva, and many family members came close and waved their goodbyes. We waited in a hall with small tables and light refreshments. The oven timer was going while family members made light conversation and ate rice crackers. The bell rang, the art deco doors opened, and out came a tray. Cremation had turned the beloved patriarch of the family into ash and charred bones. Ichiro didn't understand my resistance to the cremation ceremony. He thought I was picking the most difficult moment in his life to win a point for the Jewish scorecard because the Torah forbids cremation. Ichiro had wanted Shoshana and Akiva to pick up their grandfather's remains and place the neck bone with extra-long chopsticks into an urn. I stood with the children, close enough to see the others in Ichiro's family following this custom, but far enough so they could not participate.

"Mom, why can't we go over?" Akiva asked. I could see that he was perplexed. He craned his neck toward the tray of smoldering ashes, the remains of his grandfather. He was torn. He wanted to be by his father's side, but he wanted to have his hand in mine too.

"The Torah forbids cremations. Jews bury their loved ones because we believe in the resurrection."

"What's that?"

"Jews believe in a world to come when there isn't war or sickness, when we recognize that we are all one. The world will live in harmony, and the dead will wake up. This will happen when Moshiach, the Messiah, comes to rule the earth."

Akiva looked skeptical. "I don't believe it."

Shoshana grabbed his shoulder.

"Can't you see it's important to Mom? Let her believe what she wants."

Ichiro shot me an unforgiving look from across the hall.

Whenever times were hard, my father-in-law had kind words and deep pockets to help us through. I couldn't imagine what life would be like without him—till it dawned on me. This was Ichiro's big chance. Ichiro means first-born. He could fill those black shoes that waited in the foyer and take them to exciting new places. The beautiful thing about prayer is that you have quiet moments to visualize the life you think you want.

GOD'S WILL, in the long run, doesn't operate according to our desire. God provided us with exactly what we needed. The arrival in Tokyo of a Jewish Orthodox family from Indianapolis proved just that. Daniel, a professor and specialist in disaster recovery and Yael, his wife, had been like me at one point, raised knowing very little about Torah. Daniel and Yael were attracted to Charedi, ultra-Orthodox traditions, learned in yeshivas and seminaries in Jerusalem, and opened their home to guests for Shabbat meals just as I believe countless had done for them.

This is common in the Orthodox world, but they took their Shabbat hospitality a step further. They gave us their bedrooms to make sure we could keep Shabbat. Yael invited many guests, did the shopping and cooking, with Daniel doing his share too. The preparation of these elaborate, multi-course meals Friday night and Saturday lunch came with nifty shortcuts. One Shabbat Yael used a tuna can to hold down the lid of a crockpot simmering with coconut curry. In the middle of the night, we all awoke to a loud boom. The tuna can had lodged itself in the ceiling, and coconut curry had traveled from the kitchen to the dining room, then made a right-hand turn into the living room. Daniel, Yael, Ichiro, and I spent hours scraping curry off the counters, the ceiling, the floors, and the walls.

Until now, I had thought of Shabbat as a serious undertaking —until the coconut curry explosion. But the curry debacle got me thinking how it's the unexpected things, even minor calamities, that charge Shabbat with meaning. This family had a big heart to let us in on their lives. It took guts to let guests you hardly knew into your bedroom and bathroom, and to offer a mop and cleaning rag when required.

"I think I'm ready to learn *Halacha*, the laws. There was so much going on that I needed to process. Maybe the curry debacle happened because we're not contributing enough to the meals," I said to Ichiro when we were back in our bedroom.

"You need to finding a mentor," Ichiro said, and over Shabbat lunch, he brought up the subject with our hosts.

"What you thinking about mentors, Rabbi Daniel?"

"A mentor is good if you can relate face to face in the beginning. I attach myself to my *Rav*."

"How you picking the Rav?" Ichiro asked.

"He had the attributes I wanted to develop in myself."

"Well, Daniel, you understanding what I wish my wife understanding. My master at the White Crane Clinic teaching me that it's dangerous trying develop spiritually without a Rabbi or mentor. She refuse to finding a mentor. What do you think of that?"

"It could take years to find your Rabbi or Rebbetzin. So, what are you going to do in the meantime?" Daniel replied, answering Ichiro's question with a swift question of his own. I knew that to satisfy my spiritual hunger would take work. But my way wasn't Ichiro's way. When Shabbat was over we went across the street to fetch our car from the parking lot. I must have left the headlights on because the car wouldn't start.

"Battery dying," Ichiro announced, as he called the Japan Automobile Association. Later, behind closed doors, Ichiro paced around the dining room table, pointing a pent-up finger at me. "You jumping into Orthodoxy, but you taking only the parts you like."

"Not true," I protested. "Speak softly. The kids are trying to sleep.

"You following Shabbat, but you not taking a mentor," he persisted loudly.

"Okay, Yael is not standing in front of a whiteboard and teaching me. But in my way, I am learning."

"What you did?"

"I left her our share of the cost to get the ceiling fixed."

❀

Chapter Thirteen

NO TURNING BACK

As far as the east is from the west,
So far has he removed us from our
transgressions.
—Psalm 103

From the Rebbetzin I learned about the merits of honey. When her children turned three, they were initiated into the Torah on their first day of class by licking honey off a laminated page of Hebrew letters. This custom left an impression on me. It was a little gross, but if I could see beyond licking plastic, I would borrow the metaphor and raise my Jewish children with sweetness too.

Akiva had entered his final year of Wako, an elementary school with a strong anti-war bent. He and his classmates had spent the year learning about some of the fiercest battles in World War II, which had taken place on Naha, a tropical island known today for its luxury resort hotels on the one hand, and its US military installations on the other. The presence of those

US military bases rankles Okinawans. Akiva and his sixth-grade class would go and see with their own eyes the sites where World War II battles had taken place and the caves where islanders fled to escape massacres and bombings. My eyes glanced over the three-day itinerary without a problem until I noticed the departure date. The flight to Okinawa was scheduled on Shabbos morning. "Wait a minute. The flight is on Shabbat. I have an idea!" I said cheerfully, as a glum 12-year-old boy stared back at me.

"Why don't we travel to Okinawa the day before? We can find a hotel near the beach and meet up with your classmates after Shabbat."

Akiva's eyes lit up. "Now that's an idea!" he smiled.

"With so many US military bases, there must be a Jewish community in Okinawa. Why don't we try for Friday Shabbos services on one of the bases?"

"Mom! I'm Japanese! They're not going to let me on the base."

"Akiva, you're also an American passport carrying Jew."

I got in touch with the rabbi at Camp Foster, and she graciously picked us up so that we could attend Shabbos services with personnel out of uniform. They were friendly and curious to talk to us and answer Akiva's questions about their presence in Japan.

"Mom, they're actually nice people," Akiva said as we headed back to the hotel.

"Why does that surprise you?"

"I had only bad images of American soldiers from what I learned. I guess there are always two sides to the story."

"Yes, two sides to every story." Akiva was wise. He was growing into his identity as a Japanese Jew as a fact of life. He accepted that we did things differently. He was Jewish because I was Jewish. And soon enough, Akiva would be old enough to make his own decisions and do things his own way. I had to accept that too.

"How is life?" the Rabbi asked, as the Rebbetzin entered the dining room carrying in her arms a newborn baby swaddled in a blanket. Ichiro had called Chabad House, asking for this meeting. He hadn't been happy about the Okinawa trip involving Akiva's separate arrival and what he saw as an unnecessary splurge on a hotel and airfare that we could barely afford. We sat down stiffly in folding chairs next to each other while the Rabbi and Rebbetzin sat across from us, as relaxed and focused as we were tense. They were truly remarkable—dropping their urgent matters to attend to ours.

"Ichiro wasn't happy that I went to Okinawa with Akiva. He is saying I'm not Orthodox enough!" I began. "It's not like I'm *trying* to be Orthodox! I'm returning to *me*."

Ichiro interrupted. "It's not just Okinawa. It's Liane's way of speaking. You criticize me never helping."

"The other night, I asked you for a serving bowl. You put the chicken into a dairy dish even though I've told you a hundred times to *only* use the meat dishes."

The Rabbi giggled as he adjusted his hat. "You don't think Orthodox husbands make the same mistake? Of course, they put meat in the dairy dishes!"

"So, what do you do about it?" I asked.

"You say, *oh!* You laugh and throw the dish in the garbage because you can't use it again—or you can give it away as a gift to your non-Jewish friends."

Ichiro interrupted again. "You see—there's always a decent way that doesn't ending in an argument! What other Japanese husband observing Shabbat? I only the one." Ichiro did have a point.

I recalled what Lalenya had told me about intercultural marriages. Before she packed up in Tokyo and moved her atelier and her young daughter back to France, she introduced me to the concept of "ideological neurosis," the attachment to our beliefs as being the right and only ones. Lalenya, too, had fallen into the trap of somehow believing that "right" would prevail, especially to the partner whose beliefs were the strongest. With Ichiro and me, it was clear we were at a stalemate. Ichiro had reached his limit in my Jewish world and I'd gone as far as I could go into his.

"Maybe this marriage is more than either of us can handle," I said, as the Rebbetzin sat across from me, silently peeling apples.

"You not thinking of the children!" he said.

"I most definitely am," I replied.

The Rabbi stood and, rocking back and forth, began reading from Talmud a story about a childless king and his guest, a prophet, who had come to deliver a stern message. The prophet told the king that because he had neglected his family duties by not fulfilling the command to have children, he would not be receiving his portion in the world to come.

"The king was shocked," the Rabbi said, looking from me to Ichiro. "Everyone knew this king as a wise ruler, but he didn't have children. The king protested. 'I thought I would not have made a good father. But if what you say is true, let me marry your daughter, and then I am quite sure we will have good children.' The prophet shook his head with regret. He announced that this was impossible. 'A heavenly decree is irrevocable. You shall be with neither a wife nor children, and you will not take your place in the world to come.'"

"The king became furious," the Rabbi continued as he read. "He ordered the prophet to leave his castle. The king knew in his heart that God gives people many chances and free will to change the course of their destiny, and so he decided to take matters into his own hands."

I smiled when I recognized the message. "Yes! This king got it right! He was ready to change his destiny by taking matters into his own hands."

Ichiro offered me a look of resignation as if a change was the last thing he wanted.

CHANGE TAKES EFFORT. Sometimes a little. Sometimes a whole lot. Shabbat became a marathon day of walking to Chabad House. I filled my water bottle, and Shoshana grabbed a few granola bars. We put on our sneakers and headed out the door. Ichiro waved us off while Akiva was still upstairs asleep. "Come on. Take the bus to Chabad House. You don't needing walk three and a half hours."

Our house was threaded overhead by a tangle of power lines. Between them, I could make out a pale blue sky. "Clear day, Shoshana. No need for an umbrella."

"Mom, how many calories are we going to burn?" Shoshana asked, figuring that the long walk would offset the challah, the bowls heaped with salads, and the hot beef and potato cholent. We walked up Setagaya Dori, past the recycled clothing shops and the vintage furniture showroom. I stopped to check the price on a wicker chair.

"Mom, we don't have space for any more furniture."

"Well, you never know."

"Are you thinking about another house?"

"Making this one more comfortable—that's good enough reason, no?"

Divorce was the flittering bee in my bonnet that I had to fight off, even when the buzzing became loud. One way to stave off these thoughts was to buy furniture and barricade myself in with cabinets, closets, and bookshelves. Not that I was doing it consciously. Only in hindsight would I realize that's what I'd been doing.

We walked past one convenience store after another, stopping at traffic lights, admiring poodles and dachshunds taking their owners for walks.

"Mom, this is fun."

"What did you say?" The roar of speeding traffic made it hard to hear Shoshana.

"It's fun walking to Chabad House." We paused to drink from our water bottles under a lone birch tree. Shoshana bent down to pet a poodle.

I shook my head. "It's fine to walk to Chabad on a spring day, but it will be impossible once it gets hotter." Daniel, Yael, and their family had returned to America, and we were on our own once again with Shabbat. The difference was that we were now accustomed to observing all of Shabbat as a day of rest and couldn't imagine turning back. I paused in front of a real estate agent's window to look at apartments for rent.

"What are you thinking?" Shoshana asked in surprise.

"Don't worry. We're not moving. But how about we rent an apartment near Chabad House just for Shabbat?"

"Isn't that a big waste of money if we're only staying for Shabbat?"

"You know there's a saying: work six days and God picks up the tab on the seventh."

After Shabbat, I found a studio very close to Chabad with a purple magnolia tree blooming through sliding glass doors.

"Perfect," I smiled.

Back at home, I showed Ichiro the floor plan.

"Is this what your God wanting of you, being a good Jew for not take the bus on Shabbat? If it making you feel better, then go ahead—so long you paying for the rent."

"We must fixing our marriage for the sake of the children," he added.

"Fixing?"

"What if I becoming Jew?"

I was speechless.

"I'm ready to thinking about it. How about a walk?" he asked. He rarely asked me to accompany him.

"No, I'm busy. I have to get Akiva's lunch ready for tomorrow." The rice cooker, a daikon radish, a plate with an omelet, and condiments were spread over the counter.

Ichiro took his walk around the block alone and brought me home a cabbage from the last vegetable field left in the neighborhood. He had news, too, that the farmer had sold his property. The open sky above the rows of vegetables would disappear to make way for a new development of twenty-two houses. Then he added that he had decided he was going to become Jewish, after all.

"But how?" I asked skeptically. If I was incredulous, it was because there was no chance Ichiro could have an Orthodox conversion in Japan. There were no teachers, mentors, rabbis and fellow Orthodox converts to learn with. We would have to go overseas for an Orthodox conversion and I knew Ichiro would never leave Japan. This conversation had nowhere to go.

"Have you thought who would convert you and where? About circumcision? Learning Hebrew? The conversion process requires an official conversion Rabbinate to supervise your studies. Oh, please, don't do it for my sake."

"That's what you wanting all along. It's for the family's sake!" I wasn't against Ichiro becoming Jewish. It would have been the happiest day of my life to see him stand before the Beit Din, the court of three Rabbis, and declare with joy in his heart that he belonged with the Jewish people. The strict test was to demonstrate a convert's sincere commitment to a Torah-led way of life. It was hard enough for me as a born Jew. But for Ichiro? In Japan? It was an impossible stretch of my imagination to see how that could be possible.

"If you're ready to move to America, or Israel, where there are plenty of rabbis who you can learn with, then let's go."

"We can't. Children are still in school. It making not good result we moving them to another country."

By the time the first stars appeared in the sky, Ichiro had changed his mind and decided that he wouldn't become Jewish, after all.

That night my mother called from Florida.

"Liane, I don't understand why I have to go on Facebook to find out what's going on between you and Ichiro. I haven't seen a photograph of him on your Timeline in ages."

"Mom—I didn't want to worry you. We're up in the air. There are some things that are too painful for you to know. But I'll tell you this. Ichiro brought up the subject of conversion."

"Oh, you make me laugh. It's simply not practical, Liane. He's tied to his life in Japan. He's not going anywhere. Look at how my cousins and your cousins married out. They're all in okay marriages."

"Okay? Just okay? What if okay is no longer okay for me? By Jewish law, our marriage isn't even recognized."

"Well, fiddle it. By the civil law, in Japan and the USA, you jolly well are."

"I don't want to go on being the wife who goes against everything Ichiro values. Look at the funeral of his father! He still hasn't forgiven me for not letting Shoshana and Akiva pick up his father's ashes. He said that I had dishonored his father, and once again Shoshana and Akiva are caught in the middle."

I sniffled into a tissue and my mother tutted into the phone. "My word, this is more serious than I imagined," she said.

Ichiro made another appointment to speak to the Rabbi and Rebbetzin. We drove in a fog of silence and headlights on a highway corridor flanked with tall apartment buildings to reach Chabad House.

"How is life?" the Rabbi asked Ichiro, as he placed tall glasses of his own brand of green tea before us. I began. "He's still sore about the funeral. He called me a hypocrite, saying I'm not

Orthodox enough!" Ichiro interrupted: "Liane taking the comfortable part of being Jewish. Did you know she not let Akiva participating in Sports Day this year? It's the school year's biggest event, and all the parents participate their children."

"Was Sports Day on Shabbat?" the Rabbi asked.

"No, Yom Kippur," Ichiro said.

The Rabbi's dimples appeared when he laughed. "Yom Kippur! The day of fasting and repentance! *Oopah*! You did a great thing by allowing your son to be with other Jews on Yom Kippur and perform the mitzvah of observing the holiest day of the year."

"This was my son's last year of elementary school, the biggest Sports Day of his life. You know, Rabbi, he is my son, too, and he's just as much Japanese as he a Jew. You see—there's a decent way that doesn't have to end in an argument!"

But the Rabbi wouldn't discuss the subject. He couched his words in a friendly suggestion: "How about pressing the reset button?"

Chapter Fourteen

A FAMILY RESET IN ISRAEL

From one end of the skies is its rising
and its circuit is to the other end;
there is no escaping its heat.
—Psalm 19

Pressing the reset button sounded like a very good idea. With Akiva's bar mitzvah approaching, I proposed that we go on a family trip to Israel, and Ichiro agreed. He sold a watch that he had inherited from his father and bought four tickets to Israel with the profit. I had relatives in Givatayim to visit, too, the cousins of my father's wife, Sidi. The Tuchfelds observed Shabbat and practiced an Orthodox way of life. Maybe they could help us find a bar mitzvah tutor for Akiva, too.

Most of what I knew about Israel had been crafted by the Japanese media, their selective reporting and the government's agenda to present Israel through the narrative of the Palestinian conflict. That Israeli Arabs arrived at the same airport, took the same buses, made their purchases at the same shopping malls and grocery stores, visited the same post offices, parks, zoos and museums was a revelation.

We started our trip by heading up to Tsfat, the ancient Kabbalistic center of learning in northern Israel. Tsfat was built on a mountaintop, its covered alleys leading to steep steps, stone archways, and sweeping views across mountains. It was impossible to know where Israel ended and Lebanon began.

On our first day in Tsfat, we arrived in the early afternoon, with plenty of time to get settled into a room painted lavender with vaulted ceilings. I left the door open for some fresh air because the room had no windows, but our host stopped by to tell us to close it because missiles were threatened to arrive from Lebanon after nightfall. Suddenly the hostility across the borders felt very real. But not to worry. You get used to it, our host told us. He showed us how to shelter if we heard sirens. We were to stand with our faces to a stone wall should we come under attack. It was our first night together in Tsfat and we were learning how to holiday in a war zone.

"Now you understanding why I never moving to Israel?" Ichiro said.

"If we were back in Japan, you think we'd be any safer? Earthquakes, volcanoes, and North Korea threatening to attack us?"

There was weird normalcy to Tsfat under missile threat. The Artist Colony was open for business. I stepped into galleries and jewelry shops crowded with tourists passing along narrow alleys under stone archways. Around dusk, just as Shabbat was coming in, we headed to the Old Jewish Quarter. The soldiers were out in full force with their rifles slung over their shoulders. They stood around casually, chatting and smoking cigarettes, and just before prayers began, the soldiers broke into a circle dance.

A man with a long beard approached us. He took one look at Akiva's kippah, spelling out in gold letters Chabad of Tokyo, and he cried out: *"Baruch Hashem*! Thank God! How's the Rabbi? I worked in Japan many years ago as a *basta*, a street vendor. I met the Chabad rabbi when I was selling jewelry on the streets, and I came back to Israel a changed man." He pulled on his side-locks. "Look what became of me!"

I looked into his light blue eyes. His nose rose like Mount Fuji. I would have loved to know more about this man's trans-formation to pious Jew, but a pink sunset gave way to an ultra-marine sky. Shabbat had begun, and the holy man merged into the crowd.

A woman approached me with a scarf over her wig.

"Where are you from?" she asked as she scrutinized my Asian family.

She clasped her hands to her heart when I explained that we were from Japan. *"Min Hashamayim!"* Literally, From Heaven.

"What do you mean?" I asked.

"My grandson just announced his engagement to a Japanese woman. I don't usually leave the house on the eve of Shabbat. But tonight, I said to myself, Ruthie, go out. There's no point staying at home alone and worrying about missiles. Tell me, do Japanese believe in God?"

Ichiro was happy to join the conversation.

"We Japanese having one God with many names. But every God same at the source. We connecting altogether here," he said, pointing to his heart.

"What do Japanese people believe?" Ruthie continued.

"We believe everything happening for a reason."

"You're a brave man to accompany your Jewish wife to Israel," Ruthie said, whispering under her breath, "Ach, that man, Obama."

"I admiring my wife. She having courage to live with uncer-tainty. She needing risk-take. It's like her air. But me, I'm Japanese. I can live without to take risks."

My first and only trip to Israel prior to this one had been in

December of 1979. I had arrived with a backpack and was stunned to see teenagers my own age chewing gum and carrying guns in army fatigues. I couldn't imagine myself ever living in Israel then and taking risks with my life.

"I discovered that what you avoid comes back to bite you in the *tuchus*."

"Bite you in *tuchus*?"

"That's Yiddish for rear end," I translated.

"Never happening when you find your master," Ichiro guffawed.

We followed a map to the five-hundred-year-old Ashkenazi Ari Synagogue, rebuilt after a major earthquake, and hidden behind walls in a small courtyard. Like much of the Israeli landscape, this ancient synagogue had been built from sand-colored stones. The interior was crafted like a jewel, painted the colors of sapphires, with emerald greens, lemony yellow, with ruby red accents. The ark housing the Torah was elevated on an octagonal platform. I had been praying in a Chabad House kitchen for so long that I had almost forgotten how stunning a synagogue could be.

The Ashkenazi Ari Synagogue of Tsfat is one of the oldest in Israel, tracing its history back to a disciple of Rabbi Yitzchak Luria, the mystic who would take his rabbinical students to the fields to welcome the Shabbat with breathtaking sunsets over distant hills, singing *Lecha Dodi* in sweet harmony. Most of these Torah scholars were refugees from the Spanish Inquisition. They had lost contact with their families, who faced expulsion or death for not converting to Christianity in late 15th century Spain.

Curiously enough, there may have been a Japan connection here too. Among the first sea merchants to arrive in the early 1600s to Nagasaki, the only port in all of Japan to accept foreigners, were Marranos. These concealed Jews, forced to convert to Christianity, were also refugees from the Spanish

Inquisition. In Nagasaki their Jewish identity resurfaced and they buried their dead in a Jewish graveyard; Chabad Rabbi Edery visited right after he was shown photographs of its existence.

I returned to the Ashkenaz Synagogue on Shabbat morning while Ichiro slept in with Shoshana and Akiva. Men covered in white and black striped *tallitot*, prayer shawls, led the service from the ornate pulpit. I couldn't keep my eyes off pillars that had been carved and decorated with hands brought together in an inverted heart shape. I had drawn a pastel picture long ago with two hands in those exact positions, oblivious that they had anything to do with Judaism. It was here that I discovered that the hand position belongs to the *Kohanim*, a lineage of high priests descended from Aaron, appointed by his brother Moses to lead the daily prayers and rites for all Israelites. To this day, only the priestly class can bless the congregation. I tried to imagine my great grandfather, Avraham Cohen, raising his hands to bless his congregation. This was the closest I would come to know him—through what he might have done if only I could verify his priestly status. If only it were so.

Judaism comes with deep roots, and its own operating manual, the Torah. The chances that my children would want to know what was inside the Torah and want to follow it, after being educated in the Japanese system, were getting slimmer with each passing year. But it was on this Shabbat in Tsfat under missile threats, that the seed was planted. It occurred to me that I could actually imagine myself one day living in Israel. The proverb, "Change your location, change your luck," came to mind.

I wore a loose white blouse buttoned up over a long, navy-blue skirt as if I had been born to a father with a full beard and to a mother who had taught me *tzniut*, the laws of modesty. Until I got to Israel and saw Jews dress in many ways, I had no idea that I had adopted the Chabad House costume of the Rebbetzin herself!

Pogroms had driven my mother's grandparents out of Latvia to England at the end of the nineteenth century. My father had escaped from Romania after the Communists established their anti-Semitic regime in 1949. Jews in my family uprooted when the soil became hostile to growth. Both my parents came from Jewish stock that identified with the Haskalah, the romantic movement in Europe, otherwise known as the Jewish Enlightenment. It was a 19th century intellectual movement that sought the impossible: to preserve Jewish identity while integrating into surrounding societies, with their enticing sophistication, and advanced education. The women in my family dressed as they pleased, got educated, danced on the stage, navigated the stock market, and married out. They became matriarchs when their husbands died young, as my great aunt Vicky did, and gathered the family around fine bone china, ruby red crystal glasses, and lavish Sunday feasts.

Our trip to Israel occurred over the Jewish new year, Rosh Hashanah. My father's wife Sidi had introduced me to her wonderful cousins, Michael and Devora, who welcomed us to their home and their synagogue in Givatayim, graced by impressive tetrahedrons that formed a three-dimensional Star of David high above the seating. This would make a fine venue for Akiva's bar mitzvah, for sure. But was I out of my mind? Michael thought it possible and there's nothing as powerful as somebody whom you barely know making an implausible dream into reality. Michael found Akiva a tutor who could prepare him online for his bar mitzvah. When we got back to Tokyo, the bar mitzvah lessons began. Akiva would sit in front of the computer, learning his *haftorah*, his Torah portion, from Rabbi Moshe Shmaryahu, a choir member in the Israeli Philharmonic.

This is how Akiva prepared for his bar mitzvah at Givurat

Mordechai Synagogue in Givatayim. My mother traveled from Florida to see her grandson with a Torah in his arms. It had been no easy trip for her, flying from West Palm Beach to Tel Aviv just weeks after losing Leon, her husband of twenty-three years. Uncle Graham from London, the Maidenhead branch of the family, Sir Hugh and Justine, and from Manchester, Sir Gordon and Carole joined us.

"I wouldn't have missed this for the world," my mother whispered, as the Rabbi blessed the wine over Kiddush lunch. Waiters carried in a beautiful Moroccan buffet. We sipped *bissara* soup and dipped our challah into humus with fragrant black olives, chicken tagine, and pumpkin streaked with honey and raisins. Ichiro ate in silence. When he posed for pictures after Shabbat, he couldn't bring himself to smile for the camera. I was reminded of that awkward shot at our wedding when he bowed deeply, and I missed my cue. In Israel, I was at home and he was on the high end of the seesaw.

"Well, I do think you and Ichiro both deserve medals for all you've done to give the children two belief systems. Buddhist Orthodoxy and Conservative Chabadism," my mother joked.

She made him laugh. Ichiro leaned in from across the table. "What else can I do?" he said, as he refilled my mother's glass with sparkling wine.

"Well, like I always said to my stubborn daughter, marriage counseling wouldn't do you both any harm. Not that it worked for her father and me! But her father was impossible. Nothing I could do was ever enough."

I approached Ichiro in our hotel room after the children had gone to bed. "While we're here in Israel, how about we visit a few schools in the Naale program? The government offers free high school education for Jewish kids raised outside of Israel." Ichiro stopped with a toothbrush in his mouth.

"I fine we did Akiva's bar mitvah in Israel and he can coming to Israel after he finish high school in Japan."

"He's also Jewish. He's been in your system all his life. Why not let him go experience the other half of his identity?"

"Israel! Look how dangerous country! Everywhere missiles raining down. I never consenting!" Ichiro raised his voice. Akiva came wandering into the room in his pajamas, rubbing his eyes. "What are you guys fighting about now?"

"Your high school education," I answered.

"You guys can choose," he shrugged. Then Shoshana hollered from the next room. She had awoken too. "When we get back to Tokyo, why don't you go get counseling from Incho?" Shoshana reminded us that Incho, the master of the acupuncture clinic where we had met, was still there to help us.

INCHO'S OFFICE hadn't changed much over the years. From behind a desk piled high with patients' charts, he examined Ichiro and me with x-ray eyes. We sat awkwardly on a loveseat, surrounded by a scrolled painting of Buddha in fine draped robes, shelves containing crystals, gongs, and books flowing onto the floor. A naked mannequin, tattooed in meridian lines and acupuncture points, guarded the door.

Incho complimented me on my black cloche. He told me I looked like a madam in this hat. Ichiro explained what a madam was, so he corrected himself. A woman of elegance, he said. The receptionist offered us cups of green tea, and Incho waited for us to sip before speaking. I found myself tongue-tied. I didn't know where to begin. Whether through intuition or whatever Ichiro had told him, Incho knew about the difficulties between us. He pointed to the two *bizen yaki*, rough-hewn brownish teacups from which Ichiro and I were drinking, and wrapped a piece of newspaper carelessly and noisily around his empty cup.

"You and Ichiro have become like this messy wrapping, covering up the beauty inside. This is not good for Shoshana and Akiva. Both kids have great potential, but there must be harmony to reach it. This is the Taoist way."

I listened carefully, taking notes, and when I looked over at Ichiro, I saw that he was writing the words down too. Gift wrapping is very important in this society. I had learned from Ichiro's mother that it's disrespectful, if not a downright insult, to present a gift or money unwrapped. Crumbled newspaper wrapping around a cup was Incho's way of reminding us that we were not living in our two-seater world, but our children were deeply affected by our every word and act. I nodded in agreement.

Ichiro had shed every trace of association with the White Crane clinic's dress code. Long gone were the kimono and ponytail he wore when I had met him. With his grey blazer, navy slacks, and his hair cut short, I hardly recognized him in his familiar surroundings. Yet he came to Incho with humility, for counseling like old times, a disciple dressed like a salesman yet sitting on the edge of his seat ready to breathe in the words of his master. Ichiro took this relationship as a lifelong contract of respect, but no easy friendship. Incho tore at the paper wrapped around the cup noisily, almost comically, to bring the metaphor home. Ichiro sat across from him mesmerized by what our relationship must have looked like from his master's point of view. But I wasn't all that convinced.

Thoughts flittered in and out of my mind. A harsh voice said it was a big mistake to have dragged Ichiro out of this Taoist world with its archaic codes and metaphors. But a kinder voice said what I felt in my heart. *He would have lost you, and you would have lost the chance to bring Shoshana and Akiva into this world.* The kinder voice continued: *The children may be offering you a chance to draw closer and make peace.*

Ichiro prodded me. "You're okay? You not listen to my trans-lation." He was selectively translating what he wanted to convey. I shook my head. My Japanese was good enough now to know what he had left out. He hadn't translated what I'd just said about the handicap our children were experiencing at school, of being regarded as *ha-fu*, a triple threat. To be bicultural, biracial, and bilingual conferred on our children, awe, envy, pity, and discrimination.

Ichiro tossed his pen into the crease in his notebook. "Well, you can doing your own translation." Incho waited till the pen came to a rest. "Ichiro is not well. He has heart problems. Could you be more compassionate for his sake, and for the kids' sake?"

"Ichiro hasn't told me about his heart problems." I was shocked.

"Who gets ill and who recovers? It's the patient who can let go of anger," Incho said as he rested his hands on his knees, looking from Ichiro to me.

I blinked back tears. A marriage doesn't just fall apart. It self-destructs, word by unkind word, and, God forbid, organ by organ. Incho was speaking the truth. I had low thyroid functioning and hypertension to contend with, fibromyalgia that came and went, and worst of all, the low flame of anger of feeling trapped in a marriage far from home.

I gazed at the rough-hewn cup, still messily half-wrapped in newspaper. The wrapping was coming undone. If this was how we presented ourselves to the world, it was not pretty. We were covering up who we were, layered up to protect ourselves from each other. Like the ugly wrapping, we had walled ourselves off from each other and had stopped communicating.

Not long after this meeting, my mother had been driving her car and missed the stop sign a block away from her home. Her car had plowed head-on into a neighbor. Her knee jerked up to the steering wheel to cover her face as the airbag inflated. But glass flew and she gashed her leg so badly it would take months till the bleeding stopped. On the day of the accident, she had been racing home to interview Cindy Ramkelawan from

Trinidad. Cindy's arrival in my mother's life as her dear friend and helper was a gift from heaven. She nursed my mother back to health.

Because of Cindy, my mother remained cheerful when she called. She gave me regular movie updates. I simply must see *La La Land*, a musical masterpiece—she called it. "I do agree with the critics. It should sweep the Academy Awards." So, I went to see *La La Land* and she was right. I loved imagining my Mom as a younger version of herself, when she had aspired to become an actress after graduating from the Guildhall School of Drama in London.

Over subsequent phone calls, I noticed she had a nagging cough. "Have you seen a doctor?"

"Yes, I must."

Over my mother's left lung X-rays revealed a dark shadow. Emergency surgery was necessary to remove half the cancerous lung. My mother had just turned eighty-two, and both of us wanted to believe even a horrible diagnosis like cancer would progress slowly at her age. She asked me to say the prayer for healing, the *mi sheberach,* which surprised me. I didn't know that she had been going to synagogue for Shabbat for quite some time.

My mother recovered pretty well, or maybe it was her way to fit in one last cruise along the canals of France, taking chemotherapy pills with her. After returning to Florida, she ordered tickets to see *Hamilton* long before the musical had opened on Broadway. That was my mother—planning her life at least nine months in advance, as if New York theater tickets for a Broadway show could stave off death.

THE PHONE RANG JUST after I had lit the candles. Akiva was lounging on the sofa, reading a *manga* comic book, and he ignored the ringing because Shabbat had started. But Shoshana was bothered, and she hollered down from her room: "Aren't you going to pick it up?"

I was busy slicing lemons. Ichiro knew better than to call after sundown when Shabbat had begun, so it couldn't be him unless something unexpected had happened. He would have been in the car now driving with his mother so she could join us too. Maybe they had hit heavy traffic on the raised highway over Roppongi Dori. Turning off the phones before Shabbat had become a habit, but with the phone ringing persistently, my imagination went wild with worry. My heart was in my stomach when I picked up the phone.

"*Moshi moshi* to you, dear."

For goodness's sake—it was my mother. "Are you okay?"

"Yes, I'm okay dear."

"Why are you calling now? Mom! It's already Shabbat."

"I've been trying you all week. If I didn't know you better, I'd say you were ignoring me."

"Mom! How about we speak Saturday night—after Shabbat. I'd rather not talk on Shabbat!"

"Well, dear. You know, it irks me to always have to go to your Facebook page to find out what you're up to. It looks like you've got another trip to Israel on your mind."

Just one Facebook comment about how the Naale program in Israel offered free high school education for Jewish kids worldwide and my mother had picked up on my excitement about the prospect of sending Akiva abroad. Ichiro had refused to discuss it further.

The doorbell rang. We had recently added Cinnamon, a Doxie-poodle, to our family. She had a muppet-like cuteness, with a Dachshund's long body and a silky shag in a spicy brown color. She barked to announce Ichiro and my mother-in-law's arrival. With the phone still in my hand, I said goodbye to my mother. I hadn't picked up on the fact that my mother had called about something more serious.

. . .

My mother had marked November 7th, 2016 on her calendar. It was the first breakfast meeting of the season at Wycliffe country club, when the snowbirds from up north settle in for the winter season. Mom had herself been shuttling back and forth between Long Island and Wellington for years. Cindy was surprised that my mother was taking so long to get ready that morning. Letting herself in, she found my mother sitting on the edge of her bed clenching her stockings. She tried to speak but her words came out slurred. Cindy suspected a stroke and called for the ambulance. The paramedics confirmed Cindy's diagnosis, and once in the hospital, my mother suffered a second, more severe stroke that left her paralyzed.

I was in Tokyo when I heard that my mother was dying. No —transitioning. I tried on all sorts of words for where she was going next. Losing my mother, she was taking part of me with her. Talia and Uncle Graham were already in Florida when I arrived at her side in the Hospice by the Sea. Her eyes gradually shut when the drugs took effect.

Stay, she seemed to be saying.
But it's getting late now. Don't be afraid Mom. You'll be fine.
Where am I going? I'm going to miss you.
I'm going to miss you, too. I can't imagine life without you.
I'll be with you.
I'll be with you, too.
Please don't forget your dear Mum.
Never. Not a day.

Not a sound came from her lips or mine. I heard her goodbye in my heart. I asked the doctor how long she could be in limbo between worlds. He didn't know. With stroke victims, it could be hours, or it could be days.

Feelings resurfaced from very long ago. Perhaps I had self-ishly abandoned my mother for a family saga in Japan. Maybe

I'd be abandoning my mother again, in her final hours, if I left her bedside. But I wasn't alone. I was with Graham and my sister, and we made a joint family decision to go home, cry our eyes out, and get some sleep.

My mother clung to life that night. At six the next morning, we got a call from the hospice that my mother was going. She passed away with Cindy by her side. Darling Cindy, Mom had called her. Cindy was with my mother as she left for the next world, and I can live with that. I'm actually grateful beyond words.

Death needed time to sink in. I couldn't believe that she wouldn't burst through the bedroom door at any moment demanding to know what I was doing sitting at her desk. I sat at her oversized desk and cried. I had never gone through her drawers, and I felt uneasy doing so now, but we had to know what she had left behind. My mother had been secretive in so many ways. She had planned every last detail of her funeral without us knowing. Her body was to be flown back to New York and buried a row behind Leon's and his first wife Flo. I stood in front of a mound of dirt as her casket was lowered into the ground. No, this couldn't be happening.

But strangely, I heard my mother call cheerfully *toodleoo*. She had a charming way of making light of even grave situations. *Never mind dear. I'll be quite all right. I'll see you when Moshiach comes.* It had been her way to never let on that a situation was dire. I hadn't realized what a gift this was to me. She had saved me from excessive worry, even when there had been good cause for losing sleep over her declining health.

We finished reciting Kaddish, and Uncle Graham, Talia and her family, and a few friends and relatives shoveled dirt into the deep hole receiving my mother's casket. It was getting dark. The grave diggers came to plow a mound of dirt over the grave. Uncle Graham put his arm around my shoulder. "I'm heartbroken," he said. "Your mother and I spoke almost every day." I grabbed his hand, lost for words, because I hadn't spoken every day to my mother. I uttered the cliché of all clichés: "She is in a better place, now."

I looked up to see far in the distance two men with beards and familiar black hats—felt Borsalinos with wafer-thin rims. As they came closer my jaw dropped. It was the Rabbi, Yehezkel Binyamin Edery, who happened to be in New Jersey, attending a Kosher food trade show, when my mother died. I began to laugh. This was no normal laugh but an unstoppable guffaw of shock, amazement and bottomless gratitude.

When I returned to Tokyo, Ichiro offered his condolences with a bowed head. He handed me an envelope filled with enough yen notes to cover the flight expenses. I don't think Ichiro grasped how much my mother adored him or how I needed comforting. Perhaps there was another explanation why he hadn't been able to bring himself to attend the funeral. What if he couldn't manage the long flight with his heart condition? *Give Ichiro the benefit of the doubt,* my mother said softly. From God knows where I heard her.

Chapter Fifteen

COMING HOME TO THE WINDMILL

I meditated and realized that I am
like a bird that is alone on the roof.
—Psalm 102

I could almost see my mother sitting in a wing-tipped teak chair at the head of an oval dining room table in a caramel shade of teak.

Go on. Treat yourself, she said. But this couldn't be. I was in the lobby of Tokyo's Shinjuku Park Tower weeks after my mother's funeral. I had walked into a teak-filled wonderland with Keni. He had come to Tokyo to cheer me up as only friends who've known each other for forty years can do. He noticed a woman dressed in a Chanel suit and Prada heels examining a teak credenza, her mouth covered by a white surgical mask that he said ruined the outfit. I grinned. It was a New York thing. You take yourself seriously, and you laugh at everybody else. You say one thing, and you do another. We relished the ridiculous, deliriously unaware that the COVID virus would soon have us wearing white maskings, too.

We had entered a furniture showroom of Danish Modern straight out of the 1950s. I stood transfixed by chunky teak contours on skinny legs. My mouth dropped at the sight of teak furniture that I hadn't thought about since my parents left Great Neck after their divorce. I ran my hand over the same oval table with extensions that brought back memories of happy cooperation between my parents. They would stand at opposite ends and engage in a tug of war that would split the table apart. They would insert two leaves of the same fine teak. The procedure would end with a macho flourish from my father, a mighty shove to close the gaps. These extensions came out when my father's aunties in homemade cotton dresses, my father and his uncles dressed in dark suits and neckties, visited us. The only day of the week that my hard-working relatives came was on a Sunday. Since most of them didn't drive and lived far away on Manhattan's Upper West Side, a shared Shabbat meal or a Passover seder was unthinkable.

My mother would make her dramatic appearance straight from the beauty parlor with a fresh bouffant, light as chiffon. She was an expert at applying makeup, just enough to enhance her pretty grey-blue eyes and pink rosebud lips. As she stood at the head of the long table in a sleeveless cocktail dress, her hands gloved in oven mitts, she would hold a serving platter crowned with roast beef simmering in its juices, and my sister and I would carry in crisp potatoes and a side of peas.

"*Bon appetite*," she would say cheerfully, and my father's aunts and uncles would politely respond under their breath, "*Pofta buna*," the Romanian equivalent.

In 1971, my parents' scrimping and saving had led to the purchase of a white stucco house with blue shutters in the Old Village of Great Neck. From the windows, you could have seen my mother at the dining room table, typing up her college papers, pausing once in a while to scratch an elbow or laugh at her own jokes.

"What's so funny?" I remember asking her one night after I had finished my chore of emptying the dishwasher. It was her habit after a long day at her secretarial job in Manhattan to write after dinner while my father retired to the den to watch *Rowan & Martin's Laugh-In* with a grooming brush in hand and our Scotch Terrier on his lap.

"I'm working on an essay," she had said, as she read from a sheet of paper propped upright in the typewriter roller. "I remember the lamplighter who would come around silently before dusk to our street in Wimbledon. He couldn't bear to be spoken to in any voice above a whisper. My mother explained that he had been a soldier on the war front who had been shell-shocked. We had to be careful to humor to him."

"Mom, I think my Hebrew schoolteacher is shell-shocked, too."

"Why, darling?"

"Because everyone in my class has to humor him, too."

"I didn't go to Hebrew school like you, dear. We had a tutor who came to the house to teach us Hebrew."

"What did you learn?"

My mother's brow furrowed. "It was the war years in England—there were few books, but one thing I remember was that he always told me to hold my head high. I was one of only six Jewish girls at school and we were singled out to stand at the back of the auditorium when Christian hymns were sung. He taught me to be proud and so I dreamed of the day I could live amongst Jews."

The teak dining table in the Tokyo furniture showroom had opened up these memories and came home with me. It was an extravagant impulse purchase, but I couldn't help myself. The table connected me to my past in ways that my mother no longer could.

Chabad House had nudged me back to lighting candles and Daniel and Yael had shared the warmth of Friday night Shabbats. I started to open our home to guests too. One of the regulars was June, an older woman who lived alone and got around the neighborhood by wheelchair. We had met at a traffic light while I was walking Cinnamon, where she told me she had once been a dog trainer. Shabbat became June's time to hold our Doxie-poodle on her lap and keep her quiet.

Akiva would bless the wine—well, grape juice because Ichiro disapproved of his drinking the real thing. We shuffled in house slippers around a tall cabinet to reach the kitchen and perform a ritual washing of our hands. Akiva recited the blessing on the challah, salted the bread, and sliced it up.

One Shabbat I couldn't contain myself. I had exciting news to share. "Akiva has been accepted into the Naale program for high school education in Israel—and, drum roll, for free!"

June clapped her hands together: "*Yokata!*" Hurray!

Ichiro sat expressionless across from me. He picked up cubes from the beet bowl with his chopsticks and chewed in silence.

"Akiva, how do you feel about it?" Ichiro asked.

"Naale is fine, I guess. But you guys can choose," Akiva answered warily. He knew that one parent would be happy and one would not—whatever the decision. Akiva was the family peacemaker and wasn't going to be put on the spot to decide. Shoshana got to the point:

"Can't you see Papa doesn't want him to go?"

"Your mother not thinking practically! A free education never free. Flights costing money. He missing his friends. He missing his grandmother. "

"Yeah," I said. "And you'll miss Akiva unless we all go to Israel."

Ichiro looked at me as if I was off my rocker. Leave *his* country?

"Living outside your comfort zone may be good for you."

"Please thinking practically. I having to support the family."

June offered Cinnamon a bite of challah and a term of endearment, *kawai*, cute.

"If you want Akiva to go to Israel so much, why don't you go instead?" Shoshana asked. She had perceived the unsaid, that I was halfway out the door.

"Look, you can go. I never stopping you. It's your life," Ichiro said. But did he mean it? Did I have the nerve to get up and walk away from Japan with Akiva and Shoshana too? To go to Israel for the sake of the children's future wasn't selfish, or was it? It seemed the only one who was stopping me from going now was me.

Weeks later, Shoshana took matters into her own hands. She was showing subtle signs of instability and it terrified Ichiro as much as it did me to consider another long hospitalization in Japan. Ichiro raced us to the airport. I left with Shoshana and our two suitcases for what was to be a month-long period of study at a women's seminary on a dusty hilltop in Israel.

The week we had left, the Torah portion offered up a timely story of Moses sending out twelve spies who were to bring back a report on the promised land of Israel.

All but two of the spies told of terrible things. They spoke of fortified walled cities, warrior kingdoms, and real live giants. There will always be reasons to stay put in life, endure what will never change, and not take risks. The lesson in the story of the twelve spies is to not believe negative spin because God's hand operates from faith and trust. When Shoshana and I arrived in Bat Ayin, in Judea-Samaria, otherwise known as the West Bank, there were no giants. But I noticed immediately the grave marker where a terrorist had breached the settlement fence and killed a meditator sitting peacefully in his field.

Shoshana hated the isolation, stunned and enraged that I had taken her to Bat Ayin, separated from the Arab village on the next hill by a grove of olive trees. We awoke to amplifiers calling Muslims to prayer. When the hills became silent again, it would be my turn to pray.

While in Bat Ayin, I first learned of Jerusalem Syndrome, the name of a bonafide psychiatric disorder among travelers who become psychotic and end up in Israel's mental hospitals in delusional states. Shoshana didn't wait to get to Jerusalem for her Jerusalem Syndrome moment. From Bat Ayin, she hitch-hiked to Malcha Mall, and an Arab driver and his friend picked her up in the same area of the Gush where three teenage boys had been kidnapped and tragically executed.

Shoshana's driver was Palestinian, but in stark contrast, he was an angel incarnate who gave her cash when she confided she was penniless so that she could take the bus back from the shopping mall. Shoshana found her way back just minutes before Shabbat.

By that time, I was so worried I was practically out of my body. The brutal murder of those three Jewish teenage hitch-hikers had occurred a walking distance from the front gate of Bat Ayin. I shuddered to think what could have happened to my Jewish daughter. But then it hit me. The driver had no reason to assume that Shoshana was Jewish. She looked, to all appear-ances, like a beautiful young woman from Asia. Her Japanese appearance, profoundly, might have saved her life.

Shoshana's mania was full throttle and not knowing a thing about the Israeli mental hospital system, it was the only place where I could find emergency care. I did what I had to do. I prayed that Shoshana would get the help she needed by kind nurses and professional doctors, and that I could get some badly needed rest. I asked a friend to accompany me to the hospital. This is the thing about Israel. There is always a friend nearby. Never for a second did I feel alone thanks to a Jerusalemite I'd met at Tokyo Chabad House, Daniel Moskovich.

Shoshana spent three nights in the hospital and when she was discharged, medicated and frail, I had no idea where to go next, but I knew one thing for sure. Returning to Japan was not an option in her fragile state. We stayed overnight in a hotel in Jerusalem, then I rented a weekly apartment in the German Colony.

On the Sabbath, the entire city comes to a halt. The buses stop running, shopkeepers and restaurants shutter their businesses, and families head off to synagogue, then gather at home for dinner. I contacted my Rebbetzin in Tokyo, explained what had happened, and once again she gave me cause to believe in miracles. Rebbetzin Efrat contacted her friend Chaya, a real estate agent, who lived in the neighborhood and warmly welcomed us to a Shabbat dinner in her home.

"You belong here," she said over a beautiful meal in the first Jerusalem home I'd ever visited.

"I know. Eventually, I will make aliyah," I replied, explaining that my son Akiva was at school in Tokyo.

"Why not now?" Chaya pressed on. "Your son will join you."

I thought she had to be joking, but Chaya was not. After Shabbat, she took me to Yemin Moshe, a bougainvillea-filled community with some of the oldest homes in Jerusalem, built 150 years ago on a steep slope facing the Old City walls. I climbed step by step, breath by breath, pausing to admire the green cypress trees, pink-tiled rooftops, and cobblestone alleys.

We stopped in front of the towering Yemin Moshe windmill, and Chaya pointed out the antique stagecoach that had carried London financier Moses Montefiore to Yemin Moshe long before any buildings stood on this hill. A tour guide arrived in front of the windmill with a busload of visitors, and I stretched an ear to hear what he was saying. It had been a hard sell to convince Jews to leave the relative safety of the walled city for a hill roamed by goats and bandits. This involved a big gamble.

The Yemin Moshe neighborhood was now so upmarket that brides and grooms arrived with their photographers in chauffeured limousines just to be snapped by the windmill. Steps away, the realtor climbed a flight of stairs to enter a house with spectacular panoramic views of cypress trees, pink rooftops, ancient walls, church steeples, flourishing gardens, and far in the distance the Jordanian mountains rising above the Dead Sea. I adjusted my hat. I knew so little about Jerusalem that I had no idea that such a beautiful place existed in Israel, or on this earth. I thought about Shoshana and how this peaceful home would soothe her, how we could draw and paint together from its balcony. The house had a superb kitchen, with a dishwasher and other neat appliances that I would find in a Western-style house.

"It's a perfect kitchen. What do you think?" I winked at Shoshana.

"Mom! Get real! We can't afford to live here!"

The windmill's white blades rotated lazily through the kitchen window, reminding me of the last day I'd seen my mother in Wimbledon. The windmill appeared so close, I thought I heard my mother speak to me: *This is marvelous. You must go for it. Think of all the risk-takers who came to Yemin Moshe before you. Think of all the brides and grooms taking the most remarkable risk life of their lives—marriage itself. What have you got to lose?*

"What do you think? Would you like to live here?" I asked as Shoshana wandered onto the terrace, holding onto the rails. There were two voices vying inside me. One said: "This is crazy!" The other said more calmly, in a beautiful English accent: "Simply, my dear, it's time."

SHOSHANA and I moved into our new home in Yemin Moshe, with two suitcases.

Ichiro was stunned by the unilateral decision, but to his great credit, he didn't try to stop me. He understood that I was ready to do whatever it took for Shoshana's well-being. I missed my son Akiva with all my heart but he was strong. He could manage. There is nothing as devastating as leaving one child behind to rescue the other, but I took this as yet another of God's tests.

What got me through was prayer. Being so close to the Old City, I would walk over to the Western Wall and pour my heart out to God. I asked for the strength to make Israel my home, I asked God to heal Shoshana. I prayed for Akiva to join us, and for Ichiro's understanding and his forgiveness.

Over the summer, Akiva studied at cram school every day. It was Ichiro's wish that Akiva experience the same rite of passage he had endured, nearly a year of daily preparation in order to get accepted at a ranking high school that would put him on a trajectory to a good college and a respectable job. One day Akiva decided to have a little fun. He dyed his hair blond and he happened to be caught by his junior high school homeroom teacher who called him into school the next day with his father for a sharp rebuke. Ichiro apologized to the teacher and the school principal, and when Akiva returned home, he dyed his hair back to its original dark color. The teacher didn't ask about Akiva's home life. He had no idea that Akiva's attempt to be noticed might have been a cry for help. When school resumed on the first day of September, Akiva called me in tears. His teacher had replayed the hair dying incident in front of his entire class.

"Mom, I tried my best to do what the teacher asked. I dyed my hair back when he asked me to. I was studying hard at cram school every day for high school entrance exams, but the teacher cared only about the color of my hair," he sobbed into the phone. "You weren't here! I had to study every day, and it was hard. I wanted to please Papa too."

It's a terrible truth that Japanese society can clobber those who don't conform. But nonconformity brings out creativity. Whether it's being the only kid in school to eat kosher food, or being born through no fault of your own with bipolar disorder, my children were given a tremendous opportunity to turn their handicaps into strengths.

"Akiva, one day you're going to thank your teacher from the bottom of your heart."

He went silent. "Huh?"

"Do you realize what a gift your teacher just handed you?"

"What, by humiliating me?"

"It looks like he did something despicable. But let's not dwell on it from that angle. Your teacher actually may have strengthened you."

"I know," he said softly.

"What do you want to do?"

"Take me with you."

I bit my lip. "Are you ready to go to high school in Israel?"

"Yes," Akiva said firmly.

"Papa won't come with you. He will have to give up the lease on our house, sell off the furniture and he'll probably move in with your grandmother. You'll have to leave Cinnamon behind too."

There was a long sigh. This was harder for Akiva than he had expected. I had to be honest with him.

"Then there's learning Hebrew," I added, knowing full well that learning languages came easily to Akiva.

"Take me. I'm ready," he said calmly into the phone. While we spoke, I booked a flight back to Japan, leaving Shoshana with a new, trusted friend in Yemin Moshe. Forty-eight hours later, I was back home in Tokyo. The next morning, I accompanied Akiva to speak to the junior high school principal, and Ichiro followed us over, too. We sat around a conference table where the principal spoke to Akiva respectfully. He asked Akiva about the Israeli high school system. The principal listened thoughtfully, and I explained Shoshana's needs and our difficult circumstances. He nodded empathetically. He didn't see any reason to prevent Akiva if he wished to go to school in Israel. Ichiro, with courage, decided not to stand in the way any longer. He agreed to let Akiva go.

We packed what we could, the bare minimum, leaving behind a library, my paintings, and the hardly used teak dining room table. Stuff is just stuff. I could somehow find in Jerusalem second-hand furniture to start over. I could always paint more pictures to hang on the walls, especially from Yemin Moshe. This was the price to pay, and I could accept it. This is how my life with Ichiro ended. Our marriage was over, just like that.

I boarded the plane back to Israel with Akiva, and when we lifted off, we glanced down at the shimmering green rice paddies disappearing below the clouds. I breathed deeply and felt my soul return to my body.

"We're changing our location and changing our luck," I said, as I took Akiva's hand in mine, and Japan disappeared below the clouds.

❀

Chapter Sixteen

A FAMILY REUNION IN JERUSALEM

He puts an end to wars
throughout the earth,
He breaks the bow, He snaps the spear:
The shield he burns with fire.
—Psalm 46

Shoshana wiped the sweat off her brow in layers of heavy silk kimono, woven with delicate pastel flowers. I could barely recognize my beautiful daughter out of her baggy sweater and modest flowing skirt. Here she was, twenty years old, dressed for her Coming-of-Age ceremony. She clip-clopped in her *zori* sandals along the cobblestone streets of Yemin Moshe on a warm day in December. Three months had passed since we had moved into the neighborhood. I still had to pinch myself. I was living in Jerusalem with Shoshana, while Akiva was an hour away, boarding at Ayanot Youth Village high school.

Standing by Shoshana's side was what appeared as another

mirage—*Obaasan,* her grandmother, adjusting a crease in the butterfly-shaped *obi* sash that she had spent more than an hour wrapping several times around Shoshana's waist.

This Coming-of-Age ceremony, the *Seijinshiki,* was so important to my mother-in-law that she was ready to do whatever it took to make sure Shoshana transited into adulthood in a kimono. Even if it meant doing so in Israel.

It was a risky trip for all of us and it could have ended in a disaster. But my mother-in-law is brave and she was not going to let our separation get in the way of giving Shoshana the honor of dressing up in full kimono regalia, even if it meant coming to Israel and staying in my home to do so. It was big of her. No, it was huge. At eighty years old, Ichiro's mother put aside the tensions to bring peace to the family and keep the lines of communication open. I just had to hope she would keep the conversation in a kimono framework and not on the impossible task of convincing me to return to Japan.

She had spent hours in Tokyo preparing for this trip, watching YouTube tutorials in both kimono-dressing and learning the separate skill of tying the obi sash that can be stiff, unwieldy due to its length, but if wrapped right, a magnificent accessory to show off the kimono wearer's gentle curves. With her hair set and dyed, wearing a beautifully tailored cream jacquard coat over her polyester pants, she had arrived in the middle of the night, with Ichiro trailing her with the suitcases and the jet-setting dog, Cinnamon.

She smiled warmly when we met. "I never imagined I would have this great chance to come to Israel."

For all I was learning with my new Torah teachers, I think I learned just as much in that moment. Think well, and it will be well. She arrived with an olive branch. That way of thinking has been Ichiro's mother's lasting gift to me. She was honest, as well as curious about lots of things. She wanted to know what I was paying to rent a house with arched windows overlooking the

Old City walls. She saw the windmill through the kitchen window. But I'm sure she saw it differently, as a charming relic from another era. For me, the windmill *was* my mother, those blades were her arms, and the wind made me run.

Here in Jerusalem, such metaphors invigorate me. Harmonized voices rising as one in the synagogues, Torah study, and welcoming new friends to our Shabbat table are the joys of this new life. I count among the week's greatest accomplishments the appearance of the Arab artisan house builder, who knows how to make mosquito screens that fit into arched windows.

When Shoshana's big day came, she spent hours in the basement salon of an old stone Templar era house. Her grandmother unpacked from her suitcase a collapsible rod, straight out of Mary Poppins, designed to hang the kimono. A makeup artist thickened Shoshana's eyelashes and pulled up her hair into elaborate braids held together with red and white carnations. While Shoshana's lips were lacquered bright pink, her grandmother looked approvingly at the reflection in the salon mirror.

There is a poetic Japanese expression, *mono no aware*, an awareness of the transience of things. In Shoshana's Coming-of-Age ceremony, it dawned on me that family photographs taken on this day could be our last. Then again, there's no reason to get too sentimental about a photograph capturing a fleeting moment of reunion. Jewish and Japanese wisdom has brought us all closer to God and the temples of our ancestors.

❀

Epilogue

As my dear mother of blessed memory liked to say, while quoting Shakespeare: "All's well that ends well."

The consummate theatergoer and eternal optimist who kept her worries to herself would be pleased to know that Akiva spent the next 3 years in Israel in the company of Israelis, Europeans, Americans, and three Jewish teenagers from Japan. He sharpened his English, learned Hebrew, and refined his cooking skills by making large quantities of his favorite Japanese recipes and bring back leftovers to his dorm friends. After graduation, he returned to Tokyo and is employed by a company that introduces Kosher foods to the Japanese market.

Life for Shoshana went through a rockier and more public initiation. She became a brave Jerusalem Post Magazine cover girl for bipolar disorder after Editor Erica Schachne asked me to write about a long summer at Eitanim Hospital. My new neighbors, without judging and without asking, drove me to visit Shoshana and assure me that I was home now and that there was nothing to fear. On Shabbat these angels opened their homes to me too.

Ichiro did what he could from Japan after Shoshana's hospitalization. He made sure that I could manage financially and focus on her recovery above all else. It was admittedly not easy to take Shoshana away from her Japanese family and her Tokyo cosmopolitan life, with every imaginable convenience. But just as my soul was yearning to return to Israel, I think Shoshana's was too. She has made a beautiful life for herself, developing as a mosaic artist, while cultivating a circle of compassionate and talented friends.

To witness my children's blossoming in these ways has been the greatest joy of my life in Israel. I offer my story in hope that other parents in difficult marriages and with unfathomably hard family predicaments make the courageous decisions that their hearts are telling them to do. We are never alone. Good people are all around us wanting to help us transition to become the best versions of ourselves. God is only a prayer away. Our tribes of origin can be annoying at times, but loving souls will stick by us through thick and thin.

Acknowledgments

To Fritz Jacobi, who was my first writing teacher, my best writing teacher, my boss at the Museum of Broadcasting in 1982, and my boss for some four years at Columbia Business School. Thanks to Fritz, who inducted me into the world of public relations, journalism, and writing about Japan, my life was forever changed.

The completion of this memoir was a nine-year journey that I couldn't have done alone. It was made possible through the loving encouragement and input of many dear friends and family members.

I thank my writing tribe in Japan, the awesome women who were sharing the experience of raising children, working hard, and snatching moments to write and put their souls on paper. To the passionate author and beloved yoga teacher, Leza Lowitz, my bright light in the big city, who met me elbow to elbow at cafes around Tokyo to further anchor me in the writing life while we were juggling children at home and bringing our manuscripts to fruition. To Louise George Kittaka, who met me in Doutours and broke through my writer's block. To Rebecca Ottawa, whose marvelous books about the solitary life in the Japanese countryside moved me with the fire to write about the flip side, urban married life in the heart of busy Tokyo. To Aruna Byers, my editing partner for *To Live as We Are* (the book that changed my perspective on intuition), who urged me to continue writing about my family when the memoir was still in a fragile, embryonic form.

To all the writers who inspired me and helped me stay the course: Tracy Slater, whose success with her Japan family memoir, *The Good Shufu*, helped me believe that there was a readership for yet another niche story about a foreign wife in Japan told from a decidedly Jewish perspective. To award-winning novelist Susanna Jones, author of *The Earthquake Bird*, who reminded me in the Wiltshire countryside to write not to rush, to enjoy the process, and when in doubt, remember that words are just words. To the photographer Ed Levinson, whose life in the Chiba countryside has been the inspiration for his many books, who reminded me that living off the grid is where the growth is. To Suzanne Kamata, for publishing raw, honest memoirs and novels inspired by her wheelchair-bound daughter that gave me the courage to write about Shoshana's challenges too. To photographer Everett Kennedy Brown, for entrusting me with editing *Kyoto Dreamtime*, his memoir set in a timeless world of Japanese antiquity and higher consciousness. To Richard Holland, for taking me to Hawaii and back for the dolphin ride of a lifetime during our collaboration on his memoir, *Rich Life*. To Ann Tashi Slater, fellow Tokyo soul traveler and memoir writer, whose evocative stories about her elite Tibetan family reminded me that grandmothers can have universal appeal.

To photojournalist and art world authority, Lucy Birmingham, for being among the first to write about Genesis art Workshops for Metropolis Magazine, and for journalist Carol Akiyama, for friendship and loving support of Shoshana, and for introducing Genesis art Workshops to the expat Tokyo family community. For Esther Sanders, for sharing with me the joys of raising our unique children and making this journey to test-drive Jewish Orthodoxy in Japan feel a whole lot less lonely.

Book completion is never straightforward, and while raising children, it involved many pauses and restarts. I am deeply grateful to Andy Couturier, for being an early pioneer in teaching writing classes on Zoom and helping usher me over the finish line of a completed draft. To my champion Jill Rothenberg, who coached me to take the satellite view of my memoir and to see the potential and the joy of honoring my mother's life.

To the many friends who read various drafts of this book, offered valuable comments, advice, and proofreading: Rikki Rose Horowitz, Susan Kennedy Arenz, Bracha Din, Susanna Jones, Beth Lindsey, Leza Lowitz, Donna McLay, Gaye Rowley, Esther Sanders, Ed Levinson, Rachel Cosijins-Plump, and Karen St. Pierre. In Israel, special thanks to Shari Schwartz for organizational and strategic support, and to Rebbetzin Nechama Dina Hendel of Chabad House of Baka for essential soul support. Thank you, Robert Foreman, PhD, for wonderful encouragement and manuscript feedback offered with kid gloves.

I am very grateful to journalists and authors Michael Tuch-feld, Karen Ma, Mary King, and Yehudis Litvak, who wrote about the Wakabayashi family saga at various stages, and to the editors who took an interest in Jewish life in Japan and published excerpts from *The Wagamama Bride*: Chana Weisberg, Editor of the Women's Page of *Chabad.org*: Erica Cohen Lyons, Editor of *Asian Jewish Life Magazine*; the Community Page editors at *The Japan Times*; Erica Schachne, Editor-in-Chief of *The Jerusalem Post Magazine:* Editor Jen Teeter of *Kyoto Journal*, the editorial staff at *The Jewish Forward*, and the editors and readers of the *Journal of the Association of Foreign Wives of Japan*, whose brave stories of life outside of comfort zones inspired me to write mine.

For those who took care of my health—no small order for someone born under the Virgo sign—my deepest thanks go to Nourit Masson Sekine, my French soul sister who led me to Akahigedo Shiatsu Clinic, where the extraordinary kindness, dedication and skill of the staff led me to actually marrying one of their own. To Daniel Babu, my nutritionist in Tokyo whose vast knowledge of Chinese traditional medicine turned my kitchen into the healing heart of our home. To Jesse Lee Parker, whose Tao healing arts instruction, based on centuries of Chinese ki gong wisdom, inspires me to practice to this day. To Leza Lowitz, who generously made sure that I took the time not only to write but to stretch and breathe at her beautiful Sun and Moon Yoga Studio in Tokyo. And in Jerusalem, to the staff of the Nekeudat Maga Clinic, and to Shimon Friedlander of the Neijing Clinic, for bringing me back to balance time and again with the acupuncture needles.

To my awesome fellow soul travelers, who broke bread, drank tea, made art, and shared with me unforgettable conversations in the years that rolled into decades when our paths crossed in Japan: Clay and Khine Adler, Ofer and Zohara Amit, Wakana Ando, Pauline Ascoli, Graham Bathgate, Anne Bergasse, Sascha Beck, Rabbi Jeff and Michiko Berger, Andrew Boerger, Kumiko Brase, Astrid De Los Rios, Rachel Cosijns-Plump, Melisa Eugenio, Michael Gertler, Adriana Ginsberg, Marshall Gittler, Talia Greenberg, Rosalyn Hagiwara, Marian Hara, Mindy Harris, Donna Hepburn, Brett Iimura, Nobuko Kato, Kris Kondo, Guillaume Levy Lambert, Beth Lindsey, Hanit Livermore, Natalie Kani, Debbie Krisher-Steele, Montana and Hiroko King Ramsey, Deborah Masters, Michelle Mina, Daniel Moskovich, Yona Moskovich, Shoji and Elaine Nadaya, Sivan Nakamura, Tali Nakai, Dean Newcombe, Patrick Newell,

Dorit Noda, Ofra Maezawa, Agnes McMurrow, Eynat and Martin Molenaar, Maya Moore, Liat Luft Morita, Raymond Neil, Liora Ota, Susan Preston, Montana King and Hiroko Ramsey, Sarah Ritchie, Pauline Reich, Yon-as and Ayako Seme, Sanae Sakaba, Izumi Eynat Sato, Lindsey Sawada, Hertzel and Tiorah Simontov, Peter Serafin, Matt Snyder, Relly Bar-el Stoller, Jane Taylor, Neal Teitler, Holly Thompson, Chloe Trindall, Bob Tobin, Sue Winski, Yehudis and Yossi Yeinan, Mark Zion, Bill Ward, Takahiro Yoshioka, Hila Zino, and all the wonderful students who have attended Genesis art Workshops since the year 2000.

Thank you, Rabbi Eliezer Shore, my Great Neck North High School classmate, who helped me transform this manuscript into a beautifully designed book. To Hatsumi Tonegawa, for taking my rough sketches and calligraphy and patiently turning them into a beautiful book jacket. To Refael Miller, for making sure this memoir was called by the original name conceived in 2012, *The Wagamama Bride*. To calligrapher Sophiya Gugelev for the Goshen Books logo concept. To Xanthe Smith Serafin and Suz Kennedy for proof-reading of the final draft. To Laurence O'Bryan of BooksGoSocial, for providing essential marketing support. To Eitan Yakhin, and Pomerantz Books, for introducing *The Wagamama Bride* in and beyond Jerusalem.

Without the two Chabad Houses in Tokyo, there would not have been this book. My story is a tribute to the beloved Lubavitcher Rebbe, Menachem Mendel Schneerson, the spiritual leader of the Chabad movement, who guided thousands of newlywed couples to venture out all over the globe and set up Chabad Houses in places where Jewish life had either vanished or never taken root before. To Rebbetzin Nechama Dina Hendel of Jerusalem's Chabad of Baka for amazing Torah lessons and deep friendship. To Chabad.org for giving me a constant stream of Torah inspiration and to Chana Weisberg, editor of Chabad.org's Women's Page for publishing excerpts from this memoir on one of my favorite sites. I thank the Lubavitcher Rebbe for instilling in Chabad emissaries much love and little judgement for whomever walked in the door. I thank Tokyo Chabad Rabbi Mandi and Rebbetzin Chana Sudakevich, and Tokyo Chabad Rabbi Binyamin and Rebbetzin Efrat Edery, my anchors in Tokyo, whose contrasting approaches to Chabad hospitality led me, one Shabbat at a time, back to the Jewish faith. To Rabbi and Professor Daniel and Yael Aldrich, who sparked my love of Shabbat when they opened their home to our family for the academic year they stayed in Tokyo. And to the Jewish Community Center in Hiroo, when I had just arrived in Tokyo in the late 1980s and knew very few, my deepest thanks for the warm welcome.

Special thanks to the 1980's angels of New York City who made Japan my reality: Joan Jeffri, director of Columbia's program in arts administration, the magazine editors at Columbia Alumni, Conde Nast Traveler, and Japan Airlines, and again, Fritz Jacobi. To my dear friends Anita Karl and Jim Kemp, Karen St. Pierre, Keni Valenti, Kathleen Cuadros, Patricia Egan, and the late Ginny Marshall, whose stimulating conversations on every subject under the sun made it very easy to become a writer and very hard to leave New York City. Thank you for encouraging me to go on the trip of a lifetime to Japan with reassurance that you would be there for me whenever I returned.

With a family centered in England, thanks go to my one-and-only Uncle Graham Dennie in London, my dear cousins, Sir Hugh Bayley, Justine, Annabel, and Tony Bayley, with whom I share our mysterious great grandfather Avraham Cohen. To my sister in New York, who finally broke the family law of giving free advice when none was asked for. As only a seasoned driver could give me: "Just stay in your lane." I laugh every time I think of this.

To my father, Carol Grunberg, and his wife Sidi Tuchfeld,

I'm grateful for the annual trips they took to Israel, even when I would have preferred that they came to visit me in Japan. Those trips unwittingly created the foundation for a smooth transition for me and my children from Tokyo to Israel. Thank you, Michael and Devorah Tuchfeld, for welcoming us to Givatayim and making sure Akiva had his Bar-Mitzvah in an Orthodox synagogue under the tutelage of the big-hearted cantor and opera singer Moshe Shmaryahu. To my one-and-only first cousin Dr. Greg Grunberg, with whom I can now say I share Israeli roots. To the incomparable dentist, Dr. Les Glassman, for reading everything I've written in Israel.

Lastly, I would like to thank my mother, the late Adrianne Lebensbaum, the reason for the beginning of this story and the one person who eagerly awaited the completion of this memoir, exasperating me with her frequent phone calls late into the night to find out why the memoir wasn't ready yet. "I hope I'll be alive to read it!" still echoes in my ears. Well Mom, I just have to believe that there is a big library in Heaven and that *The Wagamama Bride* is in your hands now.

It hasn't been an easy journey. Soul growth never is. But this story is a retelling from the banquet of a married life of nearly three decades, written in loving acknowledgment of the role that Ichiro and his parents played to ensure that however rocky life became, they were ready to do whatever it took to keep this marriage going. As we head out on our separate paths, may we continue, like Noah, to remember that we are one lucky family to be given life on earth, originating from the same boat. We have our children to remind us of this blessed truth.

About the Author

Photo by Benjamin Parks

Liane Grunberg Wakabayashi is a journalist, artist, and teacher who lives in Jerusalem. She was born in Montreal on August 25th, 1959, and raised in New York City in a Conservative Jewish home by European parents who had immigrated to the USA in their thirties. A lover of art and a keeper of diaries for as long she can remember, she received a BA, magna cum laude in art history, from the University of Massachusetts, Amherst, and graduated from the MFA program in arts administration at Columbia University. She visited Japan for the first time in

1985 to research blockbuster art exhibitions in Tokyo department stores. A second assignment to Japan in 1987 led to an editing position in the newsroom of *The Japan Times*. One year in Tokyo led to marriage and permanent residency. Over more than 26 years of marriage, Liane kept written records of the Eastern lifestyle and deep spiritual conversations she had with her Japanese family. With the birth of their two children, she began documenting her three-generation life in published articles, drawings, paintings and photographs.

In 2017, Liane moved with her children to Jerusalem in pursuit of a more traditional Jewish life and Torah learning. The Jerusalem Municipal Arts Council gave her the title of Expert Artist, along with a grant that led to publication of the Hebrew edition of The Genesis Way, her signature guidebook and deck of cards for creating Genesis Art. In 2020, her landscape paintings were selected for an exhibit in the Jerusalem Mayor's office. Liane enjoys drawing, swimming, chi gong, and spoiling her doxie-poodle with long walks to Jerusalem's historic First Station. To find out more about Genesis Art Workshops or memoir coaching from Liane see: www.genesiscards.com and www.goshenbooks.com.

Also by Liane Wakabayashi

Sachiko Adachi, Edited by Liane Wakabayashi with Aruna Byers
To Live as We Are

Edythe Frese van Rhoon with Liane Wakabayashi,
Through the Eyes of Illusion

Liane Grunberg with Teruhide Kato,
Kyoto Romance

Liane Grunberg Wakabayashi
The Genesis Way: 44 Cards and Guidebook

To find out about Genesis Art Workshops, please see
www.genesiscards.com

Stay in Touch

Thank you for reading my story. It's been my honor and pleasure to welcome you to the family. I love hearing your reactions to *The Wagamama Bride*, so please don't hesitate to reach out.

Goshen Books is dedicated to spotlighting the works of contemporary memoir writers worldwide, who share uplifting stories of personal transformation and triumph far from home. I would be very grateful if you could leave a short review and a rating on Amazon or Goodreads, as this helps new readers readers find *The Wagamama Bride*, and I can find you too.

Please join our mailing list, read our blog, attend our online Zoom events, and contact us about your favorite memoir writers, who write from the heart about coming home far from home.

For publicity information, to request a speaking engagement, and other author events, please do write us directly at hello@goshenbooks.com.

Bibliography

Memoirs about International Life and Family in Japan Today

Anton, Karen Hill. *The View from Breast Pocket Mountain: A Memoir.* Senyume Press, 2020.

Holland, Richard. *Rich Life: The Navy Man, the Yogi, and the Lady of Light* (forthcoming)

Kamata, Suzanne. *Squeaky Wheels: Travels with My Daughter by Train, Plane, Metro, Tuk-Tuk and Wheelchair.* Wyatt-MacKenzie Publishing, 2019.

Kennedy Brown, Everett, *Kyoto Dreamtime* (forthcoming)

Levinson, Edward. *Whisper of the Land.* Fine Line Press, 2014.

Lowitz, Leza. *Here Comes the Sun: A Journey to Adoption in 8 Chakras.* Stone Bridge Press, 2015.

Otowa, Rebecca. *At Home in Japan: A Foreign Woman's Journey of Discovery*. Tuttle Publishing, 2017.

Pover, Caroline. *One Month in Tohoku: An Englishwoman's Memoir on Life in Japan after the Tsunami*. Alexandra Press, 2020.

Slater, Tracey. *The Good Shufu: Finding Love, Self, and Home on the Far Side of the World*. Putnam Publishing Group, 2016.

Jewish Inspiration Must-Reads

Jacobson, Simon. *Toward a Meaningful Life: The Wisdom of the Rebbe Menachem Mendel Schneerson*. William Morrow, 2019.

Kalmenson, Mendel. *Positivity Bias: Practical Wisdom for Positive Living Inspired by the Life and Teachings of the Lubavitcher Rebbe*, Ezra Press, 2019.

Meir, Israel, et al. *Chofetz Chaim, a Lesson a Day: The Concepts and Laws of Proper Speech*. Mesorah Publications, 2002.

Miller, Chaim, and Menachem Mendel Schneerson. *The Gutnick Edition Chumash, Anthologized from Classic Rabbinic Texts and the Works of the Lubavitcher Rebbe*. Kol Menachem, 2002.

Morinis, E. Alan. *Everyday Holiness: the Jewish Spiritual Path of Mussar*. Trumpeter, 2009.

Sacks, Jonathan. *Judaism's Life Changing Ideas: A Weekly Reading of the Jewish Bible*, OU Press, 2021.

Shore, Eliezer. *The Face of the Waters: Chasidic Teachings and Stories for the Twenty-First Century*. Tehiru Press, 2017.

Steinsaltz, Adin. *Koren Talmud Bavli.* Koren Publishers, 2013 (English and Hebrew edition)

Twerski, Abraham. *The First Year of Marriage: Enhancing the Success of Your Marriage Right from the Start,* Shaar Press, 2004

Weinreb, Tzvi Hersh, translator. *The Koren Tehillim.* Koren Pub, 2017.

Eastern Philosophy, Spirituality, and Healing

Accolla, Dylana, and Peter Yates. *Back to Balance: A Holistic Self-Help Guide to Eastern Remedies.* Newleaf, 1996.

Adachi, Ikuro. *The Law of Undulation: Contemporary Earth Culture and Its Future: a Message from the Universe.* Natural Spirit International, Inc., 2007.

Laotzu, and John R. Leebrick. *Tao Te Ching: Classic of the Way and Its Nature.* Afterimage Book Publishers, 1980.

Melchizedek, Drunvalo. *Living in the Heart: How to Enter into the Sacred Space within the Heart.* Light Technology, 2003.

Myss, Caroline M. *Sacred Contracts: Awakening Your Divine Potential.* Transworld Digital, 2010.

Ohsawa, Georges. *Macrobiotics: An invitation to health and happiness.* George Ohsawa Macrobiotic Foundation, 1978.